*Tony Bilson's*

# FINE
# FAMILY
# COOKING

*Tony Bilson's*

# FINE
# FAMILY
# COOKING

AUSTRALIA'S ORIGINAL MASTER CHEF

MURDOCH BOOKS

Published in 2010 by Murdoch Books Pty Limited
First published in 1994 by HarperCollins Publishers Australia

Murdoch Books Australia
Pier 8/9
23 Hickson Road
Millers Point NSW 2000
Phone: +61 (0) 2 8220 2000
Fax: +61 (0) 2 8220 2558
www.murdochbooks.com.au

Murdoch Books UK Limited
Erico House, 6th Floor
93–99 Upper Richmond Road
Putney, London SW15 2TG
Phone: +44 (0) 20 8785 5995
Fax: +44 (0) 20 8785 5985
www.murdochbooks.co.uk

Publisher: Kay Scarlett
Photographer: Rodney Weidland
Cover design: Emilia Toia
Editor: Julia Cain
Food Editor: John Fenton-Smith

Produced in association with Barbara Beckett Publishing
14 Hargrave St, Paddington, Sydney, Australia 2021.

National Library of Australia Cataloguing-in-Publication Data

Author:         Bilson, Tony
Title:          Tony Bilson's Fine Family Cooking: Australia's Original Master Chef.
ISBN:           9781741969894 (pbk.)
Notes:          Includes index.
Subjects:       Cookery
Dewey Number:   641.5

A catalogue record for this book is available from the British Library.

PRINTED IN CHINA 2010

IMPORTANT: Those who might be at risk from the effects of salmonella poisoning (the elderly, pregnant women, young children and those suffering from immune deficiency diseases) should consult their doctor with any concerns about eating raw eggs.

OVEN GUIDE: You may find cooking times vary depending on the oven you are using. For fan-forced ovens, as a general rule, set the oven temperature to 20°C (35°F) lower than indicated in the recipe.

# CONTENTS

*With thanks to my wife Amanda, Barbara Beckett,*
*John Fenton-Smith, Rodney Weidland, Julia Cain,*
*Margaret Fulton, Frank Moorhouse, Michael Vanstone,*
*Wolfgang Grimm and staff of the*
*Hotel Inter-Continental, Sydney.*

*I dedicate this book with the words of*
*Philip E. Muskett from his 100-year-old volume,*
The Art of Living in Australia:
*'To the people of Australia, with one abiding hope*
*for the development of all the great natural food*
*industries of our country.'*

# COOK'S NOTES

## Herbs, spices and seasonings

The herbs used in the recipes should always be fresh and the spices freshly ground. I haunt Indian spice shops for my ingredients and buy them in small quantities. As these shops offer specialty produce, their turnover is high and the spices tend to be fresher than supermarket varieties. It is very useful to have an electric coffee grinder, the kind with high speed blades, for grinding spices and herbs. Please remember that the pepper specified in all recipes should be freshly ground.

## Preheating the oven

Remember always to allow at least half an hour for the oven to preheat. This important precaution is sometimes overlooked, with disastrous results.

## Some suggested equipment

A **mouli** is a rotary food mill used for making purées, mousses and soups (the best domestic version is made by Vev). An **electric coffee mill** for grinding spices (Braun). An **electric hand mixer** for whisking sauces (Braun or Bamix). A **pasta-rolling machine** for rolling pasta to an equal thickness. A good **balloon whisk** for egg whites. A set of **standard measuring cups** and a **liquid measuring jug**. A set of **scales**, preferably electric (Salter is the brand I recommend). These digital scales are easy to use and read. Good **knives** are a worthwhile investment. (I prefer the carbon Sabatier brand for general use, but for filleting and serrated knives I prefer the Dick brand). The **rolling pin** I use is a heavy 4 cm diameter × 80 cm long (¾ in. × 13¼ in.) piece of sanded dowl. **Silicone paper** is a special paper used to line trays for baking. It has taken the place of greaseproof paper and is especially useful because of its ability to withstand high temperatures.

## Spoon and cup measurements

|  | *Australia* | *New Zealand* | *United Kingdom* | *United States* |
|---|---|---|---|---|
| 1 tablespoon | 20 mL | 15 mL | ½ fl oz (14 mL) | ½ fl oz (14 mL) |
| 1 cup | 250 mL | 250 mL | 8 fl oz (237 mL) | 8 fl oz (237 mL) |

All countries use the same teaspoon measurements.

## Complexity of recipes

# EASY        MEDIUM        COMPLEX

# FOREWORD

Tony Bilson has been a mentor, a tutor and a companion in my life as a restaurant diner since the days of Tony's Bon Goût in the early seventies. I have eaten hundreds of meals prepared by Tony both in his restaurants and in his home, but I owe not only gastronomic pleasures to him; I owe to him, also, an introduction to the customs and practices of restaurant life. Consequently, I owe to him my introduction to some of the great experiences of my life.

I am not a gourmet, but I am a gourmand and a restaurant habitué. Paradoxically, I am most 'at home' in a restaurant and have eaten constantly in restaurants from my days as a teenage cadet journalist.

For me, the restaurant experience involves not only food and wine—I also like the restaurant as a social and aesthetic institution. I love the ever-changing fashions of restaurant life. I delight in the special cadre which great restaurateurs such as Tony create through decor, music, art works, design, lighting, plants, external views (or their absence), napery and the whole *art de la table*.

I am enchanted that there are always new restaurants to visit and at the same time I am grateful for the classical restaurants that have remained for years as part of our heritage.

I most enjoy public eating in those restaurants where I am likely to see people I know and where diners sometimes join at some point in the meal, and where unlikely ad hoc combinations occur during the evening (but not *too* ad hoc). Tony's Kinselas was especially such a place. The genius of a restaurateur, such as Tony, can bring this about.

I like socialising in a fine bar of a fine restaurant before and after the meal. I like talking with restaurant staff about food, wine, gossip, news, life.

Although I am an infrequent eater of breakfast, I have been recently introduced to the eating of breakfast in restaurants. I now often eat all the meals of the day in restaurants.

It is because of all this—because I rarely cook and rarely eat in a domestic setting (although some of my friends who live in houses are fine cooks)—that I am utterly the most inappropriate person to write the foreword for a book titled *Fine Family Cooking* (however, I do own the book *Australian Home Cooking*, published in 1909).

Nevertheless, I have great confidence and pride in commending this book to all home cooks as a way of bringing to the home meal some of the wisdom of Tony Bilson, one of our greatest chefs. This book is not just a book of recipes; it is a book about the very art of living, of which Tony Bilson is a master.

Opposite: Terrine of
Seafood with Pastis Fumet

FRANK MOORHOUSE

# INTRODUCTION

Reading through *Fine Family Cooking*, first published more than 15 years ago, I am struck by how much the recipes have to offer the modern reader in terms of hints and insights into classical techniques that are so easily adopted into the home cook's repertoire.

When I first wrote the book, some of the equipment used was less common than it is today. Most cooks worth their salt will now have food processors, spice and coffee grinders as well as hand blenders.

Nevertheless, at the heart of good cooking is generosity of spirit and a desire to provide a special experience at the table in place of the banal. This book provides the reader with techniques and ideas that will enable their creative urges to be fulfilled while recognising that some previously unfamiliar products and methods are actually very easy and satisfying to master.

After seeing Poh using a 100-year-old egg on *MasterChef* in 2009, on prime time television, it now seems entirely realistic that children's school lunches in future will include items such as the Stuffed Rosetta Rolls (p184) or Cold Almond Soup (p185).

When familiar ingredients are presented in new contexts, they help to make a meal more interesting and they also give the family new insights into the beauty and possibilities of humble ingredients that they may have taken for granted.

Australia has such a varied range of climatic conditions and the book has dishes to suit all. From the simplicity of the summery Tomato Terrine (p51) to the soul-warming Braised Oxtail (p115) aromatically spiced with citrus, the recipes provide the family with a vast range of dishes. I have described many techniques such as making savoury jellies and consommés and how they can be used to create restaurant-quality dishes to serve at home.

The use of fats in the diet has become controversial as oxygenated fats high in triglycerides may form the basis of many manufactured food products. Natural fat, on the other hand, is an essential part of a healthy diet. This book uses a range of natural fats from oils to butter to fish and poultry. I recommend using fats seasonally and in ways that provide a healthy Mediterranean diet for family and friends.

The greengrocer section of the book provides recipes for vegetables both as accompaniments to other dishes or as individual courses. Some, such as the Cauliflower Mousse (p54) or Celeriac Puree (p53) can be used as garnishes for contemporary dishes. Others, like the Spinach Bouillabaisse (p48), provide glimpses of old Provence with flavours that spring as fresh from the plate today as they did 200 years ago.

I am particularly pleased that the young cooks in *MasterChef* enjoyed using *Fine Family Cooking*, and hope that their pleasure is mirrored in your home.

Tony Bilson 2010

# BIBLIOGRAPHY

Pierre Andrieu, *Fine Bouche: A History of the Restaurant in France.* Translated from the French by Arthur L. Hayward. Cassell, London, 1956

Tony Bilson, *Tony Bilson's Recipe Book.* William Heinemann, Australia, 1987, Mandarin Australia, 1993

Anthony Blake & Quentin Crewe, *Great Chefs of France.* Marshall Editions Ltd, London, 1978

Raymond Blanc, *Recipes from Le Manoir aux Quat' Saisons.* McDonald Orbis, London, 1988

Elizabeth David, *French Provincial Cooking.* Penguin Books, London, 1960

Auguste Escoffier *Escoffier: The Complete Guide to the Art of Modern Cookery.* Translated into English by H. L. Cracknell & R. J. Kaufmann. Heinemann, London, 1907

Michel Guérard, *La Cuisine Gourmande.* Robert Laffont, Paris, Macmillan, London

Marcella Hazan, *The Essentials of Classic Italian Cooking.* Macmillan, London, 1992

*Inoue, The Works.* Dohosha Publishing, Kyota, 1992

*Larousse Pratique.* Reed International, London, 1990

Gaston Lenôtre, *Desserts and Pastries.* Flammarion, 1975

Kyomi Mikuni, *Food Fantasy of the Hotel de Mikuni.* Tokyo, 1986, (reprinted 1990)

Philip E. Muskett, *The Art of Living in Australia.* Kangaroo Press, 1893, (reprinted 1987)

Richard Olney, *Provence the Beautiful.* Weldon/Angus&Robertson, Sydney, 1993

Patricia Wells, *Cuisine Actuelle–The Cuisine of Joel Robuchon.* Macmillan, London, 1993

# The Fish Market

*The next best thing to fish you have caught yourself is fresh fish bought from a good fish market. Truly fresh fish should be bright in colour, with flesh that is firm and rigid yet elastic to the touch. Get to know your local fishmonger to ensure that you always buy the best fish and seafoods.*

Cities like Sydney and Tokyo are blessed with good fish markets. Visiting them is always educational. To wander through these markets and choose seafoods that appeal because of their variety and freshness is inspirational.

There is, of course, nothing like the fish you have caught yourself. I do try to catch fish off the rocks around Sydney, but I have never caught a fish. However, I live in hope that my strategies will allow me to trap an old snapper one day, causing it to bite onto my hook and relieve me of the ignominy of my reputation.

It is impossible for me to speak of a favourite fish; it is the quality of a fish on the day that appeals to me. I choose fish for the occasion. Expensive fish like lobster I use as part of a composite dish or for special meals. Some fish, like red mullet (rougets), are still unusual and can provide guests with a new experience.

Freezing is a method of preserving food without altering its flavour, but in the process we lose the 'life' taste of the fish. If we salt the fish, we alter the taste drastically, but we also preserve something of that essential taste that we lose with freezing. The only prerequisite is that we salt only fresh fish.

Much of the fish that is for sale has been frozen, which is a pity but a fact of life. Local fish is less likely to have suffered this indignity, so becoming familiar with your local seafoods and knowing when they are in season is worthwhile.

When you become known by suppliers they will tell you if fish has been frozen, but until then, look to see if the gills have been removed and if the flesh is firm to the touch. The gills should be a lovely pink colour. If the gills are removed, it is usually because the fish has been frozen. Frozen fish may, in some circumstances, be the best available. If this is the case, always buy whole fish not fillets. The fillets will have had the flavour washed out of them.

Never buy frozen cooked shellfish.

Fresh fish is best cooked simply and, for me, the most complex flavours in fish cooking are simply achieved. Bouillabaisse has been made into a complex dish by writers, not by the fishermen who cooked beside their boats. If you cook a single piece of fish in a large quantity of unseasoned water you will have a flavourless soup. If you cook a variety of fresh fish in a small amount of wine with sympathetic seasonings and spices you have bouillabaisse.

Simple cooking methods are always best with fish: steaming or grilling (broiling) with some herbs and butter or oil and roasting whole fish are well within the range of an inexperienced cook. The worst sin you can commit with fish is to overcook it.

Previous pages: Salted Anchovies

# FISH STOCK

*Try to use a mixture of different fish to get the finest flavours. Snapper, whiting and John Dory are excellent for making fish stock, but a word of warning—do not overcook the fish as the stock will lose its delightful fresh quality.*

Melt the butter in a deep saucepan or stockpot over a medium heat. Add the mirepoix and leek and cook gently until the vegetables soften but do not brown. Add the rest of the ingredients and bring the stock to the boil. A white scum and some oil will float to the surface. This should be removed and discarded, using a slotted spoon. Lower the heat to a simmer and continue cooking for a further 20 minutes. Strain the stock through a fine sieve or muslin, gently pressing the juice from the bones.

Cool and then refrigerate the stock to use when required. The stock will keep, refrigerated, for 3–4 days and can be frozen.

*Makes 4 cups*

1 kg (2 lbs) fish bones and
   heads, washed and with gills
   removed
60 g (2 oz) butter
1 cup mirepoix (page 253)
1 small leek, chopped
2 thyme sprigs
2 parsley sprigs
1 bay leaf
6 black peppercorns
340 mL (11 fl oz) white wine
   (semillon or chardonnay)
6 cups (1.5 litres/ 2½ imp.
   pints) water

# SALTED ANCHOVIES

*Fresh anchovies sometimes appear at the fish market during summer. These fish are of the highest quality and are simple to prepare. The fish are first salted by being laid on a bed of sea salt for 4 hours (2 hours each side).*

Discard any broken or bruised fish. The fish should look bright and the light should catch the colour of their scales.

In a mortar and pestle or an electric coffee grinder, make the seasoning by pulverising the peppercorns, bay leaves and marjoram.

Spread the salt on a tray so that the tray is evenly covered, then lay the fish on the salt and sprinkle over the seasoning. Cover with plastic wrap (cling film).

After 2 hours, turn the fish over and cover for a further 2 hours. It may be convenient to keep the fish refrigerated during this period, but it is not necessary.

Remove any salt from the fish with a brush and pat them dry with paper towels (absorbent kitchen paper).

Layer the fish in the preserving jar and cover with a good quality olive oil. Alternatively, purée the fish by placing them whole in a blender or food processor with 1 cup (250 mL/8 fl oz) olive oil. After the fish are puréed, pass the mixture through the fine blade of a mouli grater or a sieve and store it in the preserving jar.

*Serves 6–8*

500 g (1 lb) whole fresh
   anchovies
1 teaspoon black peppercorns
2 bay leaves
1 teaspoon fresh marjoram
   leaves
500 g (1 lb) sea salt or rock
   salt
1 × 3 cup (750 mL/ 1¼ imp.
   pints) preserving jar with
   rubber seal
virgin olive oil to cover anchovies

# CURED SALMON WITH VIRGIN OLIVE OIL AND GOLDEN SHALLOTS

1 side of salmon, skin removed
(approximately
1.5–2 kg/ 3–4 lbs)

6 golden shallots, chopped
freshly ground black pepper to
taste
⁴/₅ cup (200 mL/ 6½ fl oz)
virgin olive oil

Cure
1 cup (250 g/ 8 oz) white
granulated sugar
405 g (13 oz) Maldon sea salt
2 tablespoons fresh thyme leaves
1 tablespoon freshly ground
black pepper

chervil sprigs to garnish

Blanch the shallots in boiling water for 1 minute, then refresh them under cold water and press the excess water from them in a sieve. Add the shallots and the pepper to the oil and let them steep in the oil for 24 hours.

*To cure the fish*

Use a pair of tweezers to extract the bones from along the centre of the fillet.

Mix the curing ingredients together in a bowl. Take a piece of aluminium kitchen foil half as long again as the fillet of salmon. Make a bed for the fillet with half the salt mixture in the centre of the lower half of the foil. Place the fillet on the salt mixture, skin side down. Cover the top of the fish with the rest of the mixture. Fold the foil over the fish and seal with a double fold.

Leave to marinate for 24 hours on a flat surface or tray in a convenient place. The salmon does not need to be refrigerated at this stage. The timing is critical: if the fish is left much longer it may dry out and become tough.

Remove the fish from the cure and wipe any remaining salt mixture from it with a damp cloth.

Wrap the fillet in plastic wrap (cling film) and refrigerate until needed. It will keep, refrigerated, for 2–3 weeks.

*To serve*

Cut the fish into very fine (paper-thin) slices, cutting at an angle away from the tail. As you cut a slice, press it flat with the back of the knife and then transfer it to a cold plate. Cover the bottom of each plate with the fish slices. Spoon the oil and shallot mixture over the fish and garnish with chervil sprigs and freshly ground black pepper.

*Serves 10–15*

Opposite: Cured Salmon
with Virgin Olive Oil and
Golden Shallots

# MARINATED SARDINES

20 sardines, butterflied and
    filleted
1 tablespoon Maldon sea salt
1 teaspoon freshly ground pepper
1 tablespoon chopped fresh
    thyme leaves

Marinade
4 tablespoons sherry vinegar
2 tablespoons finely chopped
    golden shallots

²⁄₅ cup (100 mL/3½ fl oz)
    extra virgin olive oil
2 tablespoons snipped chives
2 tablespoons finely chopped
    fresh parsley
1 tablespoon blanched julienne of
    lemon rind
1 tablespoon chopped capers
2 tablespoons finely chopped
    cooked egg white
1 medium tomato, cut into
    5 mm (¼ in.) dice
chervil sprigs to garnish

Place the sardine fillets on a large plate and season with the salt, pepper and thyme. Cover with plastic wrap (cling film) and refrigerate overnight. In a small container, mix together the vinegar with the shallots. Cover the container with plastic wrap and refrigerate overnight.

Two to three hours before serving, brush any excess salt from the fish and pat them dry with paper towels (absorbent kitchen paper). Brush the flesh with some of the vinegar/shallot mixture, then cover again and return to the refrigerator.

*To serve*

Half an hour before serving, mix together the oil, herbs, lemon rind, capers, egg white, chili pepper and tomato, and the remainder of the vinegar/shallot mixture. Spoon the mixture over the fish and garnish with the sprigs of chervil.

*Serves 6–8*

# DEEP-FRIED BOTTLE SQUID

600 g (1¼ lbs) squid

½ tablespoon salt
1 tablespoon freshly ground
    black pepper
1 cup (125 g/4 oz) plain (all-
    purpose) flour
virgin olive oil to cover squid

⅓ cup chopped Italian parsley
    leaves
3 tablespoons sherry vinegar
3 lemons, quartered

*These delicious little squid, five centimetres (2 inches) long, are lovely served as a first course or as a garnish for grilled fish.*

Mix the salt and pepper with the flour.

Wash the squid and dry them on paper towels (absorbent kitchen paper). Heat the oil in the deep fryer to 280°C (530°F).

Put the seasoned flour in a plastic or polythene bag and place the squid in the bag. Seal the opening of the bag and toss the squid around inside it, so that they are coated with the seasoned flour. Remove the squid, shake off any excess flour, and deep-fry them for 7–8 minutes. Place a tight cover on the fryer because the oil will spit while the squid fry. Remove the squid when they are crisp and golden and drain them on paper towels.

*To serve*

Immediately toss the squid with the vinegar and parsley and serve with the quartered lemons.

*Serves 6 as a main course*

# PROVENCAL FISH SOUP

*This simple dish is a great favourite at home. The base soup can be made in advance and the dish completed by adding and cooking the fish 15 minutes before serving.*

### To make the rouille

Rouille is a highly seasoned mayonnaise that is added to the soup when it is served, either by the cook or by each person.

Blanch the red sweet pepper (capsicum) in boiling water for 1 minute, then drain it. Cut the potato and red sweet pepper into pieces. Place all the ingredients in a blender and blend until the rouille has a shiny surface or coagulates. Put aside.

### To make the croûtons

Cut the baguette into thin slices. Place the slices of bread on a baking sheet and brown them in a preheated oven (250°C/475°F). Remove the croûtons from the oven when golden and allow to cool. Cut a head of garlic in half and rub each croûton with the cut side of the garlic.

### To make the soup

Heat the olive oil in a large heavy-based pot. Soften the onion, garlic, fennel and carrot in the oil over a medium heat. Add the tomato and tomato paste (purée) and continue to cook until the mixture begins to stick to the pan.

Add the wine and fish stock (or water) and the seasonings and bring to the boil. Add the fish, in the order in which they are listed, but adding the prawns (shrimps) and the mussels before the delicate fish (John Dory, bream, whiting and red mullet). The delicate fish should be added 3 minutes before serving. Keep the soup boiling to cook the firm fish and open the mussels, then lower the heat to a simmer to cook the delicate fish.

### To serve

Place the bowl of Gruyère and a basket of the croûtons on the table.

Warm a large soup bowl for each person. Place a few slices of cooked potato on the bottom of each bowl, add a large spoonful of the rouille and then spoon the fish soup into each bowl, giving each guest a mixture of the fish.

Sprinkle the soup with chopped parsley and serve.

*Serves 10–12*

1.5 kg (3 lbs) mixed fish fillets, cut into chunky 3–4 cm (1½ in.) pieces (choose six different fish; lobster, eel, rock cod, ling, gurnard, snapper, tuna, flathead, John Dory, bream, whiting, red mullet)
8 large green prawns (shrimps)
500 g (1 lb) cleaned mussels

Rouille
½ red sweet pepper (capsicum)
60 g (2 oz) cooked potato
2 eggs
80 mL (2½ fl oz) lemon juice
4 garlic cloves
¼ teaspoon cayenne pepper
⅘ cup (200 mL/6½ fl oz) virgin olive oil
1 teaspoon salt

Croûtons
½ baguette (French bread stick)
1 head garlic
250 g (8 oz) Gruyère cheese, grated

⅖ cup (100 mL/3½ fl oz) virgin olive oil
1 onion, chopped
4 garlic cloves, crushed
1 cup chopped fennel root
⅓ cup chopped carrot
1 cup chopped tomato
½ cup tomato paste (purée)
2 cups (500 mL/16 fl oz) white wine
4 cups (1 litre/1¾ imp. pints) fish stock (page 17)
1 tablespoon saffron threads
2 star anise pods
5 cm (2 in.) strip orange rind
2 each thyme, marjoram, oregano and basil sprigs
2 bay leaves
salt and freshly ground pepper
½ teaspoon cayenne pepper

500 g (1 lb) cooked potato
½ cup Italian parsley leaves

# STEAMED COD
# WITH CAPER SAUCE

*For this recipe, it is best to use a spacious multi-purpose steamer, preferably the high-domed Chinese variety.*

Bring the water in the bottom of the steamer to the boil. Season the fillets. Spread the onion rings and thyme in the steamer and place the fish on top, with sufficient space between the ingredients for the steam to circulate freely. Then place the container with the fish on top of the boiling water to cook. The fish should take 12–15 minutes to cook. After 10 minutes, add the zucchini (courgettes). Remove the fish, onion, thyme and zucchini from the steamer with a slotted spatula.

*To make the sauce*
Place all the ingredients for the sauce in a small saucepan and heat over a low heat until warmed through.

*To serve*
Spoon the sauce over and around the fish and serve it hot, decorated with the zucchini flowers, if available.

*Serves 6*

1 kg (2 lbs) cod fillets, cut into 155 g (5 oz) portions
salt and freshly ground black pepper
2 onions, sliced into thin rings
6 thyme sprigs
12 baby zucchini (courgettes) with their flowers or 500 g (1 lb) larger zucchini, cut into batons

Caper sauce
⅓ cup salted capers, washed
½ cup tomato dice
½ cup (125 mL/4 fl oz) virgin olive oil
2 tablespoons sherry vinegar
2 tablespoons chopped parsley
freshly ground black pepper

# STEAMED MUSSELS
# WITH SAUCE POULETTE

Wash the mussels and remove their beards under running water, then drain.

Melt the butter over a medium heat in a wide, 10 cm (4 in.) deep saucepan. Soften the mirepoix in the butter for 2–3 minutes. Do not let the butter brown. Add the garlic, herbs and pepper.

Add the wine, stock and tomato and bring to the boil over a high heat. Add the mussels and fit a tight lid to the pan. Steam the mussels for 5 minutes, then remove the lid and stir with a wooden spoon to help the mussels open. When they have opened, strain the liquid into a saucepan, ladle the mussels into a dish and sprinkle them with parsley.

Mix the egg yolks with the cream. Bring the liquid in the saucepan to the boil, and whisk in the cream/egg yolk mixture. The sauce will thicken. Remove the sauce from the heat before it boils. Strain the sauce over the mussels using a fine sieve. Serve the mussels with fresh, hot, crusty bread.

*Serves 6*

2 kg (4 lbs) small black mussels

60 g (2 oz) butter
½ cup mirepoix (page 253)
4 garlic cloves, crushed
6 thyme sprigs
2 bay leaves
½ teaspoon freshly ground pepper
½ cup (125 mL/4 fl oz) white wine (chardonnay)
½ cup (125 mL/4 fl oz) fish stock (page 17)
4 tablespoons tomato juice or fresh pulp
¼ cup chopped fresh parsley
6 egg yolks
½ cup (125 mL/4 fl oz) light (single) cream

Opposite: Steamed Mussels with Sauce Poulette

# MUSSEL RISOTTO

1 kg (2 lbs) mussels

⅓ cup (90 mL/ 3 fl oz) virgin
   olive oil
1 onion, diced small
2 garlic cloves, crushed
1 cup (155 g/ 5 oz) long grain
   rice
2 thyme sprigs
1 cup chopped tomato, peeled
   and seeded
1 bay leaf
300 mL (9½ fl oz) fish stock
   (page 17)
a good pinch of saffron threads
salt, pepper and cayenne pepper
   to taste

⅓ cup chopped Italian parsley
   leaves

Scrub the mussels and remove their beards and shells under running water, then drain.

Heat the olive oil in a deep frying pan or skillet with a lid, add the onion and garlic and soften over a medium heat for 2 minutes. Increase the heat and add the rice, cooking it until it is opaque (3–5 minutes). Add the other ingredients, except for the mussels and the chopped parsley, and continue to cook over a high heat for 5 minutes.

Add the mussels to the pan and place a tight lid over the risotto. Continue to cook for a further 7 minutes, by which time all the mussels will be open and the rice will have absorbed their liquid.

*To serve*
Sprinkle the risotto with the chopped parsley and serve immediately.
*Serves 4–6*

# CURRIED MUSSELS
# (LA MOUCLADE)

2 kg (4 lbs) mussels

⅓ cup (90 mL/ 3 fl oz) virgin
   olive oil
2 fresh red or green chili peppers
   (5 cm/ 2 in. long)
2 chopped onions
6 garlic cloves, crushed
½ cup chopped carrot
3 tablespoons chopped fresh
   ginger
2 tablespoons plain (all-purpose)
   flour
2 tablespoons curry paste
4 cups (1 litre/ 1¾ imp. pints)
   water
⅘ cup (200 mL/ 6½ fl oz)
   crème fraîche (page 252)

⅓ cup chopped fresh parsley

*This popular dish is more like a soup, as are most mussel dishes, and is suitable to serve for lunch or as a first course.*

Scrub the mussels and remove their beards. Wash them well under cold running water, then drain.

Heat the oil in a large saucepan with a tight lid over a medium heat. De-seed and chop the chili peppers. Add the onions, garlic, carrot, ginger and chili peppers to the pan and turn them continuously with a wooden spoon until softened. When the onion has become translucent, add the flour and cook for 2 minutes. Add the curry paste and mix it in with a wooden spoon. Slowly add the water, stirring vigorously to make a base without lumps. Use a wire whisk to finish the task if necessary. Add the crème fraîche, bring to the boil and simmer for 5 minutes. Bring to a rolling boil and then add the mussels, clamping the lid on tightly. Cook the mussels over a high heat, continually shaking the pot, for 5–7 minutes, until all the mussels have opened. Taste and adjust the seasoning.

*To serve*
Serve the curried mussels in deep bowls, sprinkled with the chopped parsley.
*Serves 6*

# GRILLED GARFISH

---

*A simple but delicious luncheon dish. Ask the fishmonger to remove the head and backbones from the fish.*

Place the fish flat on a cutting board, skin side down. Season with salt and pepper. Mix the remaining ingredients together in a bowl. Brush the fish generously on one side with half of the mixture.

Preheat the grill (broiler) so that it is hot. Place the fish under the grill, mixture side uppermost, and cook them close to the heat for 3–5 minutes, or until cooked. Brush the remaining mixture over the fish.

*To serve*

Serve the fish on hot plates with steamed potatoes and a salad of cooked baby green beans.

*Serves 4*

8 large garfish or 16 small fish
salt and freshly ground black
    pepper
1 garlic clove, crushed
1 tablespoon chopped fresh
    thyme leaves
1 tablespoon chopped fresh
    parsley
juice of 1 lemon
$^1/_3$ cup (100 g/ 3$^1/_2$ oz) butter,
    melted
70 mL/ 2$^1/_2$ fl oz virgin olive oil

# MUD CRAB
# WITH CHAMPAGNE SAUCE

---

*To prepare the mud crab*

Place the live mud crab in the freezer for 1 hour, to kill it. Scrub it all over with a brush under cold running water to remove any mud that may be clinging to the shell. Cut the crab in half with a large kitchen knife. Reserve the juices, together with the mustard and roe, if there are any. Remove the top 'shield' of the crab and discard it, together with the feathery gills around the top of the legs. Sever the legs and claws with the knife or a sharp cleaver. Crack the claws with sharp blows from the back of the knife or cleaver. Cook immediately, as crab tends to lose its moisture if there is any delay.

*To cook the crab*

Melt the butter in a large stockpot over a low heat, and soften the shallots. Add the mud crab, herbs and peppers. Keep turning the crab until the shells begin to colour (approximately 5 minutes). Add the Champagne and stock, cover with a tight-fitting lid and cook over a high heat for 10–12 minutes. Remove from the heat and keep warm.

*To prepare the sauce*

Strain the liquid from the cooked crab into a separate saucepan, and bring to the boil. Turn down the heat and whisk in the Cognac.

In a separate bowl, beat the crab mustard and any roe into the

4 kg (8 lbs) live mud crab

100 g (3$^1/_2$ oz) butter
6 golden shallots, finely chopped
3 thyme sprigs
1 bay leaf
freshly ground black pepper
$^1/_4$ teaspoon cayenne pepper
1 cup (250 mL/ 8 fl oz) good
    Champagne
150 mL (5 fl oz) fish stock
    (page 17)

Sauce
80 mL (2$^1/_2$ fl oz) Cognac
$^2/_5$ cup (100 mL/ 3$^1/_2$ fl oz)
    single (light) cream
2 egg yolks
salt

$^1/_3$ cup chopped Italian parsley
    leaves

cream and egg yolks. Turn off the heat. Pass this mixture through a fine sieve into the sauce. Mix thoroughly with a whisk and season with salt.

*To serve*
Pile the mud crab onto a serving plate or into a bowl, pour the sauce over and sprinkle with parsley. Place individual finger bowls on the table.

*Serves 4–6*

# SNAPPER POACHED IN SAFFRON COURT BOUILLON

2–2.5 kg (4–5 lbs) whole
    snapper

Court bouillon
4 cups (1 litre/ 1¾ imp. pints)
    clear fish stock (page 17)
3 tablespoons Pernod
2 large tomatoes, roughly diced
2 star anise pods
1 bay leaf
2 thyme sprigs
2 marjoram sprigs
1 teaspoon saffron threads
salt and freshly ground black
    pepper
⅙ teaspoon cayenne pepper

Garnish
1 leek, trimmed and cleaned
1 medium carrot, finely sliced
1 large tomato, peeled, seeded
    and diced
a few marjoram sprigs
a few stalks of Italian parsley

*The snapper should be filleted and cut into six portions. Use the head and bones to make the fish stock.*

*To make the court bouillon*
Slowly bring to the boil and then simmer the stock, Pernod, tomatoes, star anise and herbs in a large, saucepan for 10 minutes. Strain the liquid through muslin into a large, wide saucepan. Add the saffron. Leave to infuse for at least 10 minutes, then season with the salt, pepper and cayenne pepper and bring the court bouillon to just below the boil.

*To poach the snapper*
Place the snapper steaks in the liquid and poach for 10 minutes, or until cooked.

*To prepare the garnish*
Wash the leek, cut it into fine slices and blanch it in boiling water for 1 minute. Ridge the exterior of the carrot with a citrus zester before slicing it into fine pieces. Take a little of the poaching liquid and heat the garnish ingredients in a separate saucepan.

*To serve*
Spoon the garnish into warmed serving bowls, place the fish in the centre and spoon over the court bouillon.

*Serves 6–8*

Opposite: Snapper Poached
in Saffron Court Bouillon

# WHOLE BAKED SNAPPER

3 kg (6 lbs) whole snapper
salt and freshly ground black
   pepper

Herbed oil
⁴/₅ cup (200 mL/6¹/₂ fl oz)
   virgin olive oil
3 garlic cloves, peeled and
   crushed
3 golden shallots, finely chopped
1 tablespoon lemon juice
1 tablespoon Dijon mustard
2 tablespoons chopped fresh
   marjoram leaves
1 tablespoon chopped fresh
   thyme leaves
¹/₃ cup chopped fresh basil leaves
3 tablespoons Pernod with a
   pinch of saffron threads
   soaked in it overnight

*Snapper is one of the most highly regarded eating fish and also one of the most versatile. This dish is easy to cook, looks impressive, and can be served hot or cold. It is a lunch dish and should be served with salad or as part of a buffet with other seafoods and cold meats.*

### To make the herbed oil

Mix the herbed oil ingredients together. Set aside.

### To bake the fish

Wash the fish under cold running water and remove any scales. Pat dry with a cloth or paper towels (absorbent kitchen paper). Using a sharp knife, slash the fish twice diagonally on both sides, right through the flesh to the bone. Season generously with salt and pepper on both sides. Place the fish in a large oiled baking pan.

Spoon the herbed oil evenly over the fish.

Bake in a hot oven (200°C/390°F) for approximately 35 minutes, basting the snapper with the herbed oil. Take the fish out of the oven and check to make sure it is cooked by gently lifting the flesh around the dorsal fin. The flesh should be moist and come away easily from the bone. Allow the fish to stand for 10 minutes before serving.

### To serve

If serving hot, remove the fish to a large, warm, serving plate and spoon the juices over the fish. Serve the dish with spinach (page 48) cooked with a little garlic and a good olive oil.

*Serves 6–8*

# FILLETS OF WHITING WITH TOMATO AND TARRAGON

6 large whiting, approximately
   600 g (1¹/₄ lbs)
salt and freshly ground black
   pepper
125 g (4 oz) clarified butter
1 teaspoon chopped fresh thyme
   leaves
2 cups finely diced brioche

Tomato sauce
4 tablespoons virgin olive oil
1 tablespoon champagne
   vinegar

*Several varieties of the delicately flavoured whiting are readily available. The sand whiting is the best to use and is similar to the highly regarded sea bass (loup de mer). The fish should be skinned and filleted, with the central bones removed.*

### To make the tomato and tarragon sauce

Mix together the olive oil, vinegar, garlic and mustard. Add the tomatoes, tarragon leaves and the capers.

Pour the fish stock into a saucepan and reduce it over a medium heat until approximately 4 tablespoons of liquid remain. Add the saffron threads, thyme sprig and Pernod.

Mix together the tomato and fish stock mixtures and heat in a small saucepan. Set aside.

### To grill (broil) the fish

Season the fish, brush with a little of the butter and grill (broil) under the griller (broiler). When the fish has just cooked (it should break apart when gently pushed with a fork), sprinkle it generously with the finely diced brioche. Sprinkle with the remaining butter and return to the griller until golden.

### To serve

Spoon the warm sauce into the centre of each plate. Place the fish on the sauce and serve with steamed potatoes.

*Serves 6*

*3 large tomatoes, diced*
*⅓ cup fresh tarragon leaves*
*60 g (2 oz) capers (use the small salted ones, washed)*
*½ cup (125 mL/4 fl oz) fish stock (page 17)*
*a good pinch of saffron threads*
*1 thyme sprig*
*a dash of Pernod*

# FILLETS OF FLOUNDER BAKED WITH CREAM

*This dish can be partially prepared in advance and then the cooking completed very simply when you are ready to serve the fish. Keep the fish bones and skins to make the fish stock.*

### To make the stock

Wash the fish bones and skins under cold running water.

Melt the butter in a large saucepan, and add the mirepoix. Soften the mirepoix over a medium heat. Add the herbs and peppercorns and cook for a further 2 minutes. Add the bones, skins, wine and water, and bring to the boil. Skim the froth from the top of the stock and simmer for 30 minutes.

Strain the stock through a fine sieve into another saucepan. Bring to the boil and reduce to 1 cup (250 mL/8 fl oz). Add the crème fraîche and adjust the seasoning as required.

### To cook the fish

Preheat the oven to 250°C (475°F) 45 minutes before serving.

Season the flounder fillets with salt and pepper and arrange them in a ceramic baking pan, placing the larger fillets on the bottom and the smaller on top.

Pour the cream/stock mixture over the fish, dot with the butter and bake in the oven for 30 minutes.

### To serve

Glaze the dish under a salamander or griller (broiler) before serving. Serve the fish hot, accompanied by buttered boiled new potatoes.

*Serves 6*

*6 × 500 g (1 lb) flounder, filleted and skinned*

Stock
*the flounder bones and skins*
*1 tablespoon butter*
*1 cup mirepoix (page 253)*
*2 thyme sprigs*
*2 parsley sprigs*
*1 bay leaf*
*½ teaspoon black peppercorns*
*1¼ cups (310 mL/10 fl oz) white wine*
*3 cups (750 mL/24 fl oz) water*

*1 cup (250 mL/8 fl oz) crème fraîche (page 252)*
*salt and freshly ground black pepper to season*
*2 tablespoons butter*

# WHITING FILLETS
# WITH MUSSELS AND CROUTONS

*12 large whiting fillets
(80–90 g/ 3 oz per fillet),
seasoned with salt and pepper*
*24 mussels*

*90 mL (3 fl oz) virgin olive oil*
*500 g (1 lb) chopped tomatoes*
*1 garlic clove, crushed*
*1 teaspoon chopped fresh parsley*
*salt and freshly ground black
pepper*
*a pinch of caster (superfine)
sugar*

Croûtons
*½ baguette (French bread stick)*
*¼ cup (60 mL/ 2 fl oz) olive oil*
*1 garlic clove, crushed*
*2 tablespoons chopped fresh
parsley*

Heat the olive oil in a saucepan until it is smoking, add the tomatoes, garlic, parsley, salt, pepper and sugar and simmer for half an hour.

Scrub the mussels and remove their beards and shells. Wash them well under cold running water, then drain. Bring a saucepan of water to the boil and steam the mussels for 5–7 minutes, until they have opened.

Spread the tomato mixture on a shallow baking sheet. Lay the whiting on it and sprinkle with the mussels and their juices. Cover with foil and bake in a preheated oven (200°C/390°F) for 7 minutes.

*To make the croûtons*

Cut the baguette into small dice and fry in olive oil with the garlic clove. Drain on paper towels (absorbent kitchen paper) and then toss with the parsley.

*To serve*

Sprinkle the croûtons over the cooked whiting and serve hot.

*Serves 6*

# BRAISED BARRAMUNDI
# WITH ENDIVES

*6 × 225 g (7 oz) barramundi
steaks*
*salt and freshly ground pepper*
*60 g (2 oz) clarified butter*
*6 golden shallots, chopped*
*⁴/₅ cup (200 mL/ 6½ fl oz)
white wine*
*6 Belgian endives (witloof),
quartered and blanched*
*½ leek, cut in julienne strips
and blanched*
*1 cup finely sliced mushrooms*
*2 thyme sprigs*
*1 bay leaf*
*²/₅ cup (100 mL/ 3½ fl oz) light
(single) cream*
*155 g (5 oz) butter, diced*
*salt and freshly ground pepper*
*2 tablespoons chopped parsley*

*The rich flavour of the wild barramundi is preferable to the small farmed fish.*

Season the barramundi with salt and pepper.

Melt the clarified butter in a heavy frying pan or skillet over a high heat. Brown the steaks in the butter on both sides, lift from the pan with a slotted spatula and turn the heat to low. Cook the shallots in the clarified butter remaining in the pan until soft (2–3 minutes), deglaze the pan with the white wine and cook until the liquid is reduced by half. Increase the heat to high and return the fish to the pan. Add the Belgian endives (witloof), leek, mushrooms, thyme and bay leaf. Simmer for 5–7 minutes, or until the fish is cooked.

Place the fish on hot plates. Add the cream to the mixture in the pan, reduce the liquid by one-third, then beat the butter into the sauce with a whisk. Taste and correct the seasoning.

Arrange the vegetables around the fish, spoon a little of the sauce over the fish, and sprinkle over the parsley.

*Serves 6*

Opposite: Braised
Barramundi with Endives

# FLATHEAD BRAISED
# IN RED WINE

1 kg (2 lbs) flathead fillets

Sauce
60 g (2 oz) clarified butter or
   60 mL (2 fl oz) virgin olive
   oil
1 chopped onion
½ chopped carrot
2 chopped bacon rashers (slices)
1 cup diced tomato
1 tablespoon tomato paste
   (purée)
3 cups (750 mL/24 fl oz)
   good red wine (shiraz or pinot
   noir)
2 garlic cloves, crushed
2 thyme sprigs
1 bay leaf
1 tablespoon peppercorns

1 cup (125 g/4 oz) plain
   (all-purpose) flour
1 teaspoon salt
1 teaspoon ground black pepper
60 g (2 oz) clarified butter or
   60 mL (2 fl oz) olive oil
80 mL (2½ fl oz) Cognac
90 g (3 oz) butter, diced

*To make the sauce*
Melt the clarified butter or heat the olive oil in a heavy-based saucepan. Brown the onion, carrot and bacon over a medium heat, add the tomato and tomato paste (purée) and cook until the mixture begins to stick to the pan. Add the wine and seasonings and cook over a high heat until the mixture is reduced by half. Pass the liquid through a fine sieve.

*To cook the fish*
Remove the bones from the flathead and cut the fish into bite-sized pieces. Place the flour, salt and pepper in a plastic or polythene bag. Add the pieces of flathead and seal the top of the bag. Toss the fish in the bag so that it is evenly coated with the flour. Take the fish from the bag, dusting off the excess flour.

Melt the butter or heat the olive oil in a heavy-based frying pan or skillet. When it is hot, brown the fish on all sides, add the Cognac and flame the liquor, shaking the pan all the time. When the flames die out, add the sauce to the pan. Bring the dish to the boil and simmer for 5 minutes. Add the diced butter, swirling it into the sauce, and serve immediately.

*To serve*
Accompany the flathead with boiled new potatoes and green beans.
*Serves 6*

# GRILLED JOHN DORY
# WITH MARJORAM

1 kg (2 lbs) John Dory fillets,
   skinned

⅓ cup (90 mL/3 fl oz) virgin
   olive oil
1 tablespoon red wine vinegar
½ cup diced tomato
1 tablespoon chopped fresh
   marjoram
salt and freshly ground black
   pepper

Heat half the oil in a frying pan or skillet, preferably nonstick, and grill the fish in the oil over a medium heat, skin side up, for 3 minutes each side, until the flesh is becoming opaque in colour. Remove the fish to hot plates using a slotted spatula. Deglaze the pan with the vinegar, add the tomato dice and marjoram and cook for 1 minute. Add the rest of the oil, and salt and pepper to taste, mix together lightly and then spoon the mixture over the fish.

*To serve*
Serve the fish with a salad or with green beans and steamed potatoes.
*Serves 6*

# SEA SCALLOPS
# WITH SCALLOP ROE RAGOUT

Take the scallops from the shell, clean the flesh and separate the roes from the muscle. Season the scallops.

### To make the vinaigrette
Blanch the shallots in boiling water for 1 minute, then refresh under cold running water. Mix the vinaigrette ingredients together in a bowl with a whisk. Set aside.

### To make the ragoût
Heat 3 tablespoons of the vinaigrette in a small saucepan. Mix together the ragoût ingredients. Add them to the vinaigrette and cook gently until the roes stiffen. Set aside.

### To cook the scallops
Heat the olive oil in a frying pan or skillet until it smokes. Cook the scallops over a medium heat for 2 minutes (1 minute each side).

### To serve
Warm the remaining vinaigrette in a small saucepan. Arrange the scallops in a circle on a large, hot, serving plate. Spoon the warm ragoût into the centre of the plate. Divide the caviar between the scallops, garnish with chervil leaves and then spoon the warm vinaigrette around the scallops.

*Serves 6–8*

36 sea scallops with roes
salt and freshly ground black
    pepper
3 tablespoons olive oil

Vinaigrette
4 golden shallots, finely chopped
3 tablespoons red wine vinegar
½ cup (125 mL/4 fl oz) virgin
    olive oil
3 tablespoons walnut oil
1 teaspoon strong Dijon
    mustard
salt and freshly ground pepper

Ragoût
the scallop roes
1 tablespoon virgin olive oil
½ cup (1 leek) julienne of leek,
    blanched
225 g (7 oz) oyster mushrooms,
    sliced
1 diced medium tomato
3 thyme sprigs
½ cup chervil leaves

Garnish
20 chervil sprigs
6 teaspoons osetra caviar

# JOHN DORY BAKED
# WITH BRIOCHE

Mix together the ingredients for the marinade and spoon over the fish. Leave the fish covered, to marinate, in the refrigerator for 2 hours.

Brush a shallow baking sheet with some of the melted butter. Mix the remainder with the brioche crumbs.

Remove the fish from the marinade. You do not need to reserve the marinade. Place the fillets in one layer on the baking sheet and sprinkle with the brioche crumbs and butter mixture. Bake in a preheated oven (180°C/355°F) for 12–18 minutes, until toasted golden brown.

### To serve
Serve the John Dory hot with a chilled tomato and basil salad.

*Serves 6*

4 large John Dory fillets or
    8 small fillets (skin off)

Marinade
juice of 1 lemon
1 tablespoon chopped fresh
    parsley
2 golden shallots, chopped
freshly ground black pepper
¼ cup (60 mL/2 fl oz) virgin
    olive oil

100 g (3½ oz) butter, melted
2 cups brioche crumbs

# CODDLED SALMON
# WITH RED WINE SAUCE

_We call the fish 'coddled' because, just as a coddled egg is never boiled, and is cooked at a lower temperature than a boiled egg, the same technique is used in cooking the salmon to prevent the protein hardening. By cooking the salmon at a low temperature the protein remains soft and when you eat the fish it literally melts in the mouth. Goose or duck fat is available in tins from specialty shops. If it is unavailable, you can substitute a good quality virgin olive oil. Maintaining the fat at an even temperature can be a problem. I use a domestic deep-fryer set on the very low setting. Experience will tell you the method that suits you best._

### To make the sauce

Melt the butter in a frying pan or skillet over a medium heat and cook the mirepoix and the shallots until they are lightly golden. Add the fish bones and increase the heat so that some caramelisation occurs in the pan. Add the tomato paste (purée) and stir until the mixture begins to stick to the pan. Add the red wine, the herbs and peppercorns and continue cooking until the mixture is reduced by half. Strain the contents of the frying pan or skillet into a small saucepan and skim any fat from the surface. Reduce to about ⅓ cup (100 mL/3½ fl oz) liquid, add the truffle essence and then, still over a medium heat, whisk the butter into the sauce.

Taste for salt and adjust the seasoning as necessary.

### To cook the spinach

Trim and wash the spinach then blanch it in boiling water for 1 minute. Refresh it under cold running water. Melt the butter in a saucepan, add the garlic and cook gently for 3–4 minutes. Remove the garlic with a slotted spoon, add the spinach to the butter and cook, turning slowly with a wooden spoon until heated through. Season as desired.

### To cook the salmon

Heat the fat so it is tepid (70°C/160°F) in a deep saucepan or deep-fryer. Lower the fish into the fat and cook for 12 minutes. Take a piece of fish from the pan and test it to see if it is cooked. You should not be able to see any raw fish; it will be pink, translucent and tender when it is cooked.

### To serve

Spoon some of the spinach into the centre of the heated serving plate and make a bed for the salmon. Drain the salmon on paper towels (absorbent kitchen paper) and place it in the centre of the spinach. Spoon some of the sauce onto the plate and serve.

_Serves 6_

6 × 200 g (6½ oz) pieces of the best fresh salmon, skinned and de-boned
4 cups (1 litre/1¾ imp. pints) goose or duck fat

Sauce
1 tablespoon butter
½ cup mirepoix (page 253)
4 golden shallots, chopped
the bones and head of the salmon
1 tablespoon tomato paste (purée)
2 cups (500 mL/16 fl oz) red wine
2 thyme sprigs
1 bay leaf
½ teaspoon black peppercorns
½ teaspoon truffle essence (optional)
100 g (3½ oz) butter, diced
salt and freshly ground black pepper

1 bunch English spinach
2 tablespoons butter
1 garlic clove, crushed
salt and freshly ground black pepper

Opposite: Coddled Salmon with Red Wine Sauce

# COLD YABBIES A LA NAGE

1 kg (2 lbs) live yabbies
  (crayfish)

Nage
1 cup (250 mL/8 fl oz) virgin
  olive oil
2 cups mirepoix (page 253)
4 garlic cloves, crushed
2 cups (500 mL/16 fl oz) each
  white wine and water
2 each of thyme, marjoram or
  oregano sprigs
1 bay leaf
1 cup chopped tomato, peeled
  and seeded
salt, freshly ground black pepper
  and cayenne pepper
1/2 cup chopped fresh basil

*Yabbies (crayfish) cooked 'in a bath' and served cold are a wonderful buffet dish and children love them.*

Place half the olive oil and all the ingredients for the nage in a deep saucepan and bring to the boil. Reduce the heat and simmer for 10 minutes. Bring to a full rolling boil and add the yabbies (crayfish). Cover the saucepan with a tight-fitting lid and cook for 10 minutes.

*To serve*

Remove the yabbies from the pot with tongs and arrange them on a serving dish. Reduce the nage by one-third over a high heat. Add the remainder of the olive oil to the nage, mix it in and then strain the mixture over the yabbies. Season, then sprinkle the basil over the yabbies. Allow them to cool, and serve with a good garlicky salad and warm, crusty bread.

*Serves 4*

# PRAWNS SAUTEED WITH TOMATO AND TARRAGON

1.5 kg (3 lbs) raw green king
  prawns or large shrimp,
  peeled

80 g (2½ oz) butter (or
  80 mL/2½ fl oz virgin olive
  oil)
4 garlic cloves, crushed
1 teaspoon salt
½ teaspoon freshly ground pepper
⅓ teaspoon cayenne pepper
1 cup chopped tomato, peeled
  and seeded
1 tablespoon tomato paste
  (purée)
²⁄₅ cup (100 mL/3½ fl oz)
  Cognac
⅓ cup fresh tarragon leaves
1 cup (250 mL/8 fl oz) white
  wine
²⁄₅ cup (100 mL/3½ fl oz)
  crème fraîche (page 252) or
  virgin olive oil

*This dish can be prepared in two ways, one using butter and crème fraîche and the other using olive oil. If you would like to serve the prawns (shrimps) cold, use olive oil instead of the butter and crème fraîche. But don't mix the two methods. Either way the sauce is delicious and demands to be mopped up with bread.*

Melt the butter (or heat the olive oil) in a deep frying pan or skillet over a low heat. Add the garlic and cook gently without browning for 2 minutes. Increase the heat, add the prawns or shrimp, salt, pepper and cayenne pepper. Cook the prawns, tossing them continually until they turn red (5–6 minutes). Add the chopped tomato and tomato paste (purée) and continue to cook until the tomato begins to stick to the pan. Add the Cognac and light it. Toss the prawns in the sauce until the flames have died out. Add the tarragon leaves and white wine, then reduce the pan juices by one-half over a high heat. Add the crème fraîche or olive oil and reduce the mixture further, until the sauce reaches a creamy consistency and coats the prawns.

*To serve*

Heap the prawns onto individual plates and serve with finger bowls and large napkins.

*Serves 6*

# PIKE MOUSSELINE
# WITH POACHED SHELLFISH

*Choose the freshest shellfish—mussels, prawns or shrimps and crab are the most suitable. Whiting may be substituted for pike to make the mousseline.*

### To make the mousseline
Refrigerate the ingredients overnight to keep them as cold as possible, and make sure that the cream is fresh.

Purée the fish and thyme with the egg whites in a blender or food processor. Add the cream in a fast stream. Stop the blender or food processor 5 seconds after all the cream has been added. Pass the mixture through the fine blade of a food mill. Add salt and pepper to taste.

Butter 6 dariole moulds (page 252). Spoon the mousseline into the moulds, banging the bottom of the moulds on the bench-top to ensure there are no air bubbles trapped in the mixture.

Fill a baking pan two-thirds full with boiling water. Place the filled moulds in the baking pan and cover the pan loosely with foil. Bake in a slow oven at (150°C/300°F) for 15–20 minutes. When the mousselines are cooked, remove them from the baking pan and allow them to stand for 5 minutes.

### To poach the seafood
Place the ingredients for the poaching liquid (except for the olive oil, parsley leaves, salt and pepper) in a medium saucepan and bring to the boil. Add the mussels and cover the saucepan. When the mussels have opened, remove them from the liquid with a slotted spoon. Add the prawns or shrimps and poach until cooked (3–4 minutes). Remove the prawns with a slotted spoon and slice them in half lengthways. Strain the liquid into another saucepan and reduce over a high heat until the stock becomes syrupy. Return the seafood to the pan, add the olive oil and the parsley leaves, and warm through. Season to taste.

### To serve
Remove the mousselines from the moulds by loosening them with a small knife. Place a warm mousseline in the centre of each plate and spoon the warm seafood in the sauce on top.

*Serves 6–8*

24 mussels
12 large prawns or shrimps, peeled

Mousseline
310 g (10 oz) pike fillets
1 teaspoon fresh thyme leaves
3 egg whites
1²⁄₃ cups (450 mL/ 15 fl oz) heavy whipping (double) cream
salt and freshly ground black pepper

Poaching liquid
⁴⁄₅ cup (200 mL/6½ fl oz) white wine
1 bay leaf
3 golden shallots, finely chopped
½ teaspoon chopped fresh thyme leaves
1 chopped medium tomato
1 garlic clove, crushed
½ cup (125 mL/4 fl oz) virgin olive oil
36 whole leaves of Italian parsley
salt and freshly ground black pepper

# ROASTED LOBSTER
# WITH HERB BUTTER

6 × 400 g (13 oz) live lobsters

Herb butter
250 g (8 oz) butter, softened
1 tablespoon fresh thyme leaves
1 tablespoon fresh marjoram
    leaves
⅓ cup chopped Italian parsley
    leaves
⅓ cup fresh chervil leaves
4 garlic cloves, crushed
4 golden shallots, chopped
¼ cup (60 mL/2 fl oz) Cognac
⅖ cup (100 mL/3½ fl oz)
    white wine
2 tablespoons champagne vinegar
1 tablespoon strong Dijon
    mustard

Place all the ingredients for the herb butter in a food processor or blender and process until smooth. Spoon the butter into a piping bag with a 1 cm (⅓ in.) diameter nozzle.

Use a kitchen steel or a similar instrument to knock a 1 cm (⅓ in.) diameter hole in the top of the lobsters' heads, thus killing them. Pipe the butter into the hole in each lobster's head. You will notice the tail stiffening as the butter goes down the carapace. Retain some of the butter.

Place the lobsters on a baking sheet and pipe a little of the butter on top of the shells. Bake the lobsters in a preheated hot oven (200°C/390°F) for 20 minutes, then take them out of the oven and allow them to rest in a warm place near the oven for 5 minutes.

Split the lobsters in half using a large kitchen knife, pipe a little of the butter onto the flesh and return the lobsters to the oven to melt the butter (2–3 minutes).

*To serve*
Serve each lobster on a plate with a green salad.
*Serves 6*

# YABBIES PROVENCAL

1 kg (2 lbs) live yabbies
    (crayfish)
⅓ cup (100 mL/3½ fl oz)
    virgin olive oil
1 cup mirepoix (page 253)
⅖ cup (100 mL/3½ fl oz)
    Cognac
100 g (3½ oz) tomato paste
    (purée)
2 each thyme, marjoram and
    parsley sprigs
1 bay leaf
⅘ cup (200 mL/6½ fl oz)
    white wine
salt, freshly ground black pepper
    and cayenne pepper
1 chopped garlic clove
1 tablespoon chopped parsley

Heat the oil in a deep, heavy-based saucepan over a high heat. Add the mirepoix and soften briefly over a medium heat without browning. Add the yabbies (crayfish) and toss them in the oil mixture until they colour (approximately 2 minutes).

Pour the Cognac into the pan and light the alcohol as it evaporates. When the flames have died down, add the tomato paste (purée) and continue to toss the yabbies, evenly coating them with the Cognac/tomato mix. Add the herbs, white wine, seasonings and garlic and cook the yabbies for a further 8–10 minutes with the lid on.

*To serve*
Sprinkle the parsley over the yabbies and serve them with individual fingerbowls and good bread.
*Serves 4–6*

Opposite: Roasted Lobster
with Herb Butter

# POACHED SCALLOPS
# WITH CHERVIL VINAIGRETTE

1 kg (2 lbs) sea scallops

1 cup (250 mL/8 fl oz) fish
    stock (page 17)
salt and freshly ground black
    pepper
2 thyme sprigs

Dressing
1 cup fresh chervil sprigs
1 tablespoon strong Dijon
    mustard
¼ cup (60 mL/2 fl oz)
    champagne vinegar
juice of 1 lemon
⅘ cup (200 mL/6½ fl oz)
    virgin olive oil
chervil sprigs to garnish

*The scallops can be served hot or at room temperature.*

Season the fish stock with salt and pepper, add the thyme sprigs, and bring to the boil over a high heat in a deep frying pan or skillet.

Add the scallops and toss them in the stock for 2–3 minutes, or until they are just cooked. Place a strainer over a bowl and strain the stock from the scallops, leaving the scallops to cool in the strainer.

Return the stock to the frying pan or skillet and reduce it, over a high heat, to a glaze.

Place the glaze and all the dressing ingredients in a blender and blend at high speed for 30 seconds.

*To serve*

Arrange the scallops in the centre of a large serving plate and surround them with the sauce. Garnish with sprigs of chervil.

*Serves 6*

# TERRINE OF SEAFOOD
# WITH PASTIS FUMET

Fumet
⅖ cup (100 mL/3½ fl oz)
    virgin olive oil
1 cup mirepoix (page 253)
1 cup fennel root, diced
1 leek, chopped
4 cups (1 litre/1¾ imp. pints)
    fish stock (page 17)
1 cup (250 mL/8 fl oz) white
    wine
½ cup (125 mL/4 fl oz) pastis
    or pernod
1 cup chopped tomato
2 pieces star anise
1 halved head of garlic

*To make the fumet*

Heat the olive oil in a saucepan, add the mirepoix, fennel and leek and soften in the oil over a low heat for 5 minutes. Add the rest of the ingredients and bring to the boil, simmer for 20 minutes and then pass through a fine sieve into a wide pan. Bring to the boil and simmer. Poach each fish in the fumet individually until it is just cooked. The time will vary for each fish, from 2 minutes for the dory, scallops and prawns, to 5 minutes for the salmon, snapper and lobster. As each fish is cooked remove it from the fumet with a wire strainer and drain on paper towel (absorbent kitchen paper). Cover with plastic wrap (cling film) and refrigerate until cold.

*To clarify the fumet*

Allow the fumet to cool to room temperature and then whisk the egg whites through the fumet so that they are thoroughly assimilated. Return the fumet to a moderate heat and bring slowly to the boil. The egg whites will coagulate and thus clarify the fumet. Strain through muslin into another saucepan and add the saffron stamen. Allow to steep for 1 hour.

*To make the jelly*

Soften the leaf gelatin in cold water and add 2 cups (500 mL/16 fl oz) of fumet. Season with the salt and cayenne pepper. Warm the gelatin to dissolve it then whisk and strain the jelly through a fine strainer to eliminate any lumps. Cool the jelly until 'it begins to thicken.

*To make the terrine*

Line a terrine mould (6 cups/1.5 litres/2½ imp. pints) with plastic wrap (cling film) and then with the leek leaves. Leave an overlap of leek leaves to cover the finished terrine. Cover the bottom of the terrine with a little jelly and then layer the seafoods in the terrine, moistening with the jelly as you proceed. When the terrine is full, add the remaining jelly and fold the overlapping leek over the fish. Fold the plastic wrap over, leaving the ends open to allow the jelly to escape when pressed. Reserve the excess jelly.

Cut a piece of wood or plastic to fit the inside of the terrine and place it on top of the terrine, weighed down with a 1 kg (2 lbs) weight. This will press some of the jelly from the ends of the terrine. The jelly should act only to bind the fish. Refrigerate the weighted terrine overnight. Set any remaining jelly and cut into dice.

*To make the sauce*

Reduce 2 cups (5oo mL/16 fl oz) of fumet over a medium heat to ½ cup (125 mL /4 fl oz). Cool the reduced fumet, then put it in the blender and add the oil in a steady stream. Season to taste with salt and pepper.

*To serve*

Slice the terrine into 2 cm (¾ in.) slices and place in the centre of the plate. Surround with the sauce and garnish with the remaining diced jelly, tomato and chervil. Sprinkle with olive oil and serve.

*Serves 15*

Fish
(all fish skinned, boned and
  shelled)
300 g (9½ oz) fillet of salmon,
  in 3 cm (1¼ in.) wide strips
200 g (6½ oz) shelled, uncooked
  large prawns
200 g (6½ oz) uncooked lobster
  tail, cut into 4 strips
300 g (9½ oz) snapper fillet, in
  3 cm (1 in.) strips
200 g (6½ oz) scallops
300 g (9½ oz) whiting fillets

Clarification
6 egg whites
2 pinches saffron stamen

leaves of a large leek
  (20 cm/ 7 in. long), washed
  and blanched

Jelly
8 leaves (2 tablespoons
  powdered) gelatin
2 teaspoons salt
a good pinch of cayenne pepper

Sauce
1 cup (250 mL/ 8 fl oz) virgin
  olive oil
salt and freshly ground black
  pepper

Garnish
½ cup diced tomato flesh
½ cup chervil sprigs

# WHITING BRAISED
# IN SAUVIGNON BLANC

———

Place the fish fillets in a greased baking pan.

Put the wine, thyme, butter, salt and pepper in a saucepan over a medium heat and reduce the mixture by half.

Pour the hot wine mixture over the fish. Shake the baking pan so that the wine is between all the fillets. Bake in a preheated oven (220°C/425°F) for 10 minutes.

Sprinkle with the parsley and serve.

*Serves 6*

12 fillets (1 kg/ 2 lbs) sand whiting
1 tablespoon butter for greasing
3 cups (750 mL/ 24 fl oz)
  fruity sauvignon blanc
3 thyme sprigs
⅖ cup (100 g/ 3½ oz) butter
1 teaspoon salt
½ teaspoon freshly ground pepper
1 tablespoon chopped fresh
  parsley leaves

# The Greengrocer

*Seasonality in produce has largely been eliminated, but it is still a good idea to choose produce according to season. That way you can be sure you are getting the best quality, most flavoursome produce, for the best price. Vegetables are best fresh and young and should require a minimum of cooking.*

The great wholesale markets of large cities receive produce each day from all over the world. Seasonality in produce has been largely eliminated by advances in food-growing technology and transport. Some of these advances have adversely affected the quality of the food we purchase.

The most glaring example of a reduction in the quality of produce is the tomato, where flavour has been exchanged for prolonged life and ease of transport. We consumers like our food to look pretty—no spots or blemishes, no ugly bumps in the wrong places. In order to achieve this marketability, farmers have been forced to become more like factory managers than gardeners. I like ugly vegetables, even if I have to work a bit harder to make them look good on the plate.

Seasonality is, for me, an important aspect of life, and it is still a good idea to choose produce according to season. That way you will be getting the best quality for the best price.

Organic produce does have more flavour but often the price/quality factors make me think twice about purchasing it. I regard organic produce in the same way as I regard any small producers: I encourage and support them to produce specialty vegetables, but I will not buy second-class produce.

Vegetables must be fresh and young so that they require a minimum of cooking. Blanching the vegetables and then heating them in a little butter or oil is a fine way to preserve their nutritional qualities and make them appealing to the eye. It also makes it easier to ensure that everything arrives at the table on time.

Young vegetables have a natural sweetness that we should try to preserve, along with their smell of earth and fresh herbs. These qualities are ephemeral, so we need to treat vegetables with delicacy and not add complex flavours that may mask their natural qualities.

Vegetables are a wonderful counterpoint to main courses, but I prefer to have them as a separate course rather than piled on the plate with meat. Vegetarian meals are a healthy alternative to meat-based dishes. Soups are a particularly good way of incorporating vegetables in a meal and very easy to make if you have a blender or food processor.

In summer, cold vegetable soups and salads come into their own, offering a complete fresh and light summer meal. Vegetables and salads are also excellent when combined with grilled meat or fish. The main ingredient can be simply prepared and then accompanied by more complex and appealing vegetables and salads.

Wild mushrooms are becoming increasingly available and can be used to emphasise the earthy flavours that I find so attractive.

Previous pages: Salad greens

# GARLIC SOUP

*Rustic yet sophisticated, garlic soup becomes a favourite of everyone who tries it. This delicate soup goes very well with Marsanne or Roussanne wines, or a Viognier. It is simple to prepare.*

Melt the butter in a large saucepan over a moderate heat and soften the leek in the butter without browning it. Add the chicken stock, garlic, herbs, salt and pepper. Bring to the boil and simmer for 1 hour. Pass the mixture through the finest blade of a food mill, and then a fine sieve or muslin, squeezing the creamy garlic pulp through the sieve. Return the soup to a clean saucepan and bring to the boil.

Whisk together the egg yolks, cream and Madeira and mix into the boiling soup, whisking as you pour. Take the saucepan off the heat and serve immediately. Do not re-boil the soup or it will curdle and separate.

*To serve*
Ladle the hot soup into warmed bowls. Serve with toasted slices of brioche.

*Serves 6–8*

2 tablespoons butter
1 leek, washed and sliced
6 cups (1.5 litres/ 2½ imp. pints) chicken stock (page 138)
4 heads of garlic, washed, skin on
2 thyme sprigs
1 bay leaf
1 tablespoon salt
freshly ground black pepper to taste

6 egg yolks
⅘ cup (200 mL/ 6½ fl oz) light (single) cream
⅖ cup (100 mL/ 3½ fl oz) Madeira

# ONION SOUP

Brown half the onions gently in the clarified butter over a medium heat. Don't allow them to stew, but slowly caramelise them in the butter. When they are soft and light brown, remove them from the pan, add the rest of the onions and continue in the same manner until they too have softened. Season with pepper, add the wine, the remaining onions and bring to the boil. Reduce the liquid by one-third, then add the stock, bay leaf and thyme and simmer for 30 minutes. Taste and season with salt.

Mix together the egg yolks and cream.

Bring the soup to the boil and add the Madeira or sherry. Bring the soup back to the boil once again and then remove it from the heat and stir in the egg yolk/cream mixture.

*To make the croûtons*
Slice the bread into 1 cm (⅓ in.) thick rounds. Melt the clarified butter and brush the bread rounds with it. Place on a baking sheet and brown in a moderate oven (150°C/300°F).

*To serve*
The soup may be served in warmed individual bowls or in a large tureen. The charm of this winter soup is that it is served so hot that

2 kg (4 lbs) brown onions, finely sliced
100 g (3½ oz) clarified butter
freshly ground black pepper
⅘ cup (200 mL/ 6½ fl oz) white wine
8 cups (2 litres/ 3¼ imp. pints) light beef stock (page 112)
1 bay leaf
3 thyme sprigs
salt to taste

4 egg yolks
⅖ cup (100 mL/ 3½ fl oz) light (single) cream
⅖ cup (100 mL/ 3½ fl oz) good Madeira or oloroso sherry

Croûtons
½ baguette (French bread stick)
2 tablespoons clarified butter
200 g (6½ oz) grated Emmentaler cheese

any personal chill disappears as soon as it appears on the table. At home, I prefer to serve it at the table from a tureen. Ladle the soup into the tureen or bowls and float the croûtons on the surface of the soup. Cover with the grated cheese, place the tureen or bowls in the oven and bake in a hot oven (200°C/390°F) until the cheese begins to brown.

*Serves 8*

# MINESTRONE

4 cups (1 litre/ 1¾ imp. pints) chicken stock (page 138)
½ onion, sliced
2 garlic cloves, crushed
freshly ground black pepper
1 bay leaf
1 thyme sprig

100 g (3½ oz) borlotti beans
100 g (3½ oz) shredded cabbage, blanched
100 g (3½ oz) cauliflower florets, blanched
100 g (3½ oz) broccoli florets, blanched

4 baby turnips, sliced finely and blanched
1 leek, washed, cut in thin rings, and blanched
2 zucchini (courgettes), diced and blanched
100 g (3½ oz) green beans, sliced and blanched
100 g (3½ oz) carrot, sliced thinly and blanched
⅓ cup Italian parsley leaves
salt and freshly ground pepper

6 egg yolks
30 mL (1 fl oz) virgin olive oil
30 g (1 oz) grated pecorino cheese

*Minestrone is a lunch in itself when accompanied by great bread with olive oil drizzled over it. An old-fashioned minestrone would have the vegetables boiled for hours. In this version, I like to keep them fresh and vibrantly coloured. The easiest way to achieve this is to have a large pot of boiling salted water on the stove in which to blanch the vegetables. Place the vegetables in a conical strainer, dip it in the water and cook until just tender. Refresh the vegetables under cold running water, squeezing the excess water from them when they have cooled.*

Soak the borlotti beans overnight in cold water.

Cook them in simmering salted water over a low heat until tender (approximately 50 minutes).

Bring the chicken stock to the boil in a large saucepan over a medium heat, then reduce to a simmer. Simmer the onion, garlic, pepper and herbs in the stock until tender (15 minutes).

Add the beans and the vegetables to the stock mixture and bring to the boil, and then add the parsley leaves. Season to taste with salt and pepper.

Poach the egg yolks in simmering water for 2 minutes. Remove and drain.

*To serve*
Spoon the soup into generous sized bowls, place an egg yolk in the centre of each bowl, sprinkle with a little olive oil and pecorino cheese and serve immediately.

*Serves 6*

Opposite: Minestrone

# SPINACH BOUILLABAISSE

2 bunches of English spinach,
    washed and trimmed
5 tablespoons virgin olive oil
1 onion, peeled and finely
    chopped
300 g (9½ oz) waxy potatoes
salt and freshly ground black
    pepper
½ teaspoon saffron threads
½ teaspoon powdered star anise
4 cups (1 litre/ 1¾ imp. pints)
    boiling water
4 garlic cloves, crushed

6 very fresh eggs

6 slices of good crusty bread
⅖ cup (100 mL/ 3½ fl oz)
    virgin olive oil

*A century old recipe from Provence.*

Blanch the spinach leaves in boiling water for 1 minute; remove and refresh under cold running water. Chop the spinach roughly and then place it in a strainer. Press the excess water from the spinach.

Heat the oil in a deep frying pan or skillet over a medium heat. Soften the chopped onion in the oil and then add the spinach.

Cut the potatoes into 6 mm (¼ in.) slices, and add them to the spinach and onion. Season with salt and pepper. Add the saffron and star anise. Stir the mixture with a wooden spoon and then add the boiling water and the garlic. Simmer until the potatoes are tender (approximately 5 minutes) and then carefully break the eggs onto the surface of your vegetables. Cook gently until the eggs are poached (5 to 6 minutes).

*To serve*

Drizzle the olive oil over the slices of bread.

Place a slice of bread at the bottom of each serving bowl. Carefully lift a portion of the vegetables and a poached egg from the frying pan or skillet with a ladle, and spoon the mixture over the bread.

Serve the soup with knives and forks, as well as spoons.

*Serves 6*

# SPINACH FLORENTINE

2 bunches of English spinach,
    washed and trimmed
8 cups (2 litres/ 3¼ imp. pints)
    water plus 1 tablespoon salt
8 cups (2 litres/ 3¼ imp. pints)
    iced water
⅖ cup (100 mL/ 3½ fl oz)
    virgin olive oil
2 garlic cloves, crushed
salt and freshly ground black
    pepper

Bring the salted water to the boil in a large pot. Add the spinach, pushing it under the boiling water with a spoon. As soon as the leaves have wilted, strain the spinach from the water and plunge it into the iced water.

When the spinach is cold, strain it and press the excess water from it with your hands.

Heat the oil in a saucepan over a medium heat, add the garlic and cook for 2 minutes without browning it. Add the spinach, and season with salt and pepper. Stir vigorously with a wooden spoon until the oil is incorporated and the spinach is hot.

*To serve*

Serve this dish as soon as the spinach is hot.

*Serves 6*

# GREEN ASPARAGUS VINAIGRETTE

Trim and peel the tough outer skin from the asparagus. Cook the asparagus for 5 minutes in boiling salted water with two slices of lemon added. Remove the asparagus and cool in iced water; pat dry. Place the oils, garlic, shallots, lemon juice, truffle essence, vinegar and mustard in a blender and purée. Strain the mixture through a fine sieve and season with salt and pepper.

*To serve*

Arrange the asparagus on a serving platter or individual plates. Spoon the sauce over the asparagus and garnish with tomato dice, enoki and chervil.

*Serves 10*

*1.5 kg (3 lbs) asparagus
  (1 kg/2 lbs trimmed)*
*1 lemon*
*⁴/₅ cup (200 mL/6¹/₂ fl oz)
  virgin olive oil*
*²/₅ cup (100 mL/3¹/₂ fl oz)
  walnut oil*
*1 garlic clove, peeled*
*6 large golden shallots*
*60 mL (2 fl oz) lemon juice*
*¹/₂ teaspoon truffle essence*
*60 mL (2 fl oz) sherry vinegar*
*1 teaspoon Dijon mustard*
*salt and freshly ground pepper*
*4 tomatoes, diced*
*100 g (3¹/₂ oz) enoki
  mushrooms*
*1 bunch chervil (20 sprigs)*

# ARTICHOKES BRAISED
# IN OLIVE OIL

*To trim the artichokes*

Break off or trim the large outer leaves and the stem with a small knife, leaving approximately 8 cm (3 in.) attached to the heart. Use a vegetable peeler to remove the bitter fibre from the outside of the stem, leaving only the tender, pale flesh. Mix together the lemon juice and water and dip each artichoke in the mixture as you trim it, to prevent discolouration.

Heat the olive oil in a large saucepan, add the onion, carrot and garlic and cook over a very low heat. After 5 minutes, add the prepared artichokes and stir to cover with the oil and vegetables.

Season the artichokes with the salt and pepper and herbs, and continue to cook slowly. When the vegetables look as though they are about to brown, add the wine to moisten the artichokes and then cover with a tight lid. Add the water in small amounts from time to time to prevent the artichokes drying out. Continue to cook over a low heat until the artichokes are tender (approximately 1 hour) and the sauce is reduced to the consistency of a vinaigrette.

*To serve*

Serve the artichokes warm or cold. To make this dish grander, carrot and onion rings can be cooked separately and then mixed with olives and Italian parsley leaves for a fresh, colourful garnish.

*Serves 6*

*6 large globe artichokes,
  trimmed*
*60 ml (2 fl oz) lemon juice*
*4 cups (1 litre/1³/₄ imp. pints)
  water*

*155 mL (5 fl oz) virgin olive
  oil*
*1 onion, finely diced*
*1 medium carrot, finely diced*
*2 garlic cloves, crushed*
*1 teaspoon salt*
*freshly ground black pepper*
*2 parsley sprigs*
*2 thyme sprigs*
*2 bay leaves*
*155 ml (5 fl oz) white wine*
*155 ml (5 fl oz) water*

# TOMATO TERRINE

Cut the tomatoes diagonally into quarters, remove the outside flesh in a clean piece (petal) and reserve 200 g (6½ oz) of the interior pulp for the sauce.

Spread a dishtowel on a tray and arrange the petals in rows with the outside of the tomato facing down. Season the tomatoes with salt and pepper and thyme leaves, and then turn them over and season the other side. The salt will cause the tomatoes to sweat. Leave them for 2 hours and then press lightly with another dishtowel to absorb the extra moisture. This concentrates the flavour of the tomatoes.

Place the stock, vinegar, tomato juice and seasonings in a saucepan and simmer for half an hour. Allow to cool. When cold, whisk the egg whites through the stock until they are thoroughly incorporated. Slowly bring the stock back to the boil, taking care that the egg white does not stick and cause burning on the bottom of the pan. Simmer for 15 minutes. The stock should be clear except for the coagulated egg white. Strain through muslin or a fine sieve.

Measure 4 cups (1 litre/1¾ imp. pints) of the stock mixture into a bowl. Soften the gelatin in a little cold water, remove and incorporate the gelatin (not the water) into the stock. If you are using powdered gelatin, follow the manufacturer's instructions on how to make a firm jelly.

Line a terrine mould (6 cups/1.5 litres/2½ imp. pints) with plastic wrap (cling film), spoon in some of the liquefied jelly to cover the bottom of the mould and then layer the petals tightly, moistening with the jelly as you proceed.

Start with the outside of the tomato down, then, when the mould is half filled, have the outside facing up, reversing the directions.

It is very important to ensure that there is jelly moistening each layer. When the mould is filled pour in enough jelly to cover the tomato and tap the mould to ensure that there are no air bubbles.

Wrap plastic wrap over the terrine, leaving the ends open. Cut a piece of wood to fit inside the top of the mould. Place the wood on top of the mould and weigh it down with a 1 kg (2 lbs) weight. This will force any excess jelly from the mould through the open ends of the plastic. The jelly should only act as a glue and should not be visible between the layers.

Clean away the jelly from the outside of the mould and refrigerate overnight with the weight in place.

### To make the sauce
Place all the ingredients for the sauce in a blender and purée. Pass through a fine sieve, then adjust the seasoning.

2 kg (4 lbs) ripe tomatoes, blanched and peeled
1 tablespoon Maldon sea salt
freshly ground black pepper
1 tablespoon fresh thyme leaves

Jelly
4 cups (1 litre/1¾ imp. pints) veal stock (page 112)
⅖ cup (100 mL/3½ fl oz) sherry vinegar
155 mL (5 fl oz) tomato juice
½ tablespoon salt
1 bay leaf
6 fresh basil leaves
4 egg whites
15 gelatin leaves (page 252)

Sauce
155 mL (5 fl oz) virgin olive oil
80 mL (2½ fl oz) sherry vinegar
200 g (6½ oz) tomato pulp and seeds
2 golden shallots, peeled
1 garlic clove, crushed
1 teaspoon salt
2 fresh basil leaves
freshly ground black pepper

Opposite: Tomato Terrine

*To unmould the terrine*

Remove the weight and the wood and then gently pull on the plastic wrap, easing the terrine from the mould.

*To serve*

Cut the terrine into 1 cm (⅓ in.) thick slices, surround with the sauce and serve with a little freshly ground black pepper on top.

*Serves 12*

# ARTICHOKES WITH SPINACH

6 globe artichokes, trimmed
2 bunches of English spinach,
   trimmed and washed
⅖ cup (100 mL/ 3½ fl oz)
   virgin olive oil
2 garlic cloves, crushed
salt and freshly ground black
   pepper

Blanch the artichokes in boiling water for 7 minutes. Remove and drain.

Press any excess water from the artichokes and slice them into 2 cm (¾ in.) thick rounds. Chop the raw spinach roughly.

Heat the olive oil in a heavy saucepan over a low heat. Add the garlic and cook gently for 2 minutes. Add the artichokes and season with salt and pepper. Cover with a lid and cook very gently for 5 minutes. Add the spinach and cook, covered, until the artichokes are tender (approximately 10 minutes).

*To serve*

Serve the artichokes and spinach with grilled meats or poultry.

*Serves 6*

# JERUSALEM ARTICHOKES

1 kg (2 lbs) Jerusalem
   artichokes
100 g (3½ oz) butter
freshly ground black pepper
155 mL (5 fl oz) chicken stock
   (page 138)
1 thyme sprig
1 bay leaf
3 garlic cloves, crushed

Peel and wash the artichokes, then cut them into quarters and blanch them in boiling salted water for 5 minutes. Wash them under cold water. Melt the butter in a heavy saucepan or casserole dish, add the artichokes, season with pepper and turn them with a wooden spoon, coating them with the butter. Add the chicken stock, thyme, bay leaf and garlic, and cook over a low heat. When the artichokes are nearly tender, approximately 10 minutes, increase the heat and glaze them by reducing the stock by half.

*To serve*

Jerusalem artichokes are delicious served with fish or duck.

*Serves 6*

# CELERIAC FRENCH STYLE

*Celeriac is a large, knobbly, swollen root with a distinctive celery flavour and for this reason it is sometimes known as celery root or knob celery. It is a versatile winter vegetable to add to soups as well as to grate and serve raw as an hors d'oeuvre or as part of a salad.*

Trim, pare and slice or dice the celeriac and place it in cold water to keep white. Drain and dry with paper towel (absorbent kitchen paper).

In a frying pan or skillet, heat 1 tablespoon of the butter and add the celeriac. Simmer over a slow heat for 5 minutes.

Barely cover the vegetable with hot beef stock, cover the pan and cook rapidly until the vegetable is tender and the liquid greatly reduced.

Press the egg yolk through a fine sieve and add it to the celeriac along with the capers. Blend the remaining tablespoon of butter with the flour and drop it piece by piece into the mixture, shaking the pan to blend thoroughly. Simmer until the mixture is thickened and, just before serving, add the parsley.

*Serves 6–8*

1 kg (2 lbs) celeriac
2 tablespoons butter
2 cups (500 mL/16 fl oz) hot beef stock (page 112)
1 hard-boiled egg yolk
1 teaspoon minced (ground) capers
1 tablespoon plain (all-purpose) flour
1 tablespoon finely chopped fresh parsley

# CELERIAC PUREE

*This method of cooking can also be used for Jerusalem artichokes, carrots and other root vegetables. Celeriac purée is the perfect accompaniment to a pork dish.*

Bring the water with the salt added to the boil in a large saucepan.

Add the potatoes and celeriac and cook until tender (approximately 10 minutes). Drain off the water, allow the vegetables to dry and then pass them through the fine blade of a food mill and return them to the saucepan. Beat the cream and then the butter into the purée over a low heat. Season with salt and pepper.

*Serves 6*

500 g (1 lb) celeriac, cleaned and diced
250 g (8 oz) potatoes, cleaned and diced
4 cups (1 litre/1¾ imp. pints) water
1 tablespoon salt

½ cup (125 mL/4 fl oz) heavy whipping (double) cream
½ cup (125 g/4 oz) soft butter
salt and freshly ground black pepper

53

# TART OF SPRING VEGETABLES

6 individual 23 cm (9 in.) tart
cases baked blind (page 252)

6 baby turnips, trimmed and
washed
12 baby carrots, trimmed and
washed
12 baby (pearl) onions, peeled
300 g (9½ oz) green beans
1 tablespoon butter
60 mL (2 fl oz) white wine
12 champignon mushrooms
6 shiitake mushrooms
1 bunch English spinach,
trimmed and washed
freshly ground black pepper

²⁄₅ cup (100 mL/3½ fl oz)
virgin olive oil
salt and freshly ground black
pepper
1 tablespoon blanched and
puréed basil

Cook the turnips, carrots, onions and green beans in boiling salted water until tender, approximately 7–10 minutes. Strain and set aside.

Place the butter, wine and mushrooms in a saucepan with some ground black pepper and cook until the mushrooms are tender. Set aside.

Blanch the spinach in boiling water for 1 minute. Drain and season.

Heat the olive oil in a small saucepan, and gently cook the spinach for 2 minutes.

Line the bottom of the tart cases with the spinach and then arrange the other vegetables on top. Heat in a preheated moderate oven (150°C/300°F) for 5 minutes.

*To serve*
Mix together the oil, salt, pepper and basil, and spoon around the tart.
*Serves 6*

# CAULIFLOWER MOUSSE

500 g (1 lb) cauliflower, florets
only
100 g (3½ oz) potato, peeled
and cut into 2 cm (¾ in.)
cubes

60 g (2 oz) butter
155 mL (5 fl oz) heavy
whipping (double) cream
2 tablespoons grated Parmesan
cheese
pinch cayenne pepper
salt and freshly ground black
pepper

*The same method of cooking can be used for other vegetables, particularly peas and carrots, although it is advisable to put those through a food mill after the initial cooking to avoid the texture of the pea skins and possible lumps of carrot.*

Cook the cauliflower in boiling salted water with the potato for 12 minutes, or until tender. Drain the water from the vegetables and toss them over the heat source to evaporate any excess water.

Put the vegetables in a blender. Add the rest of the ingredients and purée. Return to the saucepan, heat through and serve immediately.

*To serve*
Almost like a sauce, this mousse is wonderful with lamb or roasted fowl.
*Serves 6*

Opposite: Tart of Spring
Vegetables

# CURRIED PARSNIP SOUP

*500 g (1 lb) parsnips, peeled (4 medium parsnips)*
*1 onion*
*1 leek, white only*
*60 g (2 oz) butter*
*2 garlic cloves, peeled*
*2.5 cm (1 in.) piece fresh ginger root*
*1 tablespoon curry powder*
*600 mL (19 fl oz) chicken stock (page 138)*
*salt and freshly ground black pepper*
*⁴/₅ cup (200 mL/6½ fl oz) crème fraîche (page 252)*

Chop the parsnips, onion and leek into small pieces. Melt the butter in a large saucepan, and add the vegetables and garlic. Cook over a low heat for 5 minutes, until softened. Add the ginger and curry powder and cook gently for a further 5 minutes. Add the chicken stock and seasoning, and continue to cook until the vegetables are tender, about 15 minutes.

Pass the mixture through the blender or food processor and check the seasoning.

*To serve*

Return the soup to the saucepan and heat it through. Serve the soup hot, garnished with a dollop of crème fraîche and accompanied by cucumber sandwiches.

*Serves 6–8*

# GRATIN OF WHITE ASPARAGUS

*4 bunches thick white asparagus peeled of their tough outer skin*
*12 cups (3 litres/4¾ imp. pints) boiling salted water*

*Sauce*
*5 eggs*
*²/₅ cup (100 mL/3½ fl oz) water*
*300 g (9½ oz) butter*
*juice of 1 lemon*
*salt and freshly ground black pepper*
*⁴/₅ cup (200 mL/6½ fl oz) heavy whipping (double) cream*

Cook the asparagus in the water for 15 minutes. Remove the asparagus from the boiling water with a strainer, drain and dry with a tea towel. Retain the cooking water for the sauce.

Whisk together the eggs and the water in a stainless steel bowl. Whisk the egg mix over the boiling cooking water until it begins to thicken. Heat the butter to tepid, then whisk it into the mixture in a thin stream until it is assimilated into the egg mixture.

Remove the saucepan from the heat and whisk in the lemon juice. Season to taste, fold in the whipped cream, taste again for salt and adjust as necessary.

*To serve*

Place the asparagus on individual plates. Cover the tips halfway with the sauce and then brown under a grill (broiler).

*Serves 6*

# CREAM OF LEEK SOUP WITH CEPES

*Cèpes (porcini mushrooms) are increasingly becoming available in autumn and spring and add a complex, earthy flavour to this hearty soup.*

Melt the butter in a saucepan over a low heat, add the leeks, garlic and celery and cook gently with the lid on until the vegetables have softened (approximately 5 minutes). Sprinkle with the flour and stir constantly with a wooden spoon for 2–3 minutes.

Put the vegetables in a blender or food processor with 2 cups (500 mL/16 fl oz) of the stock and purée them. Pass the puréed vegetables through the medium blade of a food mill and return to the saucepan. Add the rest of the stock and mix thoroughly with a whisk. Bring to the boil and simmer for 5 minutes. Add the crème fraîche and season with salt and pepper. Keep the mixture hot while you prepare the sippets and cèpes.

### To make the sippets

Melt the clarified butter in a saucepan over a low heat and fry the sippets until golden brown. Drain on paper towels (absorbent kitchen paper) and then transfer to a serving bowl.

### To cook the cèpes

Melt the butter in a frying pan or skillet until it begins to brown. Add the cèpes and cook over a high heat. When the cèpes soften, add the garlic and season with salt and pepper. Add the parsley and stir in gently, toss the cèpes in the pan contents and then add them to the hot soup.

### To serve

Serve the soup hot and offer the sippets separately.

*Serves 8*

3 tablespoons butter
6 leeks, washed and sliced
3 garlic cloves, crushed
1 stick of celery, washed and finely sliced
1 tablespoon plain (all-purpose) flour
4 cups (1 litre/ 1¾ imp. pints) chicken stock (page 138)
⅖ cup (100 mL/ 3½ fl oz) crème fraîche (page 252)
salt and freshly ground black pepper

Sippets
2 tablespoons clarified butter
1 cup of bread cut into 1 cm (⅓ in.) dice

Cèpes
2 tablespoons butter
200 g (6½ oz) cèpes (porcini mushrooms), diced
1 garlic clove, crushed
salt and freshly ground black pepper
2 tablespoons chopped fresh parsley

# TOMATOES BAKED
# WITH SAFFRON

———

6 good sized vine-ripened
  tomatoes, peeled
4 golden shallots, finely chopped
3 garlic cloves, crushed
350 mL (11½ fl oz) heavy
  whipping (double) cream
1 teaspoon saffron threads
6 small thyme sprigs
2 bay leaves
½ teaspoon salt
freshly ground black pepper

Place all the ingredients except the tomatoes in a saucepan. Bring to the boil and simmer for 5 minutes.

Place the tomatoes in a baking or gratin pan, stem sides down, and spoon over the cream mixture.

Bake in a hot oven (200°C/390°F) for 12–15 minutes, until the cream has thickened slightly, and then serve.

*Serves 6*

# BRAISED BELGIAN ENDIVE

———

1 kg (2 lbs) Belgian endives
  (witloof)
4 cups (1 litre/1¾ imp. pints)
  water
⅖ cup (100 mL/3½ fl oz)
  lemon juice

**Method 1**
10 thin bacon rashers (slices)
155 g (5 oz) butter
1 garlic clove, crushed
600 mL (19 fl oz) chicken
  stock (page 138)
6 thyme sprigs
salt and freshly ground black
  pepper

**Method 2**
2 cups (500 mL/16 fl oz)
  white wine
½ cup (125 mL/4 fl oz) virgin
  olive oil
2 garlic cloves, crushed
1 cup chopped tomato, peeled
  and seeded
½ cup chopped black olives
6 thyme sprigs
6 marjoram sprigs
⅓ cup chopped Italian parsley

Opposite: Tomatoes Baked
with Saffron

*This dish can be served as a first course or as an accompaniment to roast fowls.*

Clean the endives (witloof) and remove the unsightly outer leaves. Bring the water and lemon juice to the boil in a large saucepan. Add the endives and cook for 5 minutes to wilt them and get rid of excess bitterness. Drain on paper towels (absorbent kitchen paper) and press to remove excess water.

*To cook using method 1*

Wrap each endive in bacon. Melt the butter in a heavy baking pan over a low heat. Add the garlic and cook gently without browning for 2–3 minutes. Add the endives, chicken stock and thyme. Season with salt and pepper. Bring the mixture to the boil and then cover lightly with aluminium kitchen foil and bake in a low oven (120°C/245°F) for 45 minutes.

Take the pan from the oven and place it over a high heat until the remaining liquid is reduced to a glaze. Serve immediately.

*To cook using method 2*

Precook the endives as before. Place the wine, olive oil and garlic in a heavy baking pan. Add the endives and then the tomato, olives, thyme and marjoram. Bring the mixture to the boil over a high heat and reduce the cooking liquid by half. Cover lightly with aluminium kitchen foil and finish cooking in a low oven for 30 minutes. Sprinkle with the parsley just before serving.

*Serves 8*

# CARROT SPAGHETTINI
# WITH CHERVIL

3 cups (500 g/1 lb) carrot,
  cleaned
60 g (2 oz) butter
²⁄₅ cup (100 mL/3½ fl oz)
  water
salt and freshly ground black
  pepper
2 pinches white granulated sugar
1 cup chervil sprigs

*Carrot and daikon (Japanese white radish) lend themselves to unusual decorative presentations. Implements such as a Japanese mandoline can transform them into shreds and ribbons that can be lightly steamed or tossed in stock and then flavoured with appropriate herbs and spices.*

Using the medium blade of the mandoline, run the carrots through lengthwise to make spaghettini-type strands. Place all the ingredients, except the chervil, in a small saucepan with a tight fitting lid. Bring to the boil over a high heat and cook for 3 minutes. Remove the mixture from the heat and allow to cool. Add the chervil to the cooled carrot and then form into small nests with your fingers. Warm the nests in a preheated oven (170°C/340°F) for 3–4 minutes before serving.

*Serves 6*

# WHITE RADISH SHAVINGS
# WITH CITRUS VINAIGRETTE

500 g (1 lb) white radish,
  cleaned
2 tablespoons orange juice
2 tablespoons lemon juice
¼ cup (60 mL/2 fl oz) walnut
  oil
salt and freshly ground black
  pepper

Grasp the radish in one hand and a vegetable peeler in the other hand. Twist the radish around clockwise and then proceed to take long shavings from the radish, turning it continually until the radish is reduced to a pile of shavings.

Place the radish shavings in a saucepan with the other ingredients, and season lightly with salt and pepper. Cook over a medium heat until it begins to wilt (approximately 5 minutes), then serve immediately.

*Serves 6*

# FRIED GARLIC BULBS

*Often when I cook vegetables I put a bruised clove of garlic in the cooking water to add to the flavour. You may think that garlic is a social no-no but I have found that if the garlic used is fresh, and it is boiled in some way, then the effects of garlic are only beneficial. No bad breath results when garlic is used in this way. The garlic in the following recipe is sweet and an interesting side dish for grilled beef and lamb. Green garlic has supple, moist outside skin, not the dry skin of the older garlic.*

Mix the water, milk, salt, thyme and bay leaf and bring to the boil. Add the garlic and simmer for 1 hour, until well cooked. Drain the garlic and cool. Season the flour and place it in a plastic bag. Add the cooked heads of garlic and toss them in the flour. Remove the garlic from the flour and shake any excess flour off the heads of garlic.

Heat the olive oil in a deep fryer to 160°C (315°F) and fry until golden brown and crisp on the outside. Drain on paper towels (absorbent kitchen paper) and serve.

*Serves 6*

*6 heads of green young garlic*

*2 cups (500 mL/16 fl oz) water*
*2 cups (500 mL/16 fl oz) milk*
*salt*
*2 thyme sprigs*
*1 bay leaf*

*100 g (3½ oz) plain (all-purpose) flour*
*salt and freshly ground pepper*
*virgin olive oil for frying*

# LEMON TURNIPS

*In this dish of Japanese origin, turnips marinated in the smooth tartness of lemon and in sweet vinegar are both refreshingly crisp and full of flavour.*

The sweet vinegar can be quickly prepared by mixing together half a cup (125 mL/4 fl oz) of rice vinegar with half a tablespoon of honey or white granulated sugar. Rice vinegar can be found in Asian foodstores and some supermarkets.

Halve or quarter then thinly slice the large turnips (small ones need only be sliced). Sprinkle with salt then toss until the turnip is fully coated. Let stand for 2 hours, until the slices become soft and water is given off. Firmly but gently squeeze out any remaining water.

Place the turnip slices in a bowl with the lemon and the sweet vinegar and refrigerate overnight to crispen the vegetable. It will keep for 2–3 days using this method.

*Serves 4–6*

*10 small (or 5 large) turnips, greens trimmed, peeled*
*1 teaspoon salt*
*½ lemon, quartered*
*½ cup (125 mL/4 fl oz) sweet vinegar (see method)*

# POMMES ANNA

Peel the potatoes. Cut them into equal-sized pieces using a knife or a cookie cutter. Slice them into thin rounds on a mandoline. Wash in cold water and dry with paper towels (absorbent kitchen paper).

Melt the butter in a small saucepan and simmer the garlic in the butter for 2–3 minutes. Pour half the butter and garlic mixture into a round (20 cm/8 in. diameter) baking pan. Lay the sprigs of thyme on the butter and arrange the slices of potato in overlapping circles until the baking pan is filled. Season with salt and pepper. Pour the remaining butter and garlic mixture over the potatoes, then place the baking pan over a high heat until the butter begins to fry the potatoes. Transfer the dish to a hot oven (200°C/390°F) and cook for 45 minutes, or until the potatoes are golden on top.

*To serve*

Turn out the potatoes from the baking pan and cut into wedges.

*To turn out the potatoes*

Lay a dishcloth flat on the kitchen bench. Take the pan of potatoes from the oven and place it in the centre of the dishcloth. Take a 40 cm (16 in.) diameter plate, turn it upside down and put it on top of the potatoes. Bring the edges of the dishcloth up over the plate and tighten it so that you have a firm grip on it, and the plate and the potatoes are held together firmly. Quickly turn the lot so that the potatoes are uppermost, then tap the bottom of the baking dish to loosen them. Remove the baking dish, thus exposing the golden, crisp potatoes.

*Serves 6*

*1 kg (2 lbs) long oval potatoes*
*200 g (6½ oz) clarified butter*
*2 garlic cloves, crushed*
*3–4 thyme sprigs*
*salt and freshly ground black*
  *pepper*

# GLAZED ONIONS

Put the onions and the melted butter into a saucepan. Stir over a low heat until the vegetables are coated with the butter. Add the rest of the ingredients and cook very slowly, stirring occasionally, until the onions are tender and the liquid is completely reduced (about 20 minutes).

Serve as an accompaniment to roast beef or chicken.

*Serves 6–8 as an accompaniment*

*750 g (1½ lbs) small white*
  *onions, peeled*
*4 tablespoons melted butter*
*1 cup (250 mL/8 fl oz)*
  *chicken stock (page 138)*
*2 tablespoons white granulated*
  *sugar*
*½ teaspoon salt*

Opposite: Pommes Anna

# TIAN PROVENCAL

1 kg (2 lbs) potatoes
90 mL (3 fl oz) virgin olive oil
6 garlic cloves, crushed
2 bay leaves
1 tablespoon fresh thyme leaves
salt and freshly ground black
    pepper
1¼ cups (310 mL/10 fl oz)
    water

*This recipe is similar to Pommes Anna, but it requires a little less attention to detail. It is very good with roasted lamb and beef.*

Peel, finely slice and wash the potatoes. Pour the olive oil into a baking pan and brush it around the sides. Mix together the sliced potatoes, garlic, herbs and seasonings and pile into the baking pan. Press the mixture down firmly. Boil the water and pour it over the potatoes. Bake at 180°C (355°F) for 1 hour, or until the potatoes are tender and golden on top.

*Serves 6*

# MASHED POTATO

1 kg (2 lbs) peeled potatoes,
    preferably Idaho
2 teaspoons salt
⅖ cup (100 mL/3½ fl oz) light
    (single) cream
1 teaspoon freshly ground white
    pepper
1 teaspoon meat glaze or truffle
    essence (optional)
200 g (6½ oz) butter, diced

Cut the potatoes into 3 cm (1¼ in.) cubes and place in a large saucepan. Cover with cold water, add 1 teaspoon of salt and bring to the boil. Simmer for 12 minutes. Drain the water from the saucepan and return the saucepan to the heat to briefly, to evaporate the small amount of water remaining.

Add the cream, beating it in with a strong whisk. Season with the remaining salt, and the pepper. Add the meat glaze or truffle essence and then beat in the butter over a low heat.

Serve the mashed potato very hot.

*Serves 8*

# CEPES SAUTEED
# A LA PROVENCAL

2 kg (4 lbs) cèpes (porcini
    mushrooms)
⅖ cup (100 mL/3½ fl oz)
    virgin olive oil
salt and freshly ground black
    pepper
1 tablespoon lemon juice

Persillade
4 garlic cloves, crushed and
    chopped
1 cup chopped fresh parsley

Heat the oil in a large frying pan or skillet. Add the cèpes and cook over a medium heat for 10 minutes. Season with salt and pepper. Add the persillade (garlic and parsley mixture), toss through, season with lemon juice and serve.

*Serves 6–8*

# GRILLED CEPES

*I first had this dish in Florence and asked what the herb was that the chef had used. They did not know the English name for the herb but said it was like a wild mint. The herb was marjoram, which is closely related to mint and basil. Large field mushrooms are a good substitute if cèpes (porcini) are not available.*

Steep the garlic in the oil for 2 hours before using it. Brush a nonstick frying pan or skillet with half of the oil and heat over a high heat. Season each cèpe with salt and pepper and press two marjoram sprigs on the skin. Cook each cèpe, skin side down, for 3–4 minutes, adding a little more oil if necessary.

Lay the cèpes on a baking sheet and sprinkle with chopped marjoram, the remaining oil and some extra pepper. Bake in a very hot oven (210°C/410°F) for 10 minutes.

*To serve*

Present the cèpes skin side up, sprinkled with any oil remaining in the baking dish, and with the chopped parsley.

*Serves 6*

*6 large cèpes (porcini mushrooms), (approximately 1 kg/ 2 lbs)*
*3 garlic cloves, crushed*
*⁴⁄₅ cup (200 mL/ 6½ fl oz) virgin olive oil*
*salt and freshly ground black pepper*
*12 marjoram sprigs*
*2 tablespoons chopped fresh marjoram*
*⅓ cup chopped fresh parsley*

# TIMBALE OF BROCCOLI

*A decorative way to serve George Bush's favourite vegetable. Recommended with Roasted Barbary Duck Glazed with Peppercorns (page 140) and Leg of Boar with Soured Cherries (page 160).*

Butter 6–8 cup-sized dariole moulds (page 252).

Trim the broccoli into small, 3 cm (1¼ in.) florets and cook in boiling salted water for 6–8 minutes, or until tender. Drain and cool under cold running water. Pat dry the cold broccoli with paper towels (absorbent kitchen paper).

Put the cream into a small saucepan with the bay leaf, salt and pepper. Bring to the boil and simmer for 5 minutes. Meanwhile, whisk the eggs in a bowl for approximately 2 minutes. Strain the cream and add to the eggs. Whisk continuously for 1 minute, then allow to cool.

Put the broccoli in the dariole moulds with the outside of the florets on the outside of the moulds and the stems facing towards the centre. Press more broccoli into the centre of the moulds to make sure it is not loose. Carefully pour the egg/cream mixture into the moulds.

Place the moulds in a baking pan filled to a depth of 3 cm (1¼ in.) with boiling water. Cover the pan loosely with kitchen foil and bake in a moderate oven (180°C/300°F) for 25 minutes, or until the cream is set. Turn out with the aid of a small knife and serve.

*Serves 6–8*

*1 kg (2 lbs) broccoli*

*1¼ cups (310 ml/ 10 fl oz) light (single) cream*
*1 bay leaf*
*1 teaspoon salt*
*½ teaspoon freshly ground black pepper*
*4 whole eggs*

# STUFFED EGGPLANTS

2 × 500 g (1 lb) eggplants
  (aubergines)
salt

340 mL (11 fl oz) virgin olive
  oil
1/2 cup diced onion
3 garlic cloves, crushed
1 teaspoon fresh thyme leaves
1 teaspoon ground coriander
  seeds
1 teaspoon ground cardamom
  seeds
2 bay leaves
1/3 cup chopped fresh parsley
1 cup diced tomato, peeled and
  seeded
salt and freshly ground black
  pepper
virgin olive oil

*I have always liked the original name for this Middle Eastern dish, Imam Bayeldi, which means 'The Imam swooned'. The dish was named this because of the high cost of the olive oil!*

Cut the eggplants (aubergines) in half lengthwise and scoop the flesh in one piece from the centre, leaving the skin with 1 cm (1/3 in.) of flesh remaining. Sprinkle the interior with salt and leave cut side down on a paper towel (absorbent kitchen paper). Dice the scooped flesh and sprinkle with salt, leave for 30 minutes, then press the moisture from the flesh. Rinse under cold running water.

Heat the oil in a deep frying pan or skillet and gently cook the onion and garlic. Add the eggplant flesh and cook until it is translucent. Add the herbs and spices and the tomato. Finish cooking over a high heat for approximately 2–3 minutes. Season to taste.

Wipe the interior of the eggplant halves dry with a paper towel and fill with the mixture from the frying pan. Sprinkle with olive oil and bake in a moderate oven (150°C/300°F) for 30 minutes. Serve warm.

*Serves 6*

# BRAISED PEAS

500 g (1 lb) shelled green peas

2 tablespoons butter
6 golden shallots, peeled and
  sliced
1 garlic clove, crushed
4/5 cup (200 mL/6 1/2 fl oz)
  chicken stock (page 138)

Melt the butter in a saucepan over a medium heat. Add the shallots and garlic. Cook, stirring with a wooden spoon, until soft. Add the peas and the chicken stock, bring to the boil and simmer the peas until tender (approximately 10 minutes).

Strain the stock from the peas and reduce the stock in a separate saucepan over a high heat until it is a glaze. Return the peas to the stock, heat and serve.

*Serves 6*

Opposite: Stuffed
Eggplants

# FRESH PEA SOUP

2 tablespoons butter

2 leeks, washed and sliced

freshly ground black pepper

100 g (3½ oz) peeled and
    cooked potato

500 g (1 lb) young peas, shelled
    and blanched

4 cups (1 litre/1¾ imp. pints)
    chicken stock, cooled
    (page 138)

⅖ cup (100 mL/3½ fl oz)
    crème fraîche (page 252)

salt and freshly ground black
    pepper

Melt the butter in a saucepan over a low heat. Add the leeks and cook until they are soft. Season with ground pepper.

Put the leeks in a blender or food processor with the potato and peas and half of the cold chicken stock. Purée the vegetables. If you like a fine, creamy texture, pass the purée through the fine blade of a food mill.

Return the purée to the saucepan, add the rest of the stock and the crème fraîche, bring to the boil and season.

*To serve*

Serve with slices of toasted brioche.

*Serves 6*

# WILD MUSHROOM TART

100 g (3½ oz) butter

12 golden shallots, chopped

4 garlic cloves, crushed

1 kg (2 lbs) mixed wild
    mushrooms (cèpes, slippery
    jacks, morels, champignons,
    etc) cut into 3–5 cm
    (1–2 in.) pieces

1 teaspoon fresh thyme leaves

1 tablespoon chopped fresh
    marjoram

1 tablespoon chopped fresh basil

3 tablespoons roughly chopped
    Italian parsley

salt and freshly ground pepper

6 × 15 cm (6 in.) discs of puff
    pastry (page 201)

1 egg

¼ cup (60 mL/2 fl oz) light
    (single) cream

1 cup diced tomato, peeled and
    seeded

155 g (5 oz) Roquefort or
    Meredith Blue cheese, diced

Melt the butter in a deep frying pan or skillet over a medium heat, and cook the shallots for 2 minutes. Add the garlic, then increase the heat and add the mushrooms, tossing them continually. Add the herbs and season with salt and pepper. Allow to cool. (This section may be prepared in advance.)

Prick the discs of pastry all over with a fork. Whisk the egg into the cream. Brush the discs with the egg wash and then lay them on a flat baking sheet.

Add the tomato and cheese to the mushroom mixture and divide the mixture into 6, spooning it onto the centre of the discs of pastry.

Bake in a preheated oven (180°C/355°F) for 20 minutes, or until the pastry is golden.

Serve immediately on hot plates.

*Serves 6*

# BRAISED LONG BEANS WITH BLACK MUSHROOMS

————

*A quick, simple dish which preserves the juicy character of the vegetable. Fresh green string beans may be used instead of long (yard-long) beans, which may be 30 cm (12 in.) or more in length.*

Soak the mushrooms in 1 cup (250 mL/8 fl oz) water. Reserve this liquid.

Wash and pat dry the beans thoroughly, then cut them into 4 cm (1½ in.) lengths.

Cut the mushrooms into 1 cm (⅓ in.) strips. Heat the oil in a preheated frying pan or skillet over a high heat and when it is hot, add the beans. Reduce the heat to moderately hot and stir-fry for 1½ minutes. Stir in the mushrooms. Add the reserved mushroom liquid and sprinkle the salt and soy sauce over the mixture. Reduce the heat to medium, cover, and cook, stirring frequently, until the beans are tender but still with texture (about 7 minutes). Stir in the sugar and serve.

*Serves 6*

375 g (12 oz) long (yard-long) beans
7–8 black (or shiitake) mushrooms, presoaked
3 tablespoons vegetable oil
¾ cup (185 mL/6 fl oz) soaking liquid from mushrooms
½ teaspoon salt
1½ teaspoons soy sauce
½ teaspoon white granulated sugar

# POTATOES AND ONIONS INDIAN STYLE

————

*This spicy mixture of vegetables is best served with Indian bread, such as chapatti, made from wholemeal (wholewheat) flour.*

Heat the oil in a deep pan or wok over a high heat. When the oil is very hot, add the mustard seeds and cover the pan as the seeds begin to pop. When the seeds stop popping and turn grey, after a minute or two, reduce the heat slightly and add the ginger and chili. Cook for 2–3 minutes. Add the coriander powder, turmeric and paprika. Stir, add the vegetables and sauté for 10 minutes, stirring frequently. Add the water and sprinkle the mixture with salt. Cover and simmer for a further 15 minutes. Stir in the lemon juice and sprinkle with the coriander leaves.

*Serves 8*

½ cup (125 mL/4 fl oz) vegetable oil
4 teaspoons black mustard seeds
2 tablespoons finely chopped fresh ginger
1 fresh green chili pepper, seeded and finely chopped
1 tablespoon ground coriander powder
1 teaspoon turmeric
½ teaspoon ground paprika
4 cups (500 g/1 lb) potatoes, boiled, peeled and cut into small cubes
3 cups (500 g/1 lb) chopped onions
4 cups (1 litre/1¾ imp. pints) water
1 tablespoon salt
2 teaspoons lemon juice
3 tablespoons chopped fresh coriander leaves

# The Fruiterer

*Fresh luscious fruits are a visual delight and a taste sensation. Buy the best, ripe, seasonal produce and enjoy the fruits raw, use them in delicious cooked desserts, or savour them in jams and as accompaniments to meat amd poultry dishes.*

Fruit, more than any other product, defines the seasons for me. Their colours seem to reflect the time of their ripening. The harlot red cherries, luscious peaches washed with scarlet and golden-fleshed mango all represent the sensuality of summer. The muted apples and figs, the ripened late season grapes filled with the accumulated sugar of the past summer, the arrival of quinces, mean autumn. The citrus fruits and russet pears, winter. Spring is the time for vegetables to show their best, while fruits blossom; the arrival of the first white asparagus and artichoke is just as significant for me as the first cherry of summer. I use fruit to help me emphasise the seasonality and sensuality of my cooking.

In Escoffier's day the availability of ripe seasonal fruit was more restricted than now, and so desserts that relied on preserved fruits were welcome. Pear Belle Hélène, Peach Melba and other classical desserts were happily made using preserved fruits. Today's cooks have access to fresh fruit from all over the world.

As an extreme example, I recently visited Fauchon in Paris, the most famous grocery shop in the world. In the middle of winter they had muscat grapes and peaches from Australia that were as good as those I could buy for my hotel. Their display included fruits from the tropics and exotics from South America.

They also had miniature cold area vegetables grown in Eastern Europe; tiny but perfect cabbages, kohlrabi and turnips, almost parodies of the staple diet of Europe in winter.

While it may seem luxurious to be eating mangoes in winter, I prefer to wait for the season. During winter I enjoy caremelising apples and pears, making marmalade and nibbling at the quince jelly made in autumn, but at the end of winter I hunger for the return of the early stone fruits, the red berries, the sight of the first Shanghai peach. It is this seasonal emphasis that gives a rhythm to my life and the life of the kitchen.

I commend it to you.

Previous pages: Summer
fruits

# GRILLED FIGS
# WITH MARC DE BOURGOGNE

*Marc de Bourgogne is a spirit made from the grape residues of wine; the skins and the stalks. In its early days it is raw and unpalatable, but after ageing for years in oak it develops a smoky flavour that I love, especially when teamed with fresh figs.*

Destalk the figs and cut them in half. Melt the butter in a large frying pan or skillet over a low heat. Gently brown the cut side of the figs in the butter without allowing the butter to burn. Sprinkle the sugar over the figs. Increase the heat to high, shaking the pan so that the sugar falls to the bottom and soaks up the butter. Add the orange juice and peel and then the Marc. Light the alcohol fumes and shake the pan all the time to melt the sugar into the sauce.

*To serve*

Serve the hot figs as soon as the flames die, with double or clotted cream.

*Serves 6*

12 firm, ripe, black figs
100 g (3½ oz) unsalted butter
100 g (3½ oz) white granulated sugar
¼ cup (60 mL/2 fl oz) fresh orange juice
½ teaspoon grated orange peel
⅖ cup (100 mL/3½ fl oz) Marc de Bourgogne

# CRABAPPLE AND THYME JELLY

*A sharp, clear, red jelly which, with the addition of the aromatic herb thyme, makes a wonderful accompaniment for practically any poultry or game at Christmas.*

Wash the crabapples, put them into a preserving pan with the thyme and just cover with water. Place a lid on the pan and simmer for 40 minutes. Strain the pulp through a jelly bag for 12 hours or overnight. Discard the pulp, measure the extracted juice and return it to the cleaned preserving pan. For every 2 cups (500 mL/16 fl oz) juice add 500 g (1 lb) warmed sugar. Warm the sugar by stirring it over a very low heat for 30 seconds. Stir the juice and sugar mixture over a low heat until the sugar has dissolved. Bring rapidly to the boil and maintain the boil for no more than 10 minutes, stirring occasionally until setting point has been reached. Skim the jelly before pouring it into jars that have been heated in a hot oven for 10 minutes. Seal immediately.

*Makes about 4–5 small jars (approximately 155 mL/5 fl oz per jar)*

1.5 kg (3 lbs) crabapples
1 cup thyme sprigs
white granulated sugar
(see method)

# CARAMELISED APPLE TART

*6 apples, peeled, quartered and*
*    cored*
*250 g (8 oz) white granulated*
*    sugar*
*2 tablespoons water*
*155 g (5 oz) unsalted butter*

*6 × 13 cm (5 in.) diameter ×*
*    1 cm (⅓ in.) thick discs of*
*    puff pastry*

*Egg wash*
*1 egg yolk*
*⅓ cup (90 mL/3 fl oz) light*
*    (single) cream*

*½ cup (90 g/3 oz) icing*
*    (confectioners') sugar*

### To cook the apples

Place the sugar and water in a heavy-bottomed saucepan and cook, stirring occasionally over a medium heat until the sugar has dissolved and a dark caramel is formed. Take the saucepan off the heat and allow the mixture to cool for 5 minutes, then add the butter. The butter and the caramel will not mix if the caramel is too cold. If this is the case, return the mixture to the heat before adding the apples. If the caramel is too hot, it may spit when you add the butter, so please be careful. Stir with a wooden spoon to amalgamate the two, then add the apples. Cook over a medium heat until they are tender (approximately 8 minutes).

Allow the apples to cool in the caramel. If there is a lot of caramel in the pan, it may be easier to drain the apples and caramel through a colander before using.

### To make the pastry

Prick the interior of each disc, leaving a collar 1.5 cm (½ in.) wide around the outside. Whisk the egg yolk into the cream. Brush the pastry collar with the egg wash and place each disc of pastry on a buttered pastry sheet, or on silicone paper on a baking sheet.

Pile four caramelised apple quarters in the centre of each disc and bake in a hot oven (200°C/390°F) for 20 minutes, or until the pastry has risen and is golden brown. Take the tarts from the oven and turn the oven heat to the highest setting. Turn the tarts over using a broad spatula. Sprinkle the bases generously with icing (confectioners') sugar and return the tarts to the oven for a maximum of 1 minute to glaze.

### To serve

Place the tarts (with the apple underneath the pastry) on warm plates and serve with muscat or caramel ice cream, crème anglaise (page 204) and heavy whipping (double) cream.

*Serves 6*

Opposite: Caramelised
Apple Tart

# REDCURRANT JELLY

*Clarity and colour have always been the hallmark of a good jelly. It should be firm, yet soft enough to be easily divided into spoonfuls when needed.*

### Method 1: To prepare the fruit

The fruit for making jelly should be fresh, firm and barely ripe, and with natural pectin and acid present in sufficient quantities to make a satisfactory 'gel'. Redcurrants, plums and apples are fruit high in pectin and therefore ideal for the purpose. Pips and the pith of fruit contain pectin and are sometimes cooked with the fruit but removed during the straining process.

Gently pick over the berries to remove any insects or bruised and damaged fruit but do not remove the stalks. If washing is necessary, rinse quickly in a colander and then drain.

Weigh the fruit and place it in a preserving pan that is about 10 cm (4 in.) deep, and has a good surface area for evaporation. Heat slowly until the juices start to run, then simmer very gently for 30 minutes, softly crushing the fruit occasionally. Spoon the fruit pulp into a jelly bag or muslin cloth attached to the legs of an upturned stool, and leave to strain into a large bowl for at least 12 hours.

### To make jelly

Discard the pulp, measure the extracted juice and return it to the cleaned preserving pan. For every 2½ cups (625 mL/1 imp. pint) juice allow 500 g (1 lb) sugar. Warm the sugar by stirring it over a very low heat for 30 seconds, then stir it into the reheated juice. When the sugar is dissolved, boil the mixture quickly for 1 minute, skim it, and pour it immediately into jars that have been heated in a hot oven for 10 minutes. Seal the jars immediately.

The yield will be quite small, about 3 small jars (approximately 155 mL/5 fl oz per jar), but the flavour will be intense.

### Method 2: To prepare the fruit

Prepare the fruit as in method 1 and place the redcurrants in a preserving pan with the water and cinnamon stick. Bring slowly to the boil, mashing the fruit occasionally, and gently simmer for 30 minutes. Spoon the fruit pulp into a jelly bag or muslin cloth attached to the legs of an upturned stool, and leave to strain into a large bowl for at least 12 hours.

### To make the jelly

Discard the pulp, measure the extracted juice and return it to the preserving pan. Add warmed sugar in the same quantities as in method 1 above, and the lemon juice. Heat gently, stirring until the sugar has dissolved, then bring quickly to the boil, boiling for 1 minute or until setting point is reached. Skim the surface with a slotted spoon to remove any scum that may have formed and quickly bottle in heated jars.

### Testing for setting

The spoon test is an easy method for seeing if your jelly has set. Take up a little of the jelly on a wooden spoon and if a blob forms and breaks away slowly, setting point has been reached. If a sugar thermometer is available, jelly at the setting point will register 105°C (220°F). Keep the thermometer handy in a jug of warm water.

# BAKED APPLES

*The ultimate comfort food, I have included this recipe for young cooks who may have been deprived of the sense of overindulgence these apples give.*

Core the apples and cut the skin to prevent it splitting during cooking, by scoring it with a sharp knife through to the flesh around the circumference. You can also score the apples in four small diagonals from the top of the apple in the shape of a cross.

Place all the ingredients for the stuffing in a bowl, mix together, cover with plastic wrap (cling film) and leave to macerate overnight.

Stuff the apples with the sultana mix, slightly overfilling them.

Combine the brown sugar (demerara sugar) and butter and spread the mixture over the tops of the apples.

Put the white granulated sugar, wine and vanilla bean in a saucepan and bring to the boil. Simmer for 5 minutes, take out the vanilla bean and pour the syrup into a baking pan. Place the stuffed apples in the pan and bake in a moderate oven (150°C/300°F) for 1¼ hours. Baste occasionally with the syrup. If the syrup begins to caramelise, add enough water to cover the bottom of the baking pan. As the apples cook the syrup takes on their flavour and forms their sauce.

Test to see if the apples are cooked by pricking with a metal skewer or knife. The apples should feel tender but not mushy.

### To serve

Spoon the syrup over the apples and serve with Crème Anglaise (page 204) and heavy whipping (double) or clotted cream.

*Serves 6*

6 cooking apples, Granny Smiths or Pink Ladies

Stuffing
1 cup (155 g/ 5 oz) sultanas (golden raisins)
2 dried figs cut into small dice
⅓ cup (60 g/ 2 oz) slivered almonds
1 teaspoon grated orange rind
pinch of ground cinnamon
pinch of nutmeg
¼ cup (60 mL/ 2 fl oz) Cognac or brandy
¼ cup (60 mL/ 2 fl oz) muscat

½ cup (90 g/ 3 oz) brown sugar (demerara sugar)
125 g (4 oz) softened unsalted butter

Syrup
⅓ cup (90 g/ 3 oz) white granulated sugar
350 mL/ 11½ fl oz white wine
1 vanilla bean

# SHANGHAI PEACH
# WITH FRAISES DES BOIS

6 ripe peaches, blanched
   (page 80)
500 g (1 lb) wild, alpine or
   small garden strawberries
2 tablespoons caster (superfine)
   sugar

Strawberry sauce
155 g (5 oz) strawberries
1½ tablespoons caster (superfine)
   sugar

Sabayon sauce
6 egg yolks
½ cup (125 g/4 oz) white
   granulated sugar
⅓ cup (90 mL/3 fl oz)
   Champagne or dry white
   wine

*The strawberries pictured in medieval mosaics are the small, wild woodland strawberries or fraises des bois, which are sweet and scented, their flavour best when freshly picked. The diminutive alpine strawberries, bright red in colour, are much harder to come by but well worth the hunt. Their flavour is quite intense. You might find them growing in the edging or mixed border of a herb garden. There is nothing sweeter than the golden flesh of a perfectly ripe peach, its skin flushed pink from the sun's rays. Put these beautifully fresh ambrosial flavours together and you have the best of both worlds.*

### To prepare the fruit

Blanch the peaches in boiling water for 1 minute, then drain, refresh under cold water and drain again. Peel and stone the peaches. Sprinkle them with the sugar and set them aside in a refrigerator to chill.

Strawberries will damage easily, so only give a slight rinse if necessary. Alpine strawberries especially will only last a few hours after picking. Rinse strawberries in a colander, dry thoroughly, then remove the green calyx.

### To make the strawberry sauce

Place the strawberries in a blender and purée them with the sugar.

### To make the sabayon sauce

In a stainless steel bowl, whip together the egg yolks and the sugar, then stir in the Champagne (or wine). Place the bowl over a pot of cold water, or in the top of a double boiler on a heat source, and raise the temperature to a simmer, stirring continuously with a whisk until the mixture falls in ribbons off the whisk and is thick and creamy.

### To serve

Arrange the peaches and strawberries in the centre of individual serving plates and spoon the sabayon and strawberry sauces decoratively around them.

*Serves 6*

Opposite: Shanghai Peach
with Fraises des Bois

# SPICED PEACHES

6 large, ripe, yellow peaches

Syrup
2/3 cup (155 g/5 oz) white
   granulated sugar
1½ cups (375 mL/12 fl oz)
   red wine
6 cardamom pods
4 cloves
6 peppercorns
1 cinnamon stick, freshly ground
1 star anise pod

*Spiced peaches are delicious as a dessert, served with a spoonful of crème fraîche (page 252), or as an accompaniment to roast duck.*

### How to blanch fruit

Three-quarters fill a saucepan with water and bring it to the boil. Three-quarters fill a large bowl with cold water and ice cubes. Place paper towels (absorbent kitchen paper) on a flat surface. Lower the fruit into the boiling water; a wire basket is ideal for this, otherwise use a slotted spoon. Time from the moment the water returns to the boil. After 1 minute, lift the fruit out of the boiling water and plunge it immediately into iced water for 1 minute. Drain, then place on the paper towels and pat dry.

### To make the syrup

Place the sugar in a saucepan with the red wine. Heat gently, stirring to dissolve the sugar, then add the spices. Increase the heat and boil for about 4 minutes, until syrupy. Strain to remove the spices and set the syrup to one side.

### To cook the peaches

Blanch the peaches then peel them. Place the peaches in a saucepan and pour over the syrup. Poach the peaches for 15 minutes or until just tender, keeping the syrup at a simmer level. Remove the peaches with a slotted spoon and set to one side.

Raise the heat to a slow boil and reduce the poaching liquid by half.

Place the peaches in a shallow baking pan and pour the reduced poaching liquid over them. Cook in a preheated oven at 120°C (245°F) for 10 minutes, basting frequently with the liquid, until the peaches are glazed.

### To serve

Allow the peaches to cool and serve them at room temperature, along with a spoonful of crème fraîche (page 252). Serve them slightly warm if they are to accompany a meat dish.

*Serves 6*

# PAIN PERDU
# WITH GLAZED PINEAPPLE

*This recipe can be adapted to other fruits but sympathetic spirits must replace the rum. For example, use kirsch with nectarines; Grand Marnier with strawberries; or serve oranges with Pastis, that wondrous spirit, a cousin to Pernod but flavoured with licorice rather than the aniseed base of its relative.*

### To make the brioche

Place the flour in a large bowl and make a well in the centre. Add all the other ingredients except the butter. Beat firmly with a wooden spoon until the dough becomes silky and elastic, then set it aside in a warm place to rise.

When the dough has doubled its bulk (approximately 2 hours), punch it down with the wooden spoon, then soften the butter and incorporate it into the dough, one teaspoon at a time.

Fill a buttered bread mould with the dough and allow it to rise again (approximately 45 minutes). Whip together the egg yolk and milk or cream and paint the egg wash onto the pastry with a fine brush. Bake in a preheated oven (200°C/390°F) for 25 minutes, or until golden on top.

### To prepare the pain perdu

Mix the rum with the crème anglaise. Place a sheet of silicone paper (page 253) on a baking sheet and lay twelve 1 cm (⅓ in.) slices of brioche on the paper. Brush them with the rum/crème anglaise mixture, ensuring the slices are moist but not wet. Sprinkle generously with the sugar then caramelise the sugar on the brioche under an extremely hot grill (broiler) or salamander. Turn the brioche over and repeat the process, moistening and caramelising as before. This can be done in advance but the brioche should be served slightly warmed.

### To prepare the pineapple in syrup

In a saucepan, over a low heat, warm the sugar and add the water. Increase the heat to medium and stir until the sugar is dissolved. Lay the pineapple slices in a baking pan and cover with the hot syrup. Bake in a hot oven (200°C/390°F) for 15 minutes, remove and cool.

### To make the sauce

Whisk all ingredients together until thoroughly combined.

### To serve

Arrange the pain perdu and pineapple in overlapping slices and surround with the sauce.

*Serves 6*

---

Brioche
2 cups (250 g/8 oz) plain (all-purpose) flour
7 g (¼ oz) fresh yeast
½ teaspoon salt
3 eggs
1½ teaspoons white granulated sugar
60 mL (2 fl oz) lukewarm milk
155 g (5 oz) butter

Egg wash
1 egg yolk
60 mL (2 fl oz) milk or cream

Pain perdu
1 cup (250 mL/8 fl oz) crème anglaise (page 204)
¼ cup (60 mL/2 fl oz) overproof rum
200 g (6½ oz) caster (superfine) sugar

Pineapple in syrup
1 cup (250 g/8 oz) white granulated sugar
¼ cup (60 mL/2 fl oz) water
1 pineapple, peeled, cored and sliced into 1 cm (⅓ in.) thick slices

Sauce
1 cup (250 mL/8 fl oz) crème anglaise (page 204)
¼ cup (60 mL/2 fl oz) overproof rum
⅓ cup (100 mL/3½ fl oz) crème fraîche (page 252)

# RASPBERRY GRATIN

*A perfect dish to serve with a great champagne. If you can't buy the cooking moulds required for the preparation of this dish, then show some initiative by cutting six rings, each 3 cm (1¼ in.) long from a piece of plastic water pipe of 10 cm (4 in.) diameter.*

Place a mould or ring in the centre of each plate and pile the raspberries in so that they sit high on the plate. Carefully remove the moulds so that the berries now support themselves.

Put the Champagne and sugar into a small saucepan and bring to the boil.

Place the yolks in a bowl and whisk until the mixture is light and airy. Add the hot syrup to the yolks, pouring it in a thin stream, a little at a time, and whisking all the time.

Ladle this fluffy sabayon sauce over the berries and then brown under a hot grill (broiler) or salamander to caramelise it. You can use a gas blow-torch to caramelise the sabayon but not every household has one. Be generous with the sauce as its silky, luscious quality teams perfectly with the acid of the berries.

*To serve*
Serve immediately. The dish needs no other cream.
*Serves 6*

4 cups (800 g/ 1¾ lbs) raspberries
155 mL (5 fl oz) Champagne
⅔ cup (155 g/ 5 oz) caster (superfine) sugar
8 egg yolks

# STRAWBERRIES AND MANGO WITH GALLIANO

Hull and halve the strawberries. Toss the strawberries with the caster (superfine) sugar and orange juice and leave to macerate in the refrigerator for 1 hour.

Cut the mangoes in half and deseed them. Skin the halves and cut the flesh into long strips. Toss with the Galliano and leave to macerate in the refrigerator for 1 hour.

Toss the orange sections in the Campari and refrigerate.

*To serve*
Remove the mango from the Galliano, using a slotted spoon, and retain the Galliano. Arrange the mango in the centre of a serving plate. Place the orange around the outside and sprinkle the strawberries over the mango. Spoon the Galliano over the fruits. Serve with individual bowls of crème fraîche.

*Serves 6*

2 cups (405 g/ 13 oz) small strawberries
⅓ cup (90 g/ 3 oz) caster (superfine) sugar
⅓ cup (90 mL/ 3 fl oz) fresh orange juice

3 large mangoes
155 mL (5 fl oz) Galliano

3 oranges, peeled and sectioned
2 tablespoons Campari

1¼ cups (310 mL/ 10 fl oz) crème fraîche (page 252)

Opposite: Raspberry Gratin

# RASPBERRIES ROMANOFF

3 cups (600 g/ 1¼ lbs)
  raspberries
⅔ cup (155 g/ 5 oz) caster
  (superfine) sugar
1¼ cups (310 mL/ 10 fl oz)
  heavy whipping (double)
  cream
4 drops vanilla extract
⅓ cup (90 mL/ 3 fl oz) Grand
  Marnier or framboise

Place the berries in a bowl and sprinkle with 60 g (2 oz) of the caster (superfine) sugar. Toss the berries in the sugar.

Whip the cream to firm peaks, gradually adding the rest of the caster sugar and the vanilla extract.

Take 3 tablespoons of the berries and purée them in a blender or food processor. Fold the purée into the cream.

Lightly bruise the rest of the berries with a fork to release a little of their juice and then fold them into the cream.

*To serve*

Pile the dessert into wide-necked glasses (old-fashioned champagne glasses are perfect), spoon the Grand Marnier or framboise over the cream mixture and serve.

*Serves 6*

# BLACKBERRY AND ORANGE JAM

1 kg (2 lbs) blackberries

2 cups (500 mL/ 16 fl oz)
  fresh orange juice
1 kg (2 lbs) caster (superfine)
  sugar
½ cup blanched orange rind cut
  into 3 cm (1¼ in.) julienne
  strips (page 253)

*An unusual combination of berries and citrus fruit.*

Reduce the orange juice to ½ cup (125 mL/ 4 fl oz) over a high heat. Add the sugar and cook to a soft ball stage (approximately 10 minutes). Add the berries and the rind and cook over a high heat for 10 minutes.

Heat the jars in a hot oven for 10 minutes. Fill the clean jars while still hot. When cool, cover the top of each jar with plastic wrap (cling film). Secure the tops with rubber bands and refrigerate the jars.

*Makes about 5 small jars (approximately 155 mL/ 5 fl oz per jar)*

# BERRY TART

There is now a wide range of delectable berries available in season. This recipe works best with blackberries, raspberries or wild strawberries.

### To prepare the berries

Mix the boiling water with the redcurrant jelly. Place the berries in a bowl and pour the redcurrant jelly and water over them. Quickly toss so that the berries are coated with the jelly.

### To make the shortcrust pastry

Place all the ingredients in a food processor and process for 15 seconds. Alternatively, rub the ingredients together in a bowl with your fingertips until they form a cohesive mass. Wrap the pastry in plastic wrap (cling film) and refrigerate for at least 30 minutes before using. Divide the pastry into six and roll each piece out onto a floured surface until it is very thin (about 3 mm/⅛ in.) and circular in shape. Line six individual tart cases (10 cm/4 in. diameter) with the pastry, pressing gently into the corners of the moulds. Prick the base of each tart with a fork to prevent it rising during cooking. Line each pastry case with aluminium kitchen foil and rest in the refrigerator for 1 hour. Fill each case with dried rice or beans and bake in a preheated oven at 180°C (355°F) for 20 minutes, or until the pastry is set and golden. Remove the foil containing the rice or beans and, if necessary, return to the oven to complete cooking, ensuring the cases are golden and crisp.

### To make the crème pâtissière

You will need two saucepans. Bring the milk to the boil with the vanilla bean in one, and mix the egg yolks with the sugar and flour in the other. Slowly pour the hot milk into the egg mixture, incorporating it with a whisk. Return the mixture to the heat and bring it to the boil, stirring with a wooden spoon. Simmer for 2 minutes, remove from the heat, pass through a sieve into a bowl, remove the vanilla bean, and allow to cool. Cover with plastic wrap and refrigerate.

### To make the filling

Whip the cream into soft peaks. Mix the Grand Marnier into the crème pâtissière and then fold in the cream.

### To serve

Fill the pastry cases with the filling, spooning the berries on top so that they cascade over the sides, and serve. Accompany the tarts with a jug of pouring cream, if you like.

*Serves 6*

---

**Berries**
3 cups (600 g/ 1¼ lbs) mixed berries
½ cup (125 mL/ 4 fl oz) boiling water
3 tablespoons redcurrant jelly (page 76)

**Shortcrust pastry**
2 cups (250 g/ 8 oz) plain (all-purpose) flour
200 g (6½ oz) cold butter, diced
1 teaspoon caster (superfine) sugar
pinch salt
1 egg
2 tablespoons iced water

**Crème pâtissière**
2 cups (500 mL/ 16 fl oz) milk
1 vanilla bean
6 egg yolks
1 cup (225 g/ 7 oz) white granulated sugar
½ cup (60 g/ 2 oz) plain (all-purpose) flour

**Filling**
⅓ cup (100 mL/ 3½ fl oz) heavy whipping (double) cream
3 tablespoons Grand Marnier
225 mL (7 fl oz) crème pâtissière (see above)

# COCONUT BAVAROIS
# WITH POACHED TAMARILLOS

---

Custard

1½ cups (125 g/4 oz) desiccated
   coconut
3¼ cups (825 mL/26 fl oz)
   milk
1 cup (250 g/8 oz) white
   granulated sugar
1 vanilla bean
4 leaves gelatin (page 252)
3 eggs
2 cups (500 mL/16 fl oz)
   heavy whipping (double)
   cream, whipped to soft peaks
walnut oil

200 g (6½ oz) white granulated
   sugar
1¼ cups (310 mL/10 fl oz)
   water
1 vanilla bean
12 tamarillos

*Bavarois literally means Bavarian cream, a cold, light, egg custard often served with fruit. This is an exotic variation of a traditional European dessert.*

Put the coconut, milk, sugar and vanilla bean into a saucepan and slowly bring the mixture to the boil. Simmer for 5 minutes then strain through a fine sieve, pressing the milk from the coconut with the back of a wooden spoon.

Soften the gelatin in a little water. Return the milk to the saucepan, beat in the 3 eggs and cook the custard gently over a low heat until it coats the back of the spoon.

Strain the custard through a fine sieve into a cold bowl and add the gelatin (not the water it was softened in). Stir the custard continually to help it cool. If you wish, place the bowl over ice to hasten the process. When the custard is cold and begins to thicken, fold the whipped cream through it.

Lightly oil with walnut oil six 155 mL (5 fl oz) dariole moulds or one soufflé bowl (4 cups/1 litre/1¾ imp. pints capacity). Fill with the custard and refrigerate. The bavarois should set within 2 hours.

### To poach the tamarillos

Put the sugar, water and vanilla bean into a large saucepan and bring to the boil. Add the tamarillos and simmer for 10 minutes. Take the saucepan off the heat and allow the fruit to cool in the syrup. Refrigerate until needed. When cool, peel the tamarillos and return them to the syrup.

### To serve

Unmould the bavarois by quickly dipping the mould in hot water and then running a small knife around the interior of the mould. This is more to break the seal between the bavarois and mould than to cut the cream. Turn the mould upside down and ease the bavarois onto the plate. Arrange the tamarillos around the bavarois and moisten with a little of the syrup. The dish can be served with Lacy Caramel Snaps (page 207).

*Serves 6*

Opposite: Coconut
Bavarois with Poached
Tamarillos

# CRÈME RENVERSÉE A L'ORANGE

### Custard
3 cups (750 mL/24 fl oz)
   crème fraîche (page 252)
⅔ cup (155 g/5 oz) caster
   (superfine) sugar
zest of half an orange
⅓ cup (90 mL/3 fl oz) Grand
   Marnier
3 whole eggs
3 egg yolks

### Caramel
2 cups (440 g/14 oz) caster
   (superfine) sugar
½ cup (125 mL/4 fl oz) water

### Caramelised oranges
1 cup (250 mL/8 fl oz) water
6 oranges, peeled and sectioned
rind of one orange, cut in
   julienne strips (page 253)
remaining caramel

walnut oil

*In this recipe the crème caramel has been literally turned out of its dish, or reversed. It is rich and sugary and totally delicious.*

### To make the custard
Put the crème fraîche, caster (superfine) sugar, zest and Grand Marnier into a saucepan and bring to the boil. Simmer for 5 minutes. Strain into a bowl and when cool, add the eggs and egg yolks and whisk. Strain into a jug.

### To make the caramel
Warm the sugar in a saucepan, add the water and bring the syrup to the boil. Cook until the sugar turns a dark caramel colour, and immediately pour in enough to cover the bottom of the dariole moulds.

### To prepare the caramelised oranges
Add the water to the remaining caramel and return the saucepan to the heat. Bring the mixture to the boil, remove from the heat and cool. Add the oranges and the orange julienne to the diluted caramel.

### To cook the crèmes
Lightly oil with walnut oil 6 dariole (page 252) or small soufflé moulds. Pour enough of the caramel into each one to cover the bottom. When this has cooled, fill them with the custard and cook 'au bain marie' by putting 3 cm (1¼ in.) of boiling water into a baking pan and setting the filled moulds in the water. Lightly cover the pan with aluminium kitchen foil and bake in a slow oven (125°C/250°F) for 30 minutes, or until set. Remove from the oven, cool the crèmes and then refrigerate.

### To serve
Cut the crèmes from the moulds with a sharp knife and tip them onto individual serving plates. Surround with the caramelised oranges.

### Method 2
Sometimes, if the main dessert will be a long time coming, I prepare these interesting pre-desserts. Bake the custards by the method outlined above but use demitasses (very small cups) instead of dariole moulds, and leave 1–2 cm (½–¾ in.) free at the top. Make a syrup with ¾ cup (185 mL/6 fl oz) blood orange juice and ¼ cup (60 g/2 oz) caster (superfine) sugar, reduced to ½ cup (125 mL/4 fl oz), then spoon the sauce over the cold cooked custards and serve them still in the cups.

*Serves 6*

# BLOOD PLUM AND SHIRAZ JAM

Cut the plums into 2 cm (¾ in.) chunks and place in a saucepan. Press some of the juice from the plums with a wooden spoon and bring to the boil. Reduce the liquid by half and pass the plums through a food mill.

In a separate saucepan reduce the wine over a high heat to 155 mL (5 fl oz) and add the sugar and citric acid. Cook to soft ball stage (page 253) (approximately 10 minutes). Add the puréed plums and cook for a further 10 minutes. Test for setting by putting a little of the jam on a cold saucer and letting it cool. If a skin begins to form the jam will set.

Heat jars in a hot oven for 10 minutes. Fill the clean jars while they are still hot. When cool, cover the tops with plastic wrap (cling film), secure with rubber bands and refrigerate.

*Makes 6 small jars of jam (approximately 155 mL/5 fl oz per jar)*

1.25 kg (2½ lbs) blood plums, stoned

3 cups (750 mL/24 fl oz) rich shiraz or red wine

1 kg (2 lbs) caster (superfine) sugar

½ teaspoon citric acid

# TART OF BLOOD PLUMS

*This tart is spectacular to look at and will draw sighs of admiration from your guests. The recipe can be used with cherries, or blueberries or other soft fruits.*

### To make the frangipane
Cream the eggs, butter and sugar together in an electric mixer. Add the almond meal then fold in the flour.

### To make the tart
Roll the shortcrust out to a thin sheet. Line a 30 cm (12 in.) tart case with the pastry and brush the inside of the tart case with plum jam.

Half fill the case with frangipane, and lay the plums on top. Bake in a moderately slow oven (160°C/315°F) for 40 minutes, or until golden. Serve warm.

*Serves 8–10*

15 blood plums, stoned and halved

Frangipane
3 eggs
155 g (5 oz) unsalted butter
⅔ cup (155 g/5 oz) caster (superfine) sugar
1⅓ cups (155 g/5 oz) almond meal
½ cup (60 g/2 oz) plain (all-purpose) flour, sifted

310 g (10 oz) shortcrust pastry (page 84)
plum jam (see above)

# TERRINE OF PEARS

*The best dessert pears have a grainy consistency. The brown Beurre Bosc is the most common commercial variety.*

### To cook the pears
Take two medium-sized saucepans, put the red wine in one and the white wine in the other. Add half a cup of sugar to each, together with a piece of the vanilla bean and a piece of cinnamon bark. Place half the peeled pears in one saucepan and half in the other. Add more wine to cover, if necessary. Bring both saucepans to the boil and simmer for 15–20 minutes, or until the pears are tender. Remove both saucepans from the heat and let the pears cool in the wine. Strain the pears, keeping the wines separate.

### To make the wine jelly and syrup
Measure 2 cups (500 mL/16 fl oz) of strained white wine syrup. Soften the gelatin in a little cold water, remove, then add the gelatin to the white wine. Mix thoroughly and then put to one side.

Return the red wine to the stove and reduce to 340 mL (11 fl oz). Strain through a fine sieve and refrigerate. The red wine syrup is used to garnish the terrine.

### To make the terrine
Line a 6 cup (1.5 litre/2½ imp. pints) terrine dish with plastic wrap (cling film) and then layer the pears in the terrine, moistening with the white wine jelly as you go. Have alternate layers of the pears poached in red wine and white wine. When the terrine is packed tightly and full of pear, pour in the rest of the white wine jelly. Have a piece of wood cut to the size of the top of the terrine. Fold over the plastic wrap, leaving the ends open, then press the wood down on top of the terrine so that the jelly covers the pears and any excess is forced out of the ends of the plastic wrap. Close over the plastic wrap and replace the wood. Weigh down with a 1 kg (2 lbs) weight and refrigerate overnight.

### To prepare the citrus garnish
To make the sugar syrup, boil together 1 cup (250 g/8 oz) white granulated sugar and 1 cup (250 mL/8 fl oz) water. Moisten the rind with some of the syrup. Cover the rind with plastic wrap (cling film) and refrigerate. Pour the rest of the syrup over the citrus sections then cover with plastic wrap and refrigerate.

8–10 Beurre Bosc pears, quartered, cored and peeled

2 cups (500 mL/16 fl oz) white wine
2 cups (500 mL/16 fl oz) red wine
1 cup (225 g/7 oz) caster (superfine) sugar
1 vanilla bean, cut into two
1 piece cinnamon bark, broken in two
7 leaves gelatin (page 252)

Citrus garnish (optional)
1 cup (250 mL/8 fl oz) sugar syrup (see method)
1 tablespoon rind of each of the following fruit cut into fine julienne and blanched
2 oranges, peeled and sectioned
2 grapefruit, peeled and sectioned
2 limes, peeled and sectioned

Opposite: Terrine of Pears

Loosen the pear terrine by gently pulling on the plastic wrap and easing it from the terrine dish. Unwrap the pear terrine and slice into 1.5 cm (½ in.) thick slices. This may be done in advance and the slices returned to the refrigerator until ready to serve.

Place a slice of the terrine in the centre of each plate and arrange the citrus sections decoratively around the pears, garnishing with the julienne rind or zests. Pour the red wine syrup around the terrine and serve.

*Serves 8–10*

# NOISETTES OF PORK
# WITH APRICOTS

*1 × 1.75 kg (3½ lbs) boned loin of pork, rind off*
*salt and freshly ground black pepper*
*2 tablespoons strong Dijon mustard*

*18 golden shallots, peeled and blanched (page 252)*
*3 tablespoons clarified butter*
*18 apricots, ripe but firm*
*2 chopped thyme sprigs*
*340 mL (11 fl oz) dry cider*
*155 mL (5 fl oz) reduced veal stock (page 112)*
*1 bay leaf*

*1 tablespoon butter*

Lay the loin of pork flat on the bench, trim the flap so that it is 1 cm (⅓ in.) thick, season with salt and pepper and brush with the Dijon mustard. Roll the loin tightly and tie it with string at 3 cm (1¼ in.) intervals. Cut the loin between each two pieces of string, into noisettes.

Pat dry the shallots and peel them. Place the shallots in a frying pan or skillet with half the clarified butter. Cook them over a medium heat for 5–7 minutes, or until they are caramelised and golden brown. Let the shallots cool down before stuffing the apricots.

Stone the apricots and replace each stone with a caramelised shallot.

Melt the rest of the clarified butter in a deep, heavy, baking pan. Lightly brown both sides of the noisettes in the butter. Sprinkle them with the thyme. Tip the excess fat from the pan and deglaze with the cider. Add the veal stock, bay leaf and the apricots. Place in a moderate oven (160°C/315°F) for 20 minutes.

*To serve*

Take the noisettes and apricots from the pan with a slotted spoon. Whisk the butter into the sauce and spoon it over the noisettes.

*Serves 6–8*

# APRICOT TART

Stone the apricots and cut them in half. Line a 30 cm (12 in.) tart tin with the pastry. Mix together the walnuts with the caster (superfine) sugar and spread this mixture over the bottom of the tart. Lay the apricots cut side down on the walnut meal. Dust heavily with icing (confectioners') sugar and bake at 180°C (355°F) for 25 minutes.

*To serve*

Serve fresh from the oven with a dollop of sour cream.

*Serves 8*

*1.25 kg (2½ lbs) apricots, ripe but firm*
*310 g (10 oz) shortcrust pastry (page 84)*
*155 g (5 oz) ground walnuts*
*⅓ cup (90 g/3 oz) caster (superfine) sugar*
*icing (confectioners') sugar*

# DUCK WITH NECTARINES

Rub the exterior and the cavity of the ducks with salt and pepper. Cut the onions in half and place them in the cavities with the thyme and marjoram sprigs.

Place the ducks on a rack sitting in a baking pan and roast them with the oven on full (220°C–250°C/425°F–475°F). The ducks should take 1¼ hours to cook. Baste them every 10 minutes with the fat that collects in the baking pan.

Remove the ducks from the pan. Leave them on the rack and remove them to a clean dish in a warm place to rest. Keep the baking pan and the residual fat.

Tip the fat from the baking pan and return it to the stove. Heat it over a medium heat and deglaze the pan with the white wine. Reduce the wine by half and then add the ginger, Cognac, thyme, bay leaf, vinegar, and the veal stock (or cream).

Simmer for 5 minutes, then reduce the sauce by one-third over a high heat. Reduce the heat and warm the nectarines in the sauce. Add any juices from the duck, and taste for seasoning.

*To serve*

You may find it easier to carve the duck by dismembering it first. If you do, remember to keep the skin away from the juices so that it remains crisp. Spoon the sauce over the duck and nectarines and serve on individual plates.

*Serves 8*

*2 × 2.25 kg (4½ lbs) ducks*
*salt and freshly ground black pepper*
*2 onions, peeled*
*4 sprigs each thyme and marjoram*

*155 mL (5 fl oz) white wine*
*1 tablespoon crushed fresh ginger*
*⅓ cup (90 mL/3 fl oz) Cognac*
*2 thyme sprigs*
*1 bay leaf*
*2 tablespoons sherry vinegar*
*340 mL (11 fl oz) reduced veal stock (page 112) or light (single) cream*
*6 ripe nectarines, blanched and peeled (page 80)*

# The Butcher

*A good butcher will hang his meat, do his own smoking and curing, and do special cuts of meat on request. Search out a butcher with the above qualities, and you will be rewarded with fresh, tender and flavoursome meats. For a different family dinner, try veal sweetbreads or braised oxtail.*

To choose a good butcher is not difficult. Ask the butcher the following three questions:

1. Does he hang his meat? If he does, ask to see the coolroom and ask him to tell you about his meat. If he is a good butcher he will be proud to show you and pleased that his hard work has a potential admirer. If he treats you like an unwelcome tax inspector, buy your meat elsewhere.

2. Does he do his own smoking and curing? If he does, you know you have a butcher who knows his craft and you will be able to learn from him.

3. Will he do special cuts of meat on request? A co-operative butcher makes life as a cook much easier.

There you have it—an amenable butcher who knows his trade and is interested in the quality of his meat. This butcher will not be found in supermarkets, and his prices will be higher than in those outlets, but in return the quality of life that he gives us is worth every extra cent.

Tenderness in meat is the result of many factors, including how the animal was killed, the acid levels in the meat and the proportion of fat and connective tissue (gristle) to muscle. All meat benefits from ageing; any meat is tough when first killed. Lamb, pork and veal should be hung for a week, beef and game benefit from longer periods.

By ageing the meat we allow bacteria to break down the fibres and make the meat more tender. When meat is aged in a vacuum-sealed plastic pack (cryovac) the tenderising occurs without the action of harmful bacteria that make the meat unpalatable. The bacteria are inhibited because of the exclusion of oxygen from the meat.

When meat is hung by the butcher on the bone without the benefit of these vacuum-sealed packs, bacteria and moulds grow on the exterior of the meat and water is evaporated. Over a month the meat can lose 25 per cent of its weight this way. The meat must be trimmed to ensure that none has been affected in flavour by the moulds and bacteria. These factors all lead to air-hung beef being more expensive. In return, we gain increased flavour, as the taste components are concentrated by the reduction of the water and drying of the beef, better texture and meat that is easier to cut.

Very few butchers hang their meat these days, so value those who do and, understand why they may be more expensive. If you cannot buy hung beef, ask the butcher to hang an aged rump for you for a week after it has been removed from its plastic pack.

Air-drying meat preserves it. Spoiling bacteria are unable to operate in the absence of water, and meat prepared by drying in the sun (jerky) has long been a staple in desert areas. In damper climates, salt is used to achieve the same result but, of course, it affects the flavour.

Previous pages: Roasted Rump of Beef

# VEAL SWEETBREADS

---

*Sweetbreads are a great luxury and should form part of any good cook's repertoire. Children like them crumbed but for a great home dish, braising them with peas (page 66) is hard to beat.*

### *To prepare the sweetbreads*

Use the heart-shaped sweetbreads from the throat of yearling calves, as they are white and creamy and more substantial than those from young (bobby) calves.

Soak the sweetbreads in salted water overnight to leach them of their blood. Dry the sweetbreads on a dishcloth or paper towel (absorbent kitchen paper).

### *To make the court bouillon*

Melt the butter in a large saucepan and gently soften the mirepoix and the shallots without colouring them. Add the white wine and water and bring to the boil. Add the thyme and bay leaf, season with pepper and simmer for 5 minutes.

### *To precook the sweetbreads*

Add the sweetbreads to the simmering court bouillon and continue to simmer for 7 minutes. Fill a large bowl with ice water. Lift the sweetbreads from the stock using a slotted spoon and plunge them in the ice water to cool. Strain the stock and reduce the liquid over a high heat to a glaze.

Drain the sweetbreads and lay them on a dishcloth on a tray, flat side down. Cover them with plastic wrap (cling film), place another tray on top with a weight so as to press the sweetbreads, and refrigerate overnight.

The next day, trim the sweetbreads into a regular shape and pull off any connective tissue or gristle.

The sweetbreads are then ready for use in the following recipe.

*1 kg (2 lbs) sweetbreads*

Court bouillon
*2 tablespoons butter*
*1 cup mirepoix (page 253)*
*2 golden shallots, peeled and chopped*
*⅘ cup (200 mL/6½ fl oz) white wine*
*600 mL (19 fl oz) water*
*2 thyme sprigs*
*1 bay leaf*
*freshly ground black pepper*

# VEAL SWEETBREADS
# IN PUFF PASTRY

Sweetbreads
*500 g (1 lb) prepared veal
   sweetbreads (page 97)*
*salt and freshly ground black
   pepper*
*2 tablespoons clarified butter*
*1 tablespoon golden shallots,
   chopped*
*¾ cup (185 mL/ 6 fl oz)
   Champagne*
*⅖ cup (100 mL/ 3½ fl oz) light
   (single) cream*
*1½ cups (200 g/ 6½ oz) small
   mushrooms*
*½ cup (125 mL/ 4 fl oz)
   sweetbread glaze
   (page 97)*
*3 tablespoons butter*

*puff pastry (page 201)*

Pastry glaze
*1 egg*
*¼ cup (60 mL/ 2 fl oz) light
   (single) cream*

*chervil sprigs for garnish*

*This dish has a delicate, creamy sauce in the classic French manner and makes a
deliciously rich first course.*

### To cook the sweetbreads and pastry

Divide the sweetbreads into 12 or 18 pieces and season with salt and
pepper. Melt the clarified butter in a heavy frying pan or skillet and
gently sauté the sweetbreads until just golden brown. Add the shallots
and cook gently without further browning. Add the Champagne and
increase the heat to a moderately slow level, reducing the liquid by
half. Add the cream, then the mushrooms, wilting them in the sauce.
Add the sweetbread glaze and then swirl the butter into the sauce.

### To glaze the pastry

Combine the egg with the cream and whisk. Divide the puff pastry
into six equal pieces then cut each piece in half laterally. Brush the
tops with the pastry glaze. Place the pieces onto a baking sheet and
bake at 185°C (365°F) for 20 minutes or until puffed and golden.

### To serve

Warm individual serving plates and place a pastry bottom on each one.
Spoon the sweetbreads on top and cover with the other pastry half.
Spoon the sauce around and garnish with sprigs of chervil.

*Serves 6*

Opposite: Veal Sweetbreads
in Puff Pastry

# DRY SALT CURE

2 kg (4 lbs) coarse sea salt,
   rock salt or Maldon sea salt
1 tablespoon saltpetre
155 g (5 oz) white granulated
   sugar

Herbs and spices
1 tablespoon fresh juniper berries
1 tablespoon star anise pod
1 tablespoon black peppercorns
1 tablespoon coriander seeds
1 tablespoon allspice
6 bay leaves
12 thyme sprigs
1 tablespoon fresh sage leaves

½ head bruised garlic cloves

*The making of dry salted hams is not difficult if you have a cool cellar with good air circulation. Smaller joints or pieces of meat, such as duck breasts and legs, legs of sucking pig or young boar (marcassin), are easier to salt at home. The following cure is a good all-purpose cure. Small amounts can be used to make duck and other small hams.*

Mix the salt, saltpetre and sugar. Pulverise the herbs and spices in an electric coffee grinder or mortar and pestle and add them to the salt/sugar mixture. Take a very fresh leg of pork weighing 3–4 kg (6–8 lbs). Have the chine bone removed and trim any remains of the fillet from the rump so that it looks trim and neat.

Loosen the meat around the top of the femur (thigh bone) and then prick the ham all over with a skewer. Rub the ham vigorously with the salt cure. Rub some of the cure around the exposed femur bone.

Have ready a generously proportioned flat tray. On it lay a heavy duty plastic (polythene) rubbish bag. Fold the bag back over itself so that you can make a bed at the bottom of the bag with the salt cure. Use half the cure to make a flat bed for the ham and lay the ham down on the bed, skin side up. Tip the rest of the cure over the ham and then press the bag as tightly as possible around the ham and salt. Secure the top of the bag with string and leave to cure in a cool place. (The ham does not need to be refrigerated.)

Turn the bagged ham each day for 10 days. If the bag is punctured for any reason, repair it with a sticking plaster. If you have a major disaster, replace the bag.

At the end of the 10 days take the ham from the bag and dry it with a cloth. Wrap the ham neatly in muslin. Tie a strong piece of clean twine around the shank and hang it to dry in a cool airy place for 4–6 weeks. The ham may drip moisture so you should place a tray under it. If you notice some bacterial growth on the ham rub the area with a bit of Cognac or Marc de Bourgogne.

If you have a problem with insects or flies, rub the exterior with cayenne pepper or wood ash.

It is most important that you hang the ham in a place with a bit of air movement. This in itself will eliminate most problems. However, if at the end of it all, you have some exterior spoilage, don't worry, the interior will be fine.

*Curing and drying times*
Smaller hams take less time; a duck breast will need 1–2 days curing, 1 week drying; a 1 kg (2 lbs) leg of sucking pig needs 4 days curing, 2–3 weeks drying.

# WET SALT CURE

Use the same salt, sugar, herb and spice ingredients as for the dry salt cure. Place 2 cups (500 mL/16 fl oz) of water in a large saucepan and then bring it to the boil to dissolve the salt and sugar. To check the degree of salinity, cool the brine and then float a potato in it. Add more water if the potato is buoyant, more salt if it sinks. You will need enough water to cover the meat.

The wet cure is best for small cuts of pork, including belly pork. The curing is usually done in a ceramic crock, the meat being held under the cure with a weighted piece of wood. Homemade bacons are easily make by curing the belly pork for 2 days per kilogram (2 lbs) and then slicing finely and grilling (broiling).

Salting duck before roasting in this way is a taste sensation. Put the duck in the brine for 1 day and then dry it thoroughly before roasting.

Salamis and other dried sausages are made from meats salted in the same manner and then minced (ground) or chopped before filling the sausage skins. Leave them in the air to dry and mature.

# POT ROASTED LAMB

*The purpose of this dish is not to braise the lamb but to cook it in a casserole with vegetables. It's a great dish and makes a change from serving the ubiquitous roast.*

1 × 2 kg (4 lbs) leg of lamb
2 teaspoons chopped fresh thyme
salt and freshly ground black pepper
80 mL (2½ fl oz) virgin olive oil
24 golden shallots, peeled
36 garlic cloves, peeled
2 cups (500 mL/16 fl oz) white wine
2 tablespoons sherry vinegar
1¼ cups (310 g/10 oz) tomatoes, peeled and chopped
1 bay leaf
12 baby turnips
12 baby carrots
2 cups (250 g/8 oz) cooked fresh peas
2 tablespoons chopped fresh tarragon leaves

Ask the butcher to trim the leg of fat and saw it in two at right angles to the bone. Alternatively, have the butcher de-bone the leg, cut the meat in two and tie it with string. Season with thyme, salt and pepper.

Heat the oil in a heavy casserole and brown the lamb on all sides. Add the shallots and continue cooking in the oil for 5 minutes. Boil the garlic in salted water for 10 minutes and then add it to the pan and colour it lightly in the fat. Tip off the fat that has collected in the dish and deglaze the casserole with the white wine and vinegar.

Add the tomatoes and the bay leaf, bring the mixture to the boil and then transfer the dish to bake in a preheated moderate oven (170°C/340°F) for 30 minutes.

Meanwhile, trim and wash the baby turnips and carrots, and cook them in boiling salted water for 5 minutes. Remove immediately from the pot and refresh under cold water. Add the vegetables to the casserole and cook on the stove top at medium heat for a further 10 minutes. Add the peas and tarragon.

Remove the meat and large vegetables from the casserole and keep warm. Reduce the remaining sauce over a high heat for 10 minutes. Carve the lamb and surround with the sauce and vegetables.

*Serves 8*

# RACK OF LAMB
# WITH SPRING VEGETABLES

*When you order the lamb ask your butcher to take the racks from young lambs weighing under 20 kg (40 lbs). Have him French the racks (page 252) so that there is 5–6 cm (2–2½ in.) of rib exposed, cap off and chine bone removed.*

### To make the marinade

Mix the ingredients together. Trim the lamb of any fat and brush the lamb with the marinade. Refrigerate for 1 day before cooking.

### To make the Tomato Provençal mix

Heat the olive oil in a frying pan or skillet until smoking. Add the tomatoes, stir and then add the garlic and thyme. Season with salt and pepper and reduce over a high heat until thick and standing up when spooned. Add the chopped parsley and allow to cool. (This Provençal preparation is very handy to keep in the refrigerator for emergency spaghettis for children.)

### To prepare the spring vegetables

Cook the turnips and carrots in boiling salted water for 7 minutes. Refresh under cold water and drain. Place the onions, clarified butter and wine in a small saucepan. Cook over high heat until the wine has evaporated and the onions start to caramelise. Cook the green beans in boiling salted water for 7 minutes and then refresh under cold water and drain. Toss in a little butter and pepper, and add to the turnips and carrots. Cook the green peas in unsalted boiling water for 7 minutes and then refresh under cold water and drain.

Just before serving, heat the vegetables gently in the butter, garlic and pepper mixture.

### To cook the racks

Heat the oven to 220°C (425°F). Take a heavy baking pan and heat it on top of the stove. Add the tablespoon of butter and moisten the bottom of the pan with it. When it begins to brown add the seasoned racks of lamb and place the pan in the oven. Cook for 15 minutes.

In the meantime, heat the griller (broiler) or salamander. Take the racks from the oven and allow to rest for 15 minutes. Spread the Tomato Provençal mix on top of the racks, along the fillets of meat, and place them on the grill tray. Retain the baking pan. Put the rack under the very hot grill to complete its cooking, about 5 minutes. The lamb should be medium–medium rare.

3 racks of lamb, 8 cutlets on each

Marinade
3 tablespoons strong Dijon mustard
2 teaspoons fresh thyme leaves
1 tablespoon chopped fresh marjoram
1 tablespoon chopped fresh parsley
3 garlic cloves, chopped
1 cup (225 g/ 7 oz) clarified butter or 1 cup (250 mL/ 8 fl oz) olive oil
salt and freshly ground pepper

Tomato Provençal
¼ cup (60 mL/ 2 fl oz) virgin olive oil
4 chopped tomatoes
2 garlic cloves, chopped
1 teaspoon fresh thyme leaves
salt and freshly ground pepper
2 tablespoons chopped Italian parsley

Spring vegetables
6 baby turnips, scrubbed and trimmed
12 baby carrots, scrubbed and trimmed
12 baby (pearl) onions
2 tablespoons clarified butter
⅖ cup (100 mL/ 3½ fl oz) white wine
36 baby green beans
2 cups (1 kg/ 2 lbs) green peas
3 tablespoons butter
1 garlic clove, crushed
freshly ground black pepper

1 tablespoon butter

Opposite: Rack of Lamb with Spring Vegetables

Sauce

*2 golden shallots, chopped*
*1 cup (250 mL/8 fl oz) white wine*
*⁴/₅ cup (200 mL/6½ fl oz) veal glaze (page 112)*
*1 garlic clove, crushed*
*2 sprigs thyme*
*1 bay leaf*
*freshly ground black pepper*

*To make the sauce*

Heat the baking pan on top of the stove over a medium heat. Brown the chopped shallots in the pan fat and then deglaze the baking pan with the white wine and sherry vinegar. Scrape the caramelised juices into the wine, add the veal glaze, garlic, thyme and bay leaf and some pepper. Strain into a saucepan and taste for seasoning.

*To serve*

Arrange the vegetables and Tomato Provençal on a plate. Carve the lamb and rest slices of meat against the vegetables and surround with the sauce. Serve with Pommes Anna (page 63).

*Serves 8*

# QUICK LAMB CURRY

*1 kg (2 lbs) lamb steaks, finely sliced*
*3 tablespoons virgin olive oil*
*1 large brown onion, finely sliced*
*salt*

Curry paste

*3 fresh hot red chili peppers, or powder to taste*
*1 tablespoon coriander seeds*
*1 tablespoon cardamom pods*
*½ tablespoon fennel seeds*
*½ teaspoon fresh thyme leaves*
*1 tablespoon fresh basil leaves*
*4 garlic cloves, peeled*
*1 teaspoon ground turmeric*

*1 cup (250 mL/8 fl oz) chicken, veal or beef stock (page 138 or 112)*

*A small electric coffee grinder is indispensable for making your own curry paste. It can also be used for grinding herbs and spices for marinades. A mortar and pestle is also useful for grinding herbs and spices.*

*To make the curry paste*

Grind the chili peppers until they turn into a paste. Add in all the other curry paste ingredients and grind to a thick paste.

*To cook the curry*

Heat the oil in a deep frying pan or skillet until it is smoking and sauté the onion and lamb fillets together. Season with salt.

When the meat begins to brown, add the spicy curry paste and coat the meat with it, turning constantly, over a high heat. When the paste begins to stick to the pan add the stock and simmer until tender (approximately 30 minutes).

*To serve*

Serve with steamed rice and tomato and basil salad.

*Serves 6–8*

# ROASTED RUMP OF BEEF

*Roasting beef is really only impressive if you use a large cut of beef. Sirloin is a good cut to use but because it is thinner it has a larger percentage of fat and gristle to meat than the rump, which is the cut to be preferred. Rump also has a fuller flavour than the other best cuts. I roast beef to be eaten rare to medium rare. If you like your meat cooked further it is best to lower the temperature from 200°C (390°F) to 160°C (315°F) to prevent the meat becoming tough and dry. Constant basting also helps with better done meat. Sealing the meat on top of the stove guarantees good caramelisation of the meat and seals it so that the juices are retained.*

Mix the seasonings together, rub into the outside of the rump and leave to stand for 1 hour at room temperature before proceeding.

Preheat the oven to 200°C (390°F).

Heat a heavy-based baking pan on top of the stove, and add the clarified butter. When the butter has melted and is very hot, brown the beef on all sides, along with the mirepoix. Place the beef in the oven and bake for 40 minutes. Remove the beef from the baking pan to a carving tray. Cover with a cloth and leave to rest.

### To make the gravy

Return the baking pan to the top of the stove and add the flour to the fat in the bottom of the pan. Cook over a medium heat for 2 minutes, stirring with a wooden spoon to amalgamate the flour with the fat. Deglaze with the vinegar and wine, add the mustard and stir briskly with the spoon to eliminate lumps. Add the stock and simmer for 5 minutes. Strain into a small saucepan and skim any fat from the surface with a ladle. Taste for seasoning and adjust as necessary.

### To serve

Serve with freshly grated horseradish, roasted potatoes, Spinach Florentine (page 48) and Cauliflower Mousse (page 54).

*Serves 8*

1 × 3 kg (6 lbs) piece of rump steak

Seasoning
1 tablespoon salt
1 tablespoon cracked pepper
1 tablespoon chopped fresh thyme
1 tablespoon chopped fresh marjoram
1 tablespoon crushed bay leaf
1 star anise pod
4 garlic cloves, crushed

½ cup (125 g/4 oz) clarified butter
1 cup mirepoix (page 253)

Gravy
1 tablespoon plain (all-purpose) flour
2 tablespoons sherry vinegar
⅖ cup (100 mL/3½ fl oz) white wine
1 tablespoon Dijon mustard
2 cups (500 mL/16 fl oz) beef stock (page 112)
salt and freshly ground black pepper

# RUMP STEAK WITH OLIVES

6 × 200 g (6½ oz) rump
   steaks
1 teaspoon chopped fresh thyme
   leaves
freshly ground black pepper
½ head of garlic
salt

Sauce
1½ cups (500 g/1 lb) peeled
   and seeded tomato, diced
1 cup (155 g/5 oz) pitted
   black olives
6 marjoram sprigs
1½ tablespoons red wine vinegar
2 tablespoons fresh Italian
   parsley leaves
1 cup (250 g/8 oz) artichoke
   hearts, diced
¼ cup (60 mL/2 fl oz) virgin
   olive oil
salt and freshly ground pepper

*If you like your steak rare ask the butcher to cut it into 4 cm (1½ in.) thick steaks from the middle of the rump.*

Season the steaks with the thyme and pepper. Cut the head of garlic in half laterally, leaving the cut cloves exposed. Rub the steaks with the cut side of the garlic.

Barbecue the steaks if you wish, or sauté them in olive oil in a frying pan or skillet. Sear them over a high heat to start (about 30 seconds each side), then season with salt. Continue to cook over a medium heat until they are cooked to the required degree.

*To make the sauce*
Put all the ingredients for the sauce in a large saucepan and bring to the boil. Simmer for 5 minutes and then taste for seasoning.

*To serve*
Serve steaks on individual warmed plates and spoon the sauce over the steaks.

*Serves 6*

# MEDALLIONS OF VEAL WITH TOMATO AND ARTICHOKES

1.5 kg (3 lbs) veal fillet or
   sirloin (backstrap)
¼ cup (60 mL/2 fl oz) melted
   clarified butter
80 mL (2½ fl oz) virgin olive
   oil
1 kg (2 lbs) ripe tomatoes,
   peeled, seeded and diced
3 garlic cloves, crushed
1 bay leaf
salt and freshly ground black
   pepper
1 cup (250 g/8 oz) artichoke
   hearts, quartered
2 tablespoons chopped fresh
   Italian parsley leaves

Cut the veal fillet into 6–8 steaks. Flatten the steaks by tapping them gently with a meat mallet until they are 2 cm (¾ in.) thick. Season and sauté gently in the butter in a heavy frying pan or skillet until browned and cooked medium (about 5 minutes).

Remove the veal steaks to a flat baking sheet.

Add the olive oil to the frying pan or skillet and heat until it begins to smoke. Add the tomato, garlic and bay leaf and cook for 12–15 minutes, or until reduced to a soft pulp. Season with the salt and pepper. Add the artichokes and simmer for 2 more minutes.

Spoon the sauce on top of the medallions and heat in a preheated oven (160°C/315°F) for 5 minutes.

*To serve*
Serve the medallions and sauce on warmed plates. Garnish with the chopped parsley leaves.

*Serves 6–8*

Opposite: Rump Steak with
Olives

# BEEF CONSOMME

Beef stock
1 kg (2 lbs) beef shanks
500 g (1 lb) veal shanks
125 g (4 oz) butter
¼ cup (60 mL/2 fl oz) virgin
 olive oil
60 g (2 oz) ham
2 large brown onions (skin on)
half a head of garlic
1 stick celery
1 leek
1 large carrot
90 g (3 oz) mushrooms
3 chopped tomatoes
2 tablespoons tomato paste
 (purée)
1¼ cups (310 mL/10 fl oz)
 white wine
6–8 cups (1.5–2 litres/
 2½–3¼ imp. pints) water
3 thyme sprigs
12 peppercorns

Consommé
1 kg (2 lbs) lean beef
500 g (1 lb) beef bones
3 tablespoons clarified butter
1¼ cups mirepoix (page 253)
1 tablespoon tomato paste
 (purée)
310 g (10 oz) tomatoes, cut
 into halves
2 garlic cloves, chopped
1 bouquet garni (page 252)
12 peppercorns
405 mL (13 fl oz) white wine
4 cups (1 litre/1¾ imp. pints)
 beef stock

Clarification
2 egg whites
125 g (4 oz) lean, minced
 (ground) beef

*Consommé is a clear soup which should be bright with soup, with no trace of fat. It and can be served hot or cold.*

### To make the beef stock

Ask your butcher to saw the beef and veal shanks into 2 cm (¾ in.) rounds. Put two-thirds of the butter and the oil in a large, heavy-based stock pot or saucepan over a high heat. Add the meat and brown it. In another saucepan, brown the ham, onion, garlic, celery, leek, carrot and mushrooms in the remaining butter and oil, but do not let them burn.

Combine the vegetable and ham mix with the meat, add the tomatoes and tomato paste (purée) and cook over a high heat. Continue to stir until the tomato paste starts to caramelise. Immediately add the wine and reduce by half. Pour over the water, making sure the bones are covered.

Bring the stock to the boil and skim to remove the scum and fat which floats to the surface. Add the thyme and peppercorns and simmer for 8 hours. A little trick is to place the pot to one side of the heat source so that the scum will collect on one side and is thus easier to remove.

Strain the stock through a strainer (the conical variety known as a chinois is the best piece of equipment to use) gently pressing the solids to remove the remaining juices. Cool overnight in the refrigerator. The fats that have solidified on the surface can then be easily removed.

*Makes about 4 cups (1 litre/1¾ imp. pints) of stock*

### To make the consommé

The process is much the same as for preparing the beef stock (above). Brown the meat and bones in the butter over a high heat for 10–15 minutes. Add the mirepoix and continue cooking until the vegetables are also slightly brown. Add the tomato paste (purée) and thoroughly coat the meat with it. Continue cooking until you feel the ingredients are about to burn. This process is called caramelisation and will give the consommé colour and flavour. Add the rest of the ingredients and bring to the boil. Lower the heat to a simmer and cook for 3½ hours, skimming as you go.

Strain the consommé into another saucepan and allow to cool. Remove any excess fat with a ladle or again refrigerate overnight and then remove the consolidated fats, which will have collected on the surface.

*How to clarify the consommé*

Thoroughly mix the egg whites with the minced (ground) beef and whisk the mixture through the cold consomme. Slowly bring to the boil. The egg whites will form a crust on top, leaving a crystal clear consommé beneath. Remove the crust. As a final step, strain the consommé through muslin.

*To serve*

It is best to prepare the consommé the day before the meal. When ready to serve, gently reheat the soup and pour into warmed serving bowls.

*Makes approximately 6 cups (1.5 litres/ 2½ imp. pints) of consommé, which will serve 4*

# RARE POT ROAST OF BEEF WITH RED WINE

*Cooking steaks for 6–8 people at home can be very difficult, as the stove is not usually big enough to cook them all at the same time. My solution is to cook the meat as one piece and then slice it like a roast. Using this method you can also cook the vegetables with the beef, making life a lot easier and at the same time creating a more interesting dish.*

Season the beef with the herbs and seasonings. Melt the clarified butter in a heavy casserole and brown the beef on all sides for 5 minutes. Add the onions and garlic and cook over a medium heat for 3 or 4 minutes. Add the mushrooms and allow them to absorb the butter and fat in the bottom of the casserole. Increase the heat and add the wine, the carrots and potatoes (which have been cooked in boiling water for 5 minutes). Cook over a high heat for 5 minutes, reducing the wine by half. Add the peas then turn the beef and cook for a further 5 minutes.

*To serve*

Take the beef from the sauce and slice it onto warmed plates. Add the butter to the sauce and whisk it in. Test for seasoning and then spoon the sauce and vegetables over the beef.

*Serves 6*

2 kg (4 lbs) piece of rump steak, trimmed of fat
4 thyme sprigs
2 bay leaves
salt and freshly ground black pepper

⅓ cup (90 g/ 3 oz) clarified butter

24 baby (pearl) onions
12 garlic cloves, peeled
24 button mushrooms
2 cups (500 mL/ 16 fl oz) red wine
12 baby carrots, blanched (page 252)
12 medium-sized new or boiling potatoes, cooked
2 cups (310 g/ 10 oz) blanched or frozen peas
2 tablespoons butter
salt and freshly ground black pepper

# VEAL CUTLETS
# WITH WILD MUSHROOMS

*6 × 185 g (6 oz) veal cutlets*
*salt and freshly ground pepper*
*2 tablespoons clarified butter*

Rice croûtons
*155 mL (5 fl oz) virgin olive*
  *oil*
*1 cup (220 g/ 7 oz) japonica*
  *(sticky) rice*
*3 cups (750 mL/ 24 fl oz)*
  *water*
*salt and freshly ground black*
  *pepper*

Sauce
*⅓ cup (90 mL/ 3 fl oz) white*
  *wine*
*1 teaspoon truffle essence*
  *(optional)*
*2 tablespoons veal glaze*
  *(page 112)*
*2 tablespoons sherry or*
  *champagne vinegar*
*¼ cup (60 mL/ 2 fl oz) virgin*
  *olive oil*
*salt and freshly ground black*
  *pepper*

Mushrooms
*750 g (1½ lbs) mushrooms*
*⅓ cup (90 mL/ 3 fl oz) virgin*
  *olive oil*
*4 golden shallots, chopped*
*2 garlic cloves, crushed and*
  *chopped*
*2 tablespoons chopped fresh*
  *parsley*
*salt and freshly ground black*
  *pepper*

Garnish
*12 chervil sprigs*
*4 zucchini (courgettes), cut into*
  *batons and blanched*

Opposite: Veal Cutlets with
Wild Mushrooms

*There are many varieties of fungi now available to us. Any of the following are suitable for this dish—shimejii, shiitake, champignons, cèpes (porcinis), morels or oyster.*

### To cook the rice croûtons

Heat 2 tablespoons of the oil in a large saucepan and add the rice. Over a medium heat, cook the rice, stirring all the while, until it is opaque (about 3 minutes). Add the water, season to taste and boil gently for 10 minutes with the lid on.

At this stage the water should have been absorbed by the rice. Turn the heat source to very low and cook for a further 5 minutes. Remove the saucepan from the heat and allow the rice to go cold. Turn the rice out of the saucepan and, with your hands, mould into 6 cm × 2 cm (2½ in. × ¾ in.) thick patties. Heat the remaining oil in a frying pan or skillet and fry the patties until golden or crisp. Drain on paper towels (absorbent kitchen paper) and set to one side, keeping warm.

### To cook the cutlets

Trim the meat and season with salt and pepper. Melt the clarified butter in a heavy-bottomed frying pan or skillet and sauté the cutlets gently for 10 minutes until golden brown on both sides. Remove to a baking sheet, spooning some of the butter from the pan over them. Set to one side and keep warm.

### To make the sauce

Use the white wine to deglaze the pan in which you have just cooked the cutlets, and tip the liquid into a small saucepan. Add the truffle essence, veal glaze, sherry (or vinegar) and olive oil. Stir until the mixture is thoroughly combined and season to taste.

### To cook the mushrooms

Clean and slice the mushrooms. Heat the olive oil in the frying pan or skillet and gently cook the shallots over a low heat for 3 minutes. Increase the temperature to moderately high and add the mushrooms and garlic. After approximately 7 minutes, when the mushrooms have wilted, add the parsley. Season to taste.

### To serve

Place a croûton in the centre of each plate and a cutlet on top. Surround with the mushrooms and spoon the sauce around them. Garnish with chervil and some blanched zucchini (courgette).

*Serves 6*

# BRAISED BRISKET WITH STAR ANISE

2 kg (4 lbs) trimmed brisket
90 g (3 oz) clarified butter
1 cup mirepoix (page 253)
2 brown onions, halved
⅓ cup (90 mL/ 3 fl oz) white wine
1 head of garlic, halved
1 leek, halved, trimmed and washed
6 cups (1.5 litres/ 2½ imp. pints) beef stock (see below)

Marinade
1 tablespoon cracked pepper
3 star anise pods
1 tablespoon chopped fresh thyme leaves
2 bay leaves
2 juniper berries
1 tablespoon brown sugar
1 tablespoon salt
3 tablespoons malt vinegar

*Brisket is one of the less tender, rather fatty cuts of beef, cut from the lower part of the shoulder. It can be bought on or off the bone and is suitable for stewing, braising or pot-roasting. Cold cuts of brisket are just as delicious.*

*To make the marinade*
Pulverise all the herbs and spices and add the sugar, salt and vinegar. When the ingredients have been mixed, rub the beef with the mixture and leave to marinate overnight, covered, in the refrigerator.

Heat a heavy casserole over a medium heat. Add the clarified butter and when it has melted and is hot, add the beef and mirepoix and brown on all sides. Brown the cut sides of the onions with the beef and then add the wine, garlic and leek. Reduce the mixture by half over a high heat and then add the stock. Bring to the boil and skim the scum and fat from the stock with a ladle. Cover and simmer, do not boil, for 4 hours. Allow the beef to cool in the stock and then refrigerate for 3 hours.

*To serve*
Remove the fat from the jellied stock. Slice the beef and serve it cold with a tomato and basil salad and spoonfuls of the beef jelly. If you prefer, heat the beef in the stock, serve with steamed parsley potatoes and Braised Belgian Endives (page 58).

*Serves 6–8*

# BEEF OR VEAL STOCK

2 kg (4 lbs) blade steak, bone in, in 4 cm (1½ in.) chunks, or 2 kg (4 lbs) bobby veal shanks, sawn into 4 cm (1½ in.) lengths
3 tablespoons virgin olive oil
1½ cups mirepoix (page 253)
6 parsley stalks
3 sprigs thyme
12 peppercorns
200 g (6½ oz) tomatoes
2 tablespoons tomato paste (purée)
2 cups (500 mL/ 16 fl oz) white wine
6 cups (1.5 litres/ 2½ imp. pints) water

Place the beef in a baking pan, brown it in a hot oven (220°C/425°F) and then remove it.

In a large saucepan, heat the oil and brown the mirepoix over a medium heat. Add the seasonings, tomatoes and tomato paste (purée) and continue to cook over a high heat until the tomato begins to brown. Deglaze the baking pan with the wine and add the liquid and beef to the saucepan. Add the water and bring to the boil. Skim any scum from the surface of the stock and simmer for 3 hours.

Strain the stock through a fine sieve or muslin. Cool the stock and then refrigerate it. It will keep in the refrigerater for several days and can be frozen.

To make a glaze, reduce the liquid by half over a medium heat.

*Makes 4 cups*

# ORANGE GLAZED HAM

*To make the glaze*

Boil together the glaze ingredients and reduce the liquid to 1¾ cups (435 mL/14 fl oz) liquid. Set aside.

*To make the sauce*

Place all the sauce ingredients except the veal demi-glace in a saucepan and bring to the boil over a high heat. Reduce by one-half and add the demi-glace. Bring to a simmer and remove any scum that comes to the surface with a ladle. Adjust the seasoning.

Strain through a fine strainer into a sauce boat or jug. Set aside.

*To cook the ham*

Leave the ham out of the refrigerator for a day before cooking. This is important because otherwise it will take much longer to cook through to the bone.

Remove the skin from the ham using a sharp flexible knife angled against the underside of the skin. Trim the ham of any 'dags' so that it is a good even shape. Score the fat at 4 cm (1½ in.) intervals in two directions to form a diamond pattern. Press a clove into each of the intersections.

Place the ham, fat side up, in a deep baking pan with the herbs, white wine and vegetables. Cover loosely with some aluminium foil and bake in a slow oven (150°C/300°F) for 2½ hours, basting the ham every 20 minutes.

Prepare another baking pan with a cooling rack in it on which to glaze the ham.

Take the pan from the oven, lift the ham from the baking pan to the rack, pat dry with paper towels (absorbent kitchen paper) and brush the ham with the orange glaze. Return the ham on the rack to a hot oven (250°C/475°F) and brush it with the glaze every 10 minutes until the glaze begins to caramelise. Keep basting the ham until the glaze is used up. The caramelising should take no longer than 1 hour. If your oven is slow, use the griller (broiler) to hasten the process. Since the glazing is always a bit uneven, you can, if desired, trace over the unglazed parts of the ham with the flame from a small blow torch so that it becomes evenly glazed.

*To serve*

The ham can be served hot or cold, accompanied by the sauce. Serve the sauce warm with hot ham. Serve the ham with Celeriac Purée (page 53) or Braised Peas (page 66).

*Serves 10*

1 × 3 kg (6 lbs) double smoked ham with chine bone removed
30 cloves
1 teaspoon fresh thyme leaves
3 bay leaves, broken into small pieces
1½ cups (375 mL/12 fl oz) white wine
½ onion
½ medium carrot, chopped

Glaze
1¾ cups (435 mL/14 fl oz) fresh orange juice
4 tablespoons honey
2 tablespoons sherry vinegar

Sauce
½ cup (125 mL/4 fl oz) good Madeira
1 cup (250 mL/8 fl oz) veal demi-glace (page 112)
4 tablespoons white wine
2 tablespoons fresh orange juice
1 tablespoon sherry vinegar
salt and freshly ground black pepper

# BRAISED OXTAIL

*This is my favourite winter dish. Make it in large amounts as it reheats well. Your butcher should cut the tails at the joints.*

Melt the butter in a deep, heavy, frying pan or skillet, or a baking pan. Fry the bacon (or smoked belly pork) until it is crisp, then remove with a slotted spoon to a large braising casserole or saucepan. Brown the oxtail in the remaining fat in small lots, removing the finished pieces to the braising pan. When the tail is all browned, tip out most of the fat. Gently brown the onions, mushrooms, garlic and carrot.

Add the tomato paste (purée) and cook over a high heat for 2–3 minutes, creating a little caramelisation. Now add the fresh tomatoes and the wine to deglaze the frying pan or skillet. Scrape any caramelised glaze into the liquid. Tip all the ingredients into the braising casserole or saucepan and add water to cover.

Add the seasonings and bring to the boil, then lower to a simmer. With a ladle, skim off and discard any scum that rises to the surface.

Simmer for 3 hours, or until tender. Strain the liquid, returning the vegetables to the casserole dish. Refrigerate the liquid for several hours to solidify the fat. Remove the fat. Reheat the sauce, taste and adjust the seasoning and return to the casserole. Bring to the boil and serve.

*To serve*
Serve oxtail on warm plates with creamy Mashed Potato (page 64).
*Serves 8*

3 kg (6 lbs) oxtail cut at the joints and trimmed of fat

125 g (4 oz) clarified butter
225 g (7 oz) bacon or smoked belly pork, diced
3 brown onions, peeled and chopped
405 g (13 oz) mushrooms, sliced
6 garlic cloves, crushed
1 carrot, peeled and diced
3 tablespoons tomato paste (purée)
3 large tomatoes, diced
3 cups (750 mL/24 fl oz) white or red wine

Seasonings
1/2 teaspoon grated orange peel
3 thyme sprigs
1 bay leaf
salt and freshly ground black pepper

# GRILLED HERBED PORK CHOPS

Mix together the marinade ingredients. Place the pork chops in an oval casserole or other suitable dish and cover with the marinade. Set aside in the refrigerator for 12 hours, turning the meat three or four times during this time.

Drain the chops and season with salt and pepper. Under a preheated moderately hot griller (broiler) (190°C/375°F), cook the chops until golden and well done, about 10 minutes to each side.

*To serve*
Serve with a garnish of watercress and quartered lemon.
*Serves 4*

4 × 250 g (8 oz) pork loin chops
salt and freshly ground pepper
1 lemon, quartered
watercress to garnish

Marinade
3/4 cup (185 mL/6 fl oz) virgin olive oil
2 tablespoons chopped fresh sage
1 tablespoon chopped fresh thyme leaves
1 bay leaf, crumbled
1 tablespoon chopped fresh rosemary
1 garlic clove, minced

Opposite: Braised Oxtail

# OSSO BUCCO WITH RISOTTO

1.75 kg (3½ lbs) or 6 veal
shanks, from young (bobby)
calves
½ teaspoon salt
1 teaspoon freshly ground black
pepper
½ teaspoon chopped fresh thyme
½ teaspoon chopped fresh
marjoram
2 bay leaves, crushed
2 tablespoons clarified butter

1 cup mirepoix (page 253)
1 cup (250 g/8 oz) chopped
onion
2 cups (500 mL/16 fl oz)
white wine
6 garlic cloves, crushed
600 g (1¼ lbs) ripe tomatoes,
diced
2 tablespoons tomato paste
(purée)

Gremolata
4 tablespoons chopped fresh
Italian parsley
2 tablespoons chopped fresh
parsley
2 tablespoons chopped lemon
zest

Risotto
3 tablespoons butter
1 medium-sized onion
1 cup (185 g/6 oz) Arborio
rice
3 cups (750 mL/24 fl oz) beef
or chicken stock (page 138)
salt and freshly ground black
pepper
2 tablespoons grated Parmesan
cheese

## Preparing the meat

Ask the butcher to saw off the base of the shank at right angles to the bone without touching the muscle. Then saw the bone 3 cm (1¼ in.) from the top of the bone, again at right angles. This last cut is important: it should be just where the muscle finishes before the joint. The cut then exposes the bone marrow so that it can be sucked from the bone when cooked.

Using a sharp knife, cut the muscle from around the top of the bone and push it to the base. Then secure the muscle to the base of the bone with string. The reason for this is that as the shank cooks the muscle shrinks, and so by cutting it from the top of the bone we direct the shrinkage to expose the top of the bone. As the cooking proceeds in the oven the bone will brown and the meat shrink to be braised in the sauce. By cutting the bone at right angles the bone will stand upright on the plate. The same preparation should be used for lamb shanks.

## To cook the shanks

Season with the salt, pepper and herbs. Melt the clarified butter in a heavy frying pan or skillet and gently brown the shanks in the butter. Cooking two at a time is best. Remove the shanks to a deep baking pan as they are browned. When you have finished this process, brown the mirepoix and the onion in the frying pan and tip the mixture over the base of the shanks. Deglaze the pan with white wine, add the garlic, tomatoes and the tomato paste (purée). Tip the sauce over the shanks and place the baking pan in a preheated oven (160°C/315°F). Bake for 1½ hours, basting every 5 minutes.

## To make the gremolata

The ingredients should be very finely chopped and then mixed.

## To make the risotto

Melt the butter in an earthenware casserole or saucepan. Chop the onion finely and cook in the butter over a medium heat for 2 minutes, stirring constantly. Add the rice and stir the mixture until it is slightly gilded. Add the stock, cover the casserole and simmer gently until the rice is tender and the liquid is all but absorbed (about 15 minutes). Add salt and pepper and sprinkle with the cheese.

## To serve

Sprinkle veal shanks with gremolata and serve with risotto.

*Serves 6–8*

# SPICED LAMB KEBAB

Cut all the kebab ingredients into 3 cm (1¼ in.) cubes. The sweet peppers (capsicums) will need to be de-cored and heavy membranes attached to walls removed. Mix together the marinade ingredients and, in a covered dish, thoroughly coat the lamb pieces with the marinade and refrigerate overnight. Drain the lamb from the marinade and thread the kebab ingredients onto skewers in the following order: onion, lamb, bacon, and sweet pepper.

Grill the kebabs over low heat (160°C/315°F) for 10–12 minutes, turning occasionally so that the meat is browned on all sides.

*To serve*
Serve on a bed of rice garnished with cooked peas, lemon wedges and sprigs of mint.

*Serves 4–6*

Kebab
*1 kg (2 lbs) leg of lamb, boned*
*2 onions*
*5 bacon rashers (slices)*
*4 sweet peppers (capsicums)*

Marinade
*½ cup (125 mL/4 fl oz) virgin olive oil*
*3 tablespoons sherry vinegar*
*4 garlic cloves, crushed*
*3 bay leaves*
*4 thyme sprigs*
*1 tablespoon paprika*
*1 tablespoon fennel seeds*
*freshly ground black pepper*
*½ teaspoon ground lemon rind*
*½ teaspoon ground cardamom pods*

# CROWN ROAST OF PORK

*To make the stuffing*
Sauté the onion and celery in the butter for 4–5 minutes, then add the sliced apple. Sprinkle the sugar over and add the cinnamon, nutmeg, sage and thyme. Season with salt and pepper, cover and cook very slowly for about 15 minutes, or until the apples are tender, shaking the pan to prevent scorching.

Stir into the mixture the dry breadcrumbs, parsley and chives and blend with the boiling water.

*To cook the pork*
Have the pork loin ribs trimmed and formed into a crown with the ribs outside. Scrape the flesh from the bones between the ribs as far as the lean meat and trim off. Cover the tip of each rib bone with aluminium kitchen foil to prevent burning while roasting. Rub the meat well with salt and pepper, and wrap strips of bacon around the lower part of the crown.

Fill the centre of the crown with apple and onion stuffing and roast in a moderate oven (180°C/355°F) for 1½–2 hours.

*To serve*
Allow 2–3 cutlets per person and serve accompanied by Spinach Florentine (page 48) and Pommes Anna (page 63).

*Serves 6*

Pork crown
*1.75 kg (3½ lbs) loin of pork (crown roast)*
*salt and freshly ground pepper*
*3 bacon rashers (slices)*

Stuffing
*½ cup (125 g/4 oz) finely chopped onion*
*1 celery stalk and leaves, finely chopped*
*60 g (2 oz) clarified butter*
*4 large apples, peeled and sliced*
*⅓ cup (90 g/3 oz) white granulated sugar*
*¼ teaspoon powdered cinnamon*
*¼ teaspoon grated nutmeg*
*1 teaspoon chopped fresh sage*
*1 teaspoon chopped fresh thyme leaves*
*salt and freshly ground black pepper*
*2 cups (250 g/8 oz) dry breadcrumbs*
*¼ cup finely chopped parsley*
*2 tablespoons chopped fresh chives*
*½ cup (125 mL/4 fl oz) boiling water*

# The Poulterer

*Chicken, duck, goose and turkey: these versatile meats can be prepared in a variety of ways. Low in fat yet high in protein, the inexpensive chicken can be dressed up for celebrations or simply prepared for everyday meals. For a special event, Mousse of Duck Livers with Sauternes Jelly is worth the preparation.*

Chicken is now the most popular food in Western societies. This is due more to modern husbandry techniques that have refined the chicken's ability to consume minced up leftovers and convert them into palatable protein quickly, rather than for any other reason. That is, chicken is cheap to produce and sell!

The range of different types of chicken is confusing. The most highly prized chickens are those from Bresse, a small damp area on the outskirts of Lyon. However, it is difference that makes life and eating more interesting. The most boring chicken is the one you eat three times a week cooked in the same way.

I prefer cooking large free-range chickens; as they say in the movies, 'size may not be everything but it sure helps'. The same rule applies to all poultry: small ducks have no breast and lack flavour. Small turkeys miss the point somehow. Specialty poultry shops are the place to buy large free-range chickens. Kosher poultry shops are particularly good sources of quality poultry.

A game chicken called the Belle Rouge is becoming available in America, Britain and Australia, and this has great flavour. It is particularly suitable for braised chicken dishes.

Cornfed chickens are the best for the poached dishes. I use chickens of at least 1.8 kg (3½ lbs) weight and preferably over 2 kg (4 lbs).

Three main types of duck are available: the Peking, Muscovy and Barbary ducks. The Peking is suitable for roasting and braising, the Muscovy for grilling and braising and the Barbary is suitable for all three cooking methods. While I prefer the ducks to weigh over 2 kg (4 lbs) dressed, you have to be careful that the ducks are still tender. The bottom of the breastbone should be tender and flexible.

Peking ducks must be well cooked; if they are underdone they are tough. This does not mean they should be overdone. A 2 kg (4 lbs) duck will take 1¼ hours to cook in a 200°C (390°F) oven. It should then be rested for 15 minutes before carving.

Muscovy ducks are tough when they are well done and should be served rare to medium rare. Eating ducks cooked only to this degree is unusual in English-speaking countries, but once tried is often preferred to the older method of longer cooking. Until you are used to cooking Muscovys it is better to have them boned out and then cook the breasts as one would a steak and make Confit or Salted Duck (page 131) from the legs. One way of cooking ducks that I love is to rub them with salt, herbs and seasonings (see Confit of Duck, page 131), leave them overnight and then poach the duck in a heavily salted court bouillon until tender.

The duck can be served hot with sauerkraut and mustard, or is absolutely delicious cold as a picnic food.

Previous pages: Poached Eggs with Caviar

# POACHING CHICKEN

*When poaching chicken, the poaching liquid should never boil except to set the exterior juices of the chicken at the beginning of the poach. The easiest method in modern homes is to poach only the breast, which may be purchased separately. While this method presents well on the plate, it does not have the same magic as a whole, large chicken being presented and carved at table.*

### To poach the breast

Season the boneless breast and place a sprig of basil, chervil, dill or rosemary under the outer skin. Put the breast at the bottom of a plastic polythene oven bag and press any air from the bag. Secure the bag by tying it with a piece of string.

Bring some water to the boil in a deep saucepan and lower the bag with the chicken into the water. Reduce the heat and do not reboil the water. A breast weighing 125 g (4 oz) will take approximately 10 minutes to cook; larger breasts slightly longer.

### To poach a whole chicken

Make a highly seasoned stock from some chicken bones (page 138) and add salt to taste. Bring to the boil, add the chicken and place a weight on top to ensure that it is fully submerged. A tightly clamped lid is essential. Lower the heat, and simmer for 45 minutes for a 1 kg (2 lbs) bird and 1¼ hours for a 2 kg (4 lbs) chicken.

# BREAST OF CHICKEN WITH SHALLOTS AND MUSHROOMS

Season the breasts with salt and pepper, melt the butter in a heavy frying pan or skillet over a medium heat and cook the breasts, skin side down, until the skin is crisp and golden (approximately 5 minutes). Turn the breasts over to cook the other side, add the shallots and garlic and continue to cook over a gentle heat for 5 minutes further. Add the mushrooms, thyme and bay leaf and allow the mushrooms to absorb the fat. When the mushrooms have wilted a little (approximately 2 minutes), increase the heat and add the wine, stirring it to deglaze the pan. Lower the heat and simmer for 5 minutes. Remove the chicken from the pan and keep it warm. Season the sauce with salt and pepper, add the parsley and swirl the butter into the sauce. Serve the breasts with the sauce poured over them.

*Serves 6*

*6 breasts of cornfed chicken*
*salt and freshly ground black pepper*
*2 tablespoons clarified butter*
*6 golden shallots, peeled and chopped*
*2 garlic cloves, crushed*
*36 champignon (button) mushrooms*
*2 thyme sprigs*
*1 bay leaf*
*155 mL (5 fl oz) white wine*
*2 tablespoons chopped fresh parsley leaves*
*1 tablespoon butter, diced*

# CHICKEN POT-AU-FEU WITH BRAISED ENDIVES

## Court bouillon
4 cups (1 litre/1¾ imp. pints) water
2 cups (500 mL/16 fl oz) white wine
1 medium-sized carrot, sliced
2 small onions, each stuck with 2 cloves
1 bouquet garni (page 252)
10 black peppercorns
1 teaspoon salt

## Chicken pot-au-feu
1.5 kg (3 lbs) whole chicken
2 veal knuckles, cut into 6 rounds
court bouillon, as needed
12 carrots, cut into oval shapes
12 turnips, cut into oval shapes
24 small onions
4 young leeks, trimmed and washed
12 Belgium endives (witloof), blanched
340 g (11 oz) beef fillet, cut into 6 equal pieces

## Sauce
1 teaspoon chopped golden shallots
1 teaspoon chopped Italian parsley
1 teaspoon chopped fresh tarragon
60 g (2 oz) mushrooms, sliced
¾ cup (185 mL/6 fl oz) white wine
125 g (4 oz) chopped butter
1 teaspoon freshly ground black pepper

*Pot-au-feu literally means pot on the fire and is, in fact, two dishes in one—at least two meats plus vegetables cooked in a broth. The braised Belgian endive (witloof) lifts this wonderful dish to new heights.*

### To make the court bouillon
Court bouillon is a simple stock in which meat, fish or vegetables are poached, usually to enhance the flavour of whatever is cooked in it. Place all the ingredients in a large saucepan and bring rapidly to the boil. Boil for 15–20 minutes then lower the heat and simmer until ready for use in the recipe, or store in the refrigerator.

*Makes about 8 cups (2 litres/3¼ imp. pints)*

### To cook the meat
Put the chicken and veal knuckles into a deep saucepan and add enough court bouillon to cover. Simmer the meat for 1 hour. Remove the chicken from the broth and debone it, slicing the meat into largish pieces. Remove the veal knuckles. Set all the meat to one side but keep warm.

Cook the carrots, turnips, onions leeks and Belgian endive (witloof) until cooked, but a little firm (about 15 minutes) in the same broth, then remove and keep warm. Add the beef fillet pieces to the court bouillon and poach for 3 minutes. Save ¾ cup (185 mL/6 fl oz) of the cooking liquid for the sauce.

### To prepare the sauce
Briefly cook the shallots, herbs and mushrooms in the wine and add the cooking liquid. Reduce the sauce by half over a high heat and strain. Gradually whisk in the butter, piece by piece, correct the seasoning and keep hot.

### To serve
Pour a little of the sauce onto each plate, arranging a selection of vegetables and meats on top and serve the rest of the sauce as an accompaniment.

*Serves 6*

Opposite: Chicken Pot-au-feu with Braised Endives

# CHICKEN DRUMSTICKS
# WITH MARJORAM AND GARLIC

*18 chicken drumsticks*
*3 tablespoons plain (all-purpose) flour*
*1 teaspoon freshly ground black pepper*
*½ teaspoon cayenne pepper*
*½ teaspoon Japanese pepper (Sansho)*
*1 teaspoon salt*
*3 tablespoons virgin olive oil*
*3 tablespoons clarified butter*
*4 golden shallots, chopped*
*3 garlic cloves, crushed*
*1 tablespoon chopped fresh marjoram*
*½ tablespoon chopped fresh thyme leaves*
*1 tablespoon chopped fresh parsley leaves*
*2 tablespoons sherry vinegar*
*1 tablespoon chicken glaze (optional) (page 138)*

Place the flour, peppers and salt in a large paper bag and mix them together. Place the chicken drumsticks in the bag, hold the bag closed, and toss the drumsticks around in the seasonings until they are thoroughly dusted with the mixture. Remove the chicken legs from the bag, leaving any excess seasoning in the bag.

Heat the oil and the butter in a frying pan or skillet, add the chicken legs, and gently cook over a medium heat. When they begin to brown (approximately 5 minutes), add the shallots and cook, stirring occasionally, until they begin to wilt (approximately 5 minutes). Add the garlic and cook gently for a further 5 minutes, being careful that the garlic does not burn.

Tip any excess fat from the pan, retaining a tablespoon or two. Add the herbs, sherry vinegar and chicken glaze to the pan, and toss to coat the legs evenly with the mixture (approximately 2 minutes).

*To serve*
Serve the drumsticks with Celeriac Purée (page 53) or Mashed Potatoes (page 64).
*Serves 6*

# SAUTEED CHICKEN
# WITH POTATOES AND
# MUSHROOMS

*1 plump chicken around 1.75 kg (3½ lbs)*
*plain (all-purpose) flour to dust*
*2 tablespoons peanut oil*
*155 g (5 oz) butter*
*500 g (1 lb) small new potatoes*
*225 g (7 oz) mushrooms, cut in pieces*
*salt and freshly ground black pepper*
*2 parsley sprigs, chopped*

Cut the chicken into 8 pieces and lightly flour each piece. In a heavy-based frying pan or skillet, heat the oil and the butter, making sure the butter does not brown. Place the pieces of chicken in the pan and sauté over a medium heat until they are lightly coloured (about 10 minutes). Add the potatoes, reduce the heat to a low simmer and cook for a further 10 minutes, making sure there is butter in the pan at all times. Add the mushrooms and season with salt and pepper. Continue to simmer for a further 8 minutes. Just before serving, sprinkle with the parsley.
*Serves 4*

# ROAST CHICKEN

*I hesitated to include this recipe, but I was persuaded by friends who wanted a good recipe for what is, after all, a domestic staple. I think you get a better result if you bring the chicken to room temperature before stuffing it with the still warm stuffing. Good breadcrumbs make a big difference to the stuffing. Use stale strong white bread (page 253) from French- or Italian-style breads. Remove the crusts and dry the inside of the bread and then crumb it by rubbing it between your fingers.*

### *To make the stuffing*

Melt the butter in a saucepan over a medium heat, and add two rashers (slices) of the bacon, chopped into small pieces, then add the onion and garlic. Cook gently, stirring constantly until the onion and bacon fat is translucent. Add the giblets, stir and cook briefly (20 seconds). Add the stuffing seasonings and cook for a few seconds so that they release their perfume. Add the breadcrumbs, take the pan from the heat and stir so that the breadcrumbs absorb the fat and the stuffing is well mixed. Allow the mixture to cool and then stuff the bird after seasoning the cavity with salt and pepper. Put a teaspoon of the stuffing between the skin and each breast.

Season the skin with salt and pepper and then mix together the melted butter and garlic and brush the mixture over the skin. Take the remaining two rashers of bacon, place one on each breast, and secure with string.

### *To cook the chicken*

Take a suitably sized baking pan and strew the bottom with the diced onion and carrot for the gravy. Place the chicken on top and bake in a preheated moderate oven (170°C/340°F) for 1 hour, basting with the fat as it accumulates in the baking pan.

Take the bacon off the breasts, increase the heat to 180°C (350°F) and cook for 15–20 minutes, basting frequently with the fat in the bottom of the baking pan.

When the skin is brown and crisp, take the chicken from the oven and place it on a serving dish. Rest the chicken in a warm place while you make the gravy. The onion and carrot should now have caramelised.

### *To make the gravy*

Place the baking dish over a medium heat to liquefy the fat. Pour almost all the fat from the pan, leaving 2 tablespoons. Return the pan to the heat and add the flour, sprinkling it over the caramelised carrot and onion. Cook gently for 3 minutes and then add the wine and vinegar. Deglaze the pan, scraping any caramelised juices into the

*1 × 2 kg (4 lbs) chicken*

Stuffing
*2 tablespoons butter*
*4 bacon rashers (slices)*
*1 onion, chopped*
*3 garlic cloves, crushed and chopped*
*the chopped chicken giblets (if available)*
*1 tablespoon fresh thyme leaves*
*1 tablespoon chopped fresh marjoram or basil leaves*
*½ cup chopped Italian parsley*
*1 bay leaf, crushed*
*1 tablespoon freshly ground black pepper*
*1 teaspoon salt*
*2 cups (125 g/4 oz) fresh breadcrumbs*
*extra salt and freshly ground black pepper*

Skin seasoning
*salt and freshly ground black pepper*
*2 tablespoons melted butter*
*1 garlic clove, crushed*

Gravy
*½ onion, diced*
*½ carrot, diced*
*1 tablespoon plain (all-purpose) flour*
*155 mL (5 fl oz) white wine*
*1 tablespoon red wine vinegar*
*1¼ cups (310 mL/10 fl oz) root vegetable cooking water*
*salt and freshly ground black pepper*

liquid and stirring to eliminate lumps. Reduce the liquid by one-half over a high heat, add the vegetable water and reduce the liquid further by one-third. Season the gravy with salt and pepper and strain it into a sauce boat or gravy jug.

*To serve*

If necessary, return the chicken to the oven to heat so that it is served hot. Carve the chicken and serve it with the gravy and stuffing, accompanied by Pommes Anna (page 63) and buttered spinach.

*Serves 6*

# SAUTEED CHICKEN IN VINEGAR

*A simple, inexpensive dish that can be prepared for the family in half an hour.*

2 kg (4 lbs) chicken, cut into 8 pieces
60 g (2 oz) clarified butter
125 g (4 oz) golden shallots, finely sliced
155 mL (5 fl oz) sherry vinegar
1 bouquet garni (page 252)

Chicken Stock
60 g (2 oz) butter
1 cup mirepoix (page 253) using white parts of 2 leeks; ½ onion; ½ carrot; 1 stick celery; 1 garlic clove
1 small chicken (500 g/1 lb)
1 cup (250 mL/8 fl oz) white wine
6 parsley stalks, chopped
2 thyme sprigs
6 black peppercorns
6 cups (1.5 litres/2½ imp. pints) cold water

Sauce
⅓ cup (90 mL/3 fl oz) white wine
1 chopped tomato
1 tablespoon tomato paste (purée)
½ cup (125 mL/4 fl oz) chicken stock
1 tablespoon beurre manié (page 252)
salt and freshly ground pepper
1 tablespoon parsley leaves

Opposite: Sautéed Chicken in Vinegar

*To cook the chicken*

Melt the butter in a frying pan or skillet and sauté the chicken pieces on all sides for 8 minutes or until a golden colour. Add the shallots, cooking for 1 more minute before swirling in the vinegar and adding the bouquet garni. Cover the pan and cook over a medium heat for 10 minutes. Remove the chicken from the pan and keep warm.

*To make the chicken stock*

There is a slight variation in the composition of the mirepoix mixture used in this recipe; leeks (which combine very well with chicken) and garlic have been added.

Over a low heat, melt the butter in a saucepan and soften the mirepoix. Add the chicken, turning frequently so that the skin does not colour. Add the wine, herbs and peppercorns, and cover the saucepan with a tight lid. Over a high heat, steam the chicken for 5 minutes. Add the water and simmer, skimming any fat from the surface of the liquid. Simmer for 1¼ hours, or until the chicken is tender. Strain through a fine sieve. The cold poached chicken can be used for other dishes, such as salads or soups.

*To make the sauce*

Put the wine, tomato and tomato paste (purée) into the frying pan or skillet, heat, and reduce by one-third. Add the chicken stock, whisking in the beurre manié to thicken it. More chicken stock may be added if the sauce seems too thick. Season to taste.

*To serve*

Arrange the chicken pieces on a large serving platter and pour over the sauce. Garnish with whole parsley leaves.

*Serves 4*

# SAUTEED CHICKEN LIVERS PROVENCAL

500 g (1 lb) chicken livers
  trimmed, washed and dried
90 g (3 oz) butter
2 tablespoons chopped golden
  shallots
3 garlic cloves, crushed
2 tablespoons chopped fresh
  parsley leaves
1/2 teaspoon fresh thyme
salt and freshly ground pepper
2 tablespoons lemon juice

Melt the butter in a frying pan or skillet. Add the livers and the shallots. Brown the livers quickly and then add the garlic, parsley and thyme. Season with salt and pepper and add the lemon juice. Serve very hot, cooked medium–medium rare.

*Serves 6–8 as a first course*

# RED CHICKEN AND EGGPLANT CURRY

310 g (10 oz) boneless, skinned
  chicken breasts

Red curry paste
5 dried red chili peppers,
  chopped
1½ tablespoons green spring
  onions (scallions), sliced
½ tablespoon lemon grass, sliced
½ tablespoon chopped garlic
2 teaspoons salt
1 teaspoon shrimp paste
1 teaspoon galangal or ginger
  root, sliced
½ teaspoon grated fresh lime zest
½ teaspoon chopped coriander
  (Chinese parsley) root or stem

Curry
5 cups (1.25 litres/2 imp.
  pints) thin coconut milk
1 teaspoon red curry paste
8 white peppercorns, crushed
3 tablespoons fish sauce
  (page 252)
½ tablespoon palm sugar
6 small eggplants (aubergines)
3 fresh red chili peppers
2 kaffir lime leaves, chopped
  (page 253)
10 sweet basil leaves

*The spread of Asian cuisines around the world has introduced many spicy and aromatic dishes to our tables. Thai cuisine especially has that chili hot quality which is balanced by a subtle sweetness. It is always best to make your own curry paste. Keep it in a sealed jar in the refrigerator.*

*To make the red curry paste*
Pound all the ingredients together with a pestle and mortar, or in a blender, to form a fine paste.

*To cook the curry*
In a large saucepan, heat 1 cup (250 mL/8 fl oz) of the coconut milk, add the curry paste (to taste) and white peppercorns, stir and cook for 2 minutes.

Slice the chicken breasts across into 6 mm (¼ in.) pieces, cut the eggplants (aubergines) into quarters, and quarter the chili peppers lengthwise. Add the chicken pieces to the saucepan, and stir well. Add the rest of the coconut milk. Bring the mixture to the boil and add the fish sauce and palm sugar. Boil the chicken pieces for 1 minute, then add the eggplants, chili peppers and kaffir lime leaves. Bring the mixture back to the boil and cook for a further 3 minutes.

Add the basil at the last moment, remove from the heat and serve immediately.

*Serves 6*

# GREEN CHICKEN CURRY

*To make the curry paste*

Grind the dry ingredients in an electric coffee grinder or mortar and pestle. Add the ground mixture to the lime juice and blend in a blender or food processor. Keep to one side.

*To cook the chicken*

Wash, blanch and purée the spinach. Heat the oil in a heavy saucepan. Add the onions and garlic and soften over a medium heat for 2–3 minutes. Add the chicken, turning in the onion and garlic mixture until the chicken begins to stiffen. Add the paste and coat the chicken well. Cook over a low heat for 1 hour, moistening if necessary with a little water. Add the spinach and simmer for a further 10 minutes. Serve with steamed rice.

*Serves 6–8*

1 × 2 kg (4 lbs) chicken (legs, wings and breasts cut in two)
⅓ cup (90 mL/3 fl oz) peanut or olive oil
2 onions, sliced
6 garlic cloves, crushed
water as required
1 bunch English spinach

Curry paste
3 fresh green chili peppers
3 tablespoons peeled ginger
6 cardamom pods
1 star anise pod
5 cm (2 in.) piece cinnamon
8 fresh basil leaves
2 curry leaves
2 kaffir lime leaves (page 253)
2 teaspoons salt
½ cup (125 mL/4 fl oz) lime juice

# SHREDDED SALTED DUCK AND GHERKIN SALAD

*This cold confit of duck makes a wonderful first course for lunch or dinner.*

Warm the duck, then remove and discard the skin. Cut the meat from the legs and shred it.

Blanch the onions in boiling water for 1 minute, drain, refresh under cold running water, drain and wring dry in a tea towel.

Julienne the cornichons with a sharp knife. Grind some pepper over the duck and mix the meat with the cornichons, parsley, marjoram, onions, Belgian endive (witloof) and radicchio (chicory).

*To make the dressing*

Mix together the duck fat and olive oil, whisk in the red wine vinegar and mustard. Season to taste with salt and pepper.

*To make the sippets*

Melt the duck fat and fry the bread until brown and crisp (3–4 minutes). Toss the sippets in the pan with the garlic while still hot.

*To serve*

Toss all the ingredients for the salad in a large bowl, pour over the dressing and serve, accompanied by a bowl of sippets.

*Serves 6–8*

4 legs of salted duck (page 131)
2 onions, finely sliced
6 cornichon gherkins
freshly ground black pepper
2 tablespoons chopped Italian parsley
1 teaspoon chopped fresh marjoram leaves
1 head of radicchio (chicory)
3 Belgian endives (witloof)

Dressing
2 tablespoons duck fat
3 tablespoons virgin olive oil
2 tablespoons red wine vinegar
1 teaspoon strong Dijon mustard
salt and freshly black ground pepper

Sippets
3 tablespoons duck fat
1 cup (60 g/2 oz) small diced bread
1 garlic clove, crushed

# CONFIT OF SALTED DUCK

*This classic preserved duck preparation from the Dordogne is usually served grilled with a hot potato salad, or in a cassoulet.*

Mix together the salt, juniper berries, herbs and spices. Lay the duck legs on a wooden tray or ceramic dish, rub in the salt, herb and spice mix, and cover with aluminium kitchen foil. Refrigerate the legs, turning them after 12 hours. After 24 hours, brush the salt mixture from the legs and pat them dry with a cloth. Place the legs in a heavy saucepan or casserole and cover them with the goose fat and the water. Bring the mixture to the boil over a medium heat and then turn the heat to the lowest level possible and cook without boiling until tender (2–3 hours). Lift the legs from the fat and layer them in a jar. Cover the legs with the hot fat, not allowing any water that may remain underneath the fat into the jar, then cool and refrigerate. Use when needed. The confit of duck will keep indefinitely if refrigerated.

*Serves 6*

6 duck legs (preferably from Muscovy ducks)

310 g (10 oz) Maldon sea salt (page 253)
6 juniper berries, crushed
1 teaspoon fresh thyme leaves
2 bay leaves, crushed
1 star anise pod, powdered
1 teaspoon roughly ground black pepper
2 garlic cloves, crushed

2 tins (125 g/4 oz) goose fat (page 253)
½ cup (125 mL/4 fl oz) water

# GRILLED CONFIT OF DUCK WITH POTATO SALAD

The confit of duck is already cooked and tender. All that needs to be done is to crisp up the skin under the griller (broiler). To do this, preheat the griller and lay the legs skin side up on the rack. Grill until the legs begin to brown, then turn them over and cook until the other side begins to brown, then turn again for a final crisping of the skin.

Heat the goose fat in a deep frying pan or skillet and gently soften the shallots in the fat. Cook the potatoes in boiling salted water until tender (10–15 minutes, depending on the size), then peel and cut into 1 cm (4⅓ in.) slices. Add the potatoes to the frying pan, browning them a little, then add the parsley and vinegar. Turn gently in the hot goose fat, season with salt and pepper and serve with the grilled confit of duck.

*Serves 6*

confit of duck (see above)

Potato salad
½ cup (125 g/4 oz) goose fat from the confit jar
1 kg (2 lbs) waxy potatoes
6 golden shallots, chopped
½ cup Italian parsley, chopped
3 tablespoons sherry vinegar
salt and freshly ground black pepper

Opposite: Grilled Confit of Duck with Potato Salad

# BAKED GOOSE WITH CHESTNUTS

*1 × 3 kg (6 lb) goose*
*1 tablespoon salt*

Stuffing
*600 g (1¼ lbs) minced pork*
*(½ fat, ½ lean)*
*1 onion*
*3 garlic cloves, crushed*
*24 peeled chestnuts*
*225 g (7 oz) goose or duck liver*
*4 fresh sage leaves*
*1 teaspoon fresh thyme leaves*
*2 teaspoons salt*
*1 teaspoon freshly ground black*
*pepper*
*¾ cup (185 mL/6 fl oz) white*
*wine*
*⅓ cup (90 mL/3 fl oz) Cognac*
*2 eggs*

Roasting
*1 cup mirepoix (page 253)*
*125 g (4 oz) butter, softened*
*freshly ground black pepper*

Sauce
*1 tablespoon plain (all-purpose)*
*flour*
*¾ cup (185 mL/6 fl oz) white*
*wine*
*2 cups (500 mL/16 fl oz) veal*
*glaze (page 112)*
*1 tablespoon redcurrant jelly*
*(page 76)*
*2 tablespoons red wine vinegar*

The chestnuts are prepared by slashing them along the curved side and then poaching them in salted water for 10 minutes. Strain them and allow to cool in cold water before peeling.

On the morning of the dinner, rub the goose with the salt and leave it to stand until late afternoon.

Dry the goose with paper towels (absorbent kitchen paper).

### *To make the stuffing*
Mix the pork with the onion, garlic, chestnuts, liver and herbs. Stir the salt, pepper, wine, Cognac and eggs into the mince mixture. Stuff the goose with this stuffing, forcing the mixture into the cavity.

### *To roast the goose*
Arrange the mirepoix on the bottom of a large baking pan. Place the stuffed goose on the bed of mirepoix. Coat the goose with the butter, season with the pepper and roast in a hot oven (180°C/355°F) for 1 hour. Reduce the temperature to 150°C (300°F) and cook for a further 1½ hours. Baste the goose frequently.

Take the goose from the pan and rest it in a warm place.

### *To make the sauce*
Tip the excess fat from the pan, leaving 2 tablespoons. Heat the fat over a medium heat, sprinkle with the flour and cook for a few minutes. Add the wine and reduce by one-third. Add the veal glaze, redcurrant jelly and vinegar. Simmer for 5 minutes and then strain the sauce through a fine strainer.

### *To serve*
Carve the goose and surround the slices of goose on individual plates with the sauce. Serve with Braised Peas (page 66) and Mashed Potato (page 64).

*Serves 6–8*

# CHICKEN PIE

*Chicken pie is a great domestic meal. I have reduced the quantity of cream I previously used, but it is still a rich dish.*

### To make the pastry

Make the pastry first. Sift the flour and salt into a bowl. Add the egg and the butter and rub the mixture together with the tips of your fingers, or process to a sandy consistency in a food processor. Add the water until the mass becomes cohesive. Dust with the flour and roll the pastry out into an oblong shape. Fold over into three sections and roll again. Rest the dough, covered in plastic wrap (cling film), in the refrigerator for 20 minutes and then repeat the folding and rolling stages twice. This pastry is a quick puff pastry. It does not rise like full puff pastry but is perfect for pies.

### To make the filling

Melt the butter in a heavy saucepan, add the bacon and cook it until it has given up its fat (a few minutes). Remove the bacon from the pan with a slotted spoon. Season the chicken with the salt and pepper and brown it in the bacon fat over a medium heat. Remove the chicken from the pan with a slotted spoon and add it to the bacon. Add the onions, leeks, garlic and mushrooms to the pan and cook until softened. Sprinkle with the flour and cook for a further 3 minutes. Add the white wine, tomatoes, thyme and bay leaf and stir until smooth. Add the cream and return the chicken and bacon to the saucepan. Simmer for 1 hour, season with salt and pepper, and allow to cool.

### To make the pie

Take a suitably sized pie plate (23 cm/9 in. diameter). Roll the pastry to cover the top, allowing for a 2 cm (¾ in.) overlap. Brush the underside of the overlapping section with the egg wash. Pile the chicken filling into the pie plate and cover with the pastry. Press the pastry down around the edge of the plate and seal it by using the pressure of your thumbs. Trim the pastry and use the trimmings to make decorative shapes for the top of the pie, remembering to brush them with egg wash to make them stick.

Brush the top of the pie with the egg wash and bake in a moderate oven (180°C/355°F) for 45 minutes, or until golden brown. Serve immediately.

*Serves 6–8*

1 kg (2 lbs) chicken leg meat, without skin

Pastry
500 g (1 lb) strong (baker's) or plain (all-purpose) flour
1 teaspoon salt
1 egg
405 g (13 oz) cold butter, cut in 6 mm (¼ in.) dice
1 cup (250 mL/8 fl oz) water
flour for dusting

90 g (3 oz) butter
6 bacon rashers (slices), chopped
salt and freshly ground black pepper
2 onions, chopped
2 leeks, washed and sliced
4 garlic cloves, chopped
310 g (10 oz) mushrooms, sliced
2 tablespoons plain (all-purpose) flour
600 mL (19 fl oz) white wine
2 tomatoes, diced
1 teaspoon fresh thyme leaves
1 bay leaf
½ cup (125 mL/4 fl oz) light (single) cream

egg wash (page 252)

# MOUSSE OF DUCK LIVERS WITH SAUTERNES JELLY

Duck liver mousse
*500 g (1 lb) duck livers,*
*  cleaned*
*90 g (3 oz) tinned foie gras*
*185 g (6 oz) butter, softened*
*1 cup (250 mL/8 fl oz) light*
*  (single) cream*
*½ teaspoon truffle essence*
*  (optional)*
*salt and freshly ground black*
*  pepper*
*⅓ cup (90 g/3 oz) goose fat*
*  (page 253)*

Sauternes jelly
*2 cups (500 mL/16 fl oz)*
*  duck or veal stock*
*  (page 140 or 112)*
*340 mL (11 fl oz) Sauternes*
*salt and freshly ground black*
*  pepper*
*6 leaves of gelatin (page 252)*

Sauce
*2 tablespoons sherry vinegar*
*2 tablespoons reduced duck*
*  stock (page 140)*
*1 cup (250 mL/8 fl oz)*
*  walnut oil*
*salt and freshly ground black*
*  pepper*

*To make the Sauternes jelly*

Soften the gelatin in ½ cup (125 mL/4 fl oz) of cold water. Place the stock and Sauternes in a large saucepan, bring to the boil and reduce the liquid to 2 cups (500 mL/16 fl oz). Remove gelatin from water, and whisk it into the liquid. Season with salt and pepper. Strain the jelly and allow to cool.

Line a terrine mould 6 cups (1.5 litres/2½ imp. pints) with plastic wrap (cling film) and pour in enough jelly to cover the bottom to a depth of 1.5 cm (½ in.). Refrigerate for 2 hours, or until the jelly is set. Retain the extra jelly.

*To make the mousse*

Sit a large pot of boiling salted water (approximately 3 cups/ 750 mL/24 fl oz) over a high heat. Place the livers in a sieve and lower it into the boiling water. Leave for exactly 3 minutes, then remove and wash the livers thoroughly under cold running water. When they are cold, place them in a bowl with some ice for 15 minutes to chill them.

Dry the livers and purée them in a food processor or blender. Add the tinned foie gras and the softened butter and incorporate them into the purée. Add the cream in a steady stream and turn off the food processor or blender the instant the surface of the pâté starts to gloss. Pass the pâté through the finest blade of a food processor, add the truffle essence (optional) and adjust the seasoning with salt and pepper.

Pour the cool mousse on top of the set jelly in the terrine mould. Tap the terrine on the bench top to settle the mousse. Melt the goose fat and pour it onto the top of the mousse. Refrigerate to set (approximately 2 hours).

*To serve*

Loosen the mousse in the terrine by tugging gently at the overlap of plastic wrap, then turn it out onto a cold plate so that the jelly is on top. Slice onto cold plates and garnish with some of the leftover jelly cut into dice.

Whisk together the sauce ingredients, seasoning with salt and pepper, and spoon the sauce around the mousse. Serve with toasted brioche.

*Serves 6–8*

Opposite: Mousse of Duck
Livers with Sauternes Jelly

# ESCALOPES OF TURKEY BREAST WITH ARTICHOKES

12 thin escalopes (scallops) of
    turkey, cut from the breast
salt and freshly ground pepper
12 thin slices of prosciutto
3 fresh cooked Jerusalem
    artichokes, diced, or 6 tinned
    artichoke hearts, washed and
    diced
½ cup (125 mL/4 fl oz) virgin
    olive oil
1 cup (90 g/3 oz) sliced
    champignon (button)
    mushrooms
3 fresh sage leaves
2 thyme sprigs
1 bay leaf
185 mL (6 fl oz) white wine
2 tomatoes, diced

Beat the escalopes (scallops) of turkey between layers of plastic wrap (cling film) until flat, and then remove from the plastic wrap. Season with salt and pepper. Lay a slice of prosciutto on top of each escalope and then add some diced artichoke. Fold over the two longest sides of the turkey escalopes and then roll them up. Secure with toothpicks.

Heat the oil in a deep frying pan or skillet and brown the rolled escalopes in the hot oil for 7 minutes. Add the champignon (button) mushrooms and herbs and cook until the mushrooms have wilted (5 minutes). Increase the heat and add the white wine and tomatoes. Reduce until the sauce coats the meat and then serve.

*Serves 6*

# BLANQUETTE OF TURKEY

1 kg (2 lbs) turkey breast
8 cups (2 litres/3¼ imp. pints)
    boiling salted water

Base
1½ cups (375 mL/12 fl oz)
    white wine
¼ cup (60 mL/2 fl oz) lemon
    juice
24 baby (pearl) onions, peeled
1 baby onion stuck with 4
    cloves
24 champignon (button)
    mushrooms
2 thyme sprigs
1 bay leaf

Liaison
155 mL (5 fl oz) light (single)
    cream
4 egg yolks
¼ cup (60 mL/2 fl oz) brandy
    (optional)
1 teaspoon salt
½ teaspoon ground white pepper

*A quick and delicious creamy turkey stew.*

### To make the base
Place all the base ingredients in a large saucepan. Bring the mixture to the boil, cover and simmer for 20 minutes.

### To cook the turkey
Meanwhile, cut the turkey breast into 3 cm (1¼ in.) cubes. Blanch the turkey by adding it to the boiling water over a high heat. As soon as the water returns to the boil strain off the water and add the turkey to the base. Cover and simmer the turkey/base mixture for 20 minutes.

### To make the liaison
In a separate bowl, whisk together the ingredients for the liaison. Remove the cover from the saucepan with the turkey and reduce the liquid by one-third over a high heat. Add the liaison to the saucepan and stir briskly to coat the meat. Do not boil the mixture or the sauce will curdle.

### To serve
Serve the blanquette of turkey immediately, with boiled rice or new potatoes.

*Serves 6–8*

# BAKED DUCK
# WITH TOMATO AND HERBS

*This dish is based on one that I had at the Restaurant de la Pyramide in Vienne, south of Lyons, in the mid-1970s. It has remained a favourite at home because it can be prepared well in advance and then heated just before dinner.*

Season the cavities of the ducks with salt and pepper and stuff with the herbs and onions. Season the outside of the ducks with salt and pepper and cut the skin with a sharp knife in a diamond pattern to a depth of 2 cm (¾ in.). Prick the skin around the base of the legs with the point of a knife or fork.

Melt the butter in a heavy baking pan and brown the ducks on all sides. Place them in a preheated oven (220°C/425°F) and roast for 1 hour, basting with the fat every 10 minutes.

Take the ducks from the oven and allow to cool. Tip the fat from the pan and reserve. Do not clean the pan as it will be used to finish the dish.

The duck flesh should still be pink and the skin crisp. When cool, carve the ducks, dividing them in the following manner: the legs into one drumstick and the thighs cut in half; the wings cut into two and each breast cut into two.

Heat 2 tablespoons of the duck fat in a saucepan over a medium heat. Add the onions and garlic and stir gently until soft. When they are translucent, add the tomatoes, increase the heat and cook briskly. Add the herbs, vinegar and salt and pepper. Cook for a further 5 minutes over a high heat to evaporate the liquid. The tomato mixture should be thick, with pieces of the tomato still a little firm.

Heat the baking pan and add the tomato mix to it, using the tomatoes to deglaze the pan, and pulling any caramelised juices into the sauce. Lay the duck pieces on the tomato mix, skin side up. Mix together the breadcrumb ingredients and sprinkle the duck with the breadcrumb mix. Bake in a 180°C (350°F) oven for 15 minutes, or until the crumbs are golden.

Serve with Tian Provençal (page 64).

*Serves 6–8*

2 × 2 kg (4 lb) Peking or
  Barbary ducks
salt and freshly ground black
  pepper
2 marjoram sprigs
2 thyme sprigs
2 onions, chopped
2 tablespoons clarified butter

3 onions, peeled and sliced
6 garlic cloves, crushed
6 tomatoes, peeled and seeded
1 teaspoon fresh thyme leaves
½ tablespoon chopped fresh
  marjoram leaves
2 bay leaves
2 tablespoons red wine vinegar
½ teaspoon salt
½ teaspoon freshly ground black
  pepper

Breadcrumbs
90 g (3 oz) butter, melted
2 cups (125 g/4 oz)
  breadcrumbs
2 golden shallots, chopped
2 garlic cloves
1 teaspoon fresh thyme leaves
2 teaspoons chopped fresh
  marjoram leaves
1 tablespoon chopped fresh
  parsley

# CHICKEN STOCK

1 kg (2 lbs) chicken bones
2 tablespoons butter or virgin
    olive oil
1 leek, washed and chopped
1 onion, sliced
½ carrot, diced
1 stick celery, diced
6 parsley stalks
3 thyme sprigs
12 peppercorns
2 cups (500 mL/ 16 fl oz)
    white wine
6 cups (1.5 litres/ 2½ imp.
    pints) water

Wash the chicken bones under running water. In a large saucepan, heat the butter or oil, add the vegetables and cook over a medium heat until softened. Add the chicken bones and seasonings and turn with a spoon for a minute or so. Add the wine and water and bring to the boil. Skim any scum from the surface of the stock and simmer for 1 hour.

Strain the stock through a fine sieve or muslin. Cool the stock and then refrigerate it. It will keep in the refrigerator for several days and can be frozen. To make a glaze, reduce the liquid by half over a medium heat.

*Makes 4 cups*

# BREAST OF MUSCOVY DUCK WITH ORANGE AND FIGS

4 muscovy duck breasts
salt and freshly ground black
    pepper
1 teaspoon chopped fresh thyme
    leaves
3 tablespoons clarified butter

Glaze
juice of 1 orange
½ teaspoon grated orange rind
2 tablespoons honey
2 tablespoons sherry vinegar

Sauce
¾ cup (185 mL/ 6 fl oz) duck
    stock (page 140)
2 tablespoons sherry vinegar
2 tablespoons Cassis
1 tablespoon butter

Garnish
6 black figs, quartered
2 oranges, peeled and segmented

Opposite: Breast of
Muscovy Duck with
Orange and Figs

*To make the glaze*
Boil the ingredients together in a small saucepan until the quantity is reduced by one-half.

*To cook the duck*
Season the duck breasts with salt, pepper and thyme. Melt the clarified butter in a heavy frying pan or skillet over a medium heat. Place the duck breasts flesh side down in the pan. When they are well browned, turn and cook for 5 minutes on the skin side. Remove the breasts to a flat baking sheet and brush the skin with the glaze. Cook the breasts under a griller (broiler) at a medium heat for another 5 minutes, then set aside in a warm place for 10 minutes.

*To make the sauce*
Deglaze the frying pan or skillet with the stock, vinegar and Cassis and reduce the liquid by one-third. Pass the sauce through a fine strainer into a saucepan. Whisk the butter into the sauce.

*To serve*
Serve the duck breasts medium to medium rare. Carve into 1 cm (⅓ in.) slices and arrange them in a fan shape on the plates. Spoon the warm sauce around the meat. Heat the figs and orange segments in the oven or under a griller and arrange them decoratively on the plates. Puréed spinach, sweetened with a little pear purée, makes an excellent accompaniment.

*Serves 8*

# ROASTED BARBARY DUCK GLAZED WITH PEPPERCORNS

1 × 2–2.5 kg (4–5 lbs)
    Barbary duck
salt and freshly ground black
    pepper
1 onion, peeled
3 thyme sprigs
3 marjoram sprigs
½ cup mirepoix (page 253)

Glaze
1 teaspoon black peppercorns
1 teaspoon white peppercorns
1 teaspoon green peppercorns
1 teaspoon pink peppercorns
1 tablespoon honey
2 tablespoons red wine vinegar
½ cup (125 g/4 oz) duck fat
    (from the roast)

Sauce
⅓ cup (90 mL/3 fl oz) white
    wine
3 tablespoons red wine vinegar
½ teaspoon freshly ground black
    pepper
2 cups (500 mL/16 fl oz) veal
    glaze (page 112)

*Peking duck may be substituted for the Barbary duck.*

Preheat the oven to 220°C (425°F). Season the duck generously inside and out with salt and pepper and stuff it with the onion and herbs. Place a wire rack in a baking pan and lay the duck breast-side down on the rack. Arrange the mirepoix in the bottom of the pan. Roast the duck in the hot oven for 25 minutes and then turn it over. Roast for a further 25 minutes. Mix the glaze ingredients with the duck fat from the roast. Continue cooking the duck, brushing it with the glaze every 5 minutes until it is used up. When the duck is crisp and golden (approximately 1¼ hours in total) remove it from the oven. Tip the fat out of the baking pan, and tip any juices in the duck into the baking pan. Rest the duck in a warm place for 15 minutes while you make the sauce.

Deglaze the baking pan with the wine and vinegar over a medium heat, add the pepper and veal glaze, taste for seasoning and then strain into a sauce boat or gravy jug.

*To serve*
Carve the duck onto hot plates and serve with Mashed Potato (page 64).

*Serves 6–8*

# DUCK STOCK

1 kg (2 lbs) duck bones
    (carcass)
2 tablespoons duck fat
½ onion, diced
½ carrot, diced
1 stick celery, diced
1 chopped tomato
1 tablespoon tomato paste
    (purée)
3 thyme sprigs
1 bay leaf
2 cups (500 mL/16 fl oz)
    white wine
4 cups (1 litre / 1¾ imp. pints)
    water

In a large saucepan, heat the fat and brown the bones over a high heat. Add the vegetables and brown over a medium heat. Add the tomato paste (purée), thyme and bay leaf, and cook until the tomato begins to brown.

Add the wine and water and bring to the boil. Skim any scum from the surface of the stock and simmer for 1½ hours. Strain the stock through a fine sieve or muslin. Cool the stock and then refrigerate it. It will keep in the refrigerator for several days and can be frozen.

To make a glaze, reduce the liquid by half and add an equal amount of Veal Glaze (page 112).

*Makes 4 cups*

# POACHED EGGS WITH CAVIAR

*The ultimate breakfast.*

In a large saucepan, bring the water and vinegar to a rolling boil. Break the eggs onto saucers so that you will be able to quickly slide them into the water. While the water is boiling, stir with a spoon or whisk to create a whirlpool. Slide the eggs, one by one, into the outside of the whirlpool, bring back to the boil, reduce the heat and simmer for 3 minutes. Take the eggs from the water with a slotted spoon and lay them on paper towels (absorbent kitchen paper). Trim the eggs into a good egg shape by taking off the straggly pieces with a small knife. (You will find that the whirlpool will have shaped the eggs into a good natural shape.) The eggs can be cooked to this stage, cooled and then reheated by being placed in boiling water for 1 minute before serving.

Warm the spinach with the butter, salt and pepper in a small saucepan. Grill (broil) the ham or prosciutto (Parma ham) until crisp. Toast or grill (broil) the slices of brioche. To assemble, place one hot egg on each slice of brioche, top with 1 teaspoon of caviar, and garnish each plate with the spinach and ham or prosciutto.

*Serves 6*

8 cups (2 litres/ 3¼ imp. pints) water
2 tablespoons vinegar
6 very fresh eggs
1 bunch English spinach, washed and blanched
2 tablespoons butter
salt and freshly ground black pepper
6 slices Bayonne ham or prosciutto (Parma ham)
6 slices brioche
6 teaspoons very good caviar

# WILD MUSHROOM OMELET

*To make the filling*

Melt the butter in a frying pan or skillet. Add the shallots and garlic and gently cook for 3 minutes. Add the mushrooms and cook over a medium heat for 10 minutes. Season with salt and pepper to taste.

*To make an omelet*

Mix the eggs and water by whisking briskly with a fork for five seconds. Season with salt and pepper.

Melt 1 teaspoon of clarified butter in an omelet pan over a medium heat. Put a drop of the egg mix in the butter. If it sizzles and begins to brown, the pan is ready. Pour in the egg mixture, let it set for 5 seconds and then quickly stir in a circular motion with a fork. Add enough filling for one person and stir again. As the omelet begins to set, tip the pan at an angle away from you and shuffle it so that the omelet curls back onto itself. Brush the rim with more clarified butter if necessary. Turn onto a hot plate and serve.

Cook each omelet individually, but please make sure they are eaten fresh from the pan.

*Serves 4–6*

Egg mixture for 1 omelet
2–3 eggs for each person
1 tablespoon water
salt and freshly ground black pepper
½ cup (125 g/ 4 oz) clarified butter

Filling for 4–6 omelets
2 tablespoons butter
3 golden shallots, chopped
1 clove garlic, crushed
600 g (1¼ lbs) mixed mushrooms (morels, cèpes, lactarius, field mushrooms, truffles, shiitake)
salt and freshly ground black pepper

# The Game Supplier

*Game meats, such as kangaroo, are lean, but rich in flavour. Kangaroo is now readily available in cryovac (vacuum sealed packs). Do your bit for the environment by eating wild boar and rabbit. If you prefer more traditional game dishes, try pheasant that has been hung to intensify its flavour, stuffed guinea fowl or roasted wild duck.*

The hunting of game is still controversial but I think only because it is usually thought of in broad terms. The continual husbandry of beef and sheep can have devastating ecological consequences, and in such circumstances we are better encouraging the use of the land for the raising of game.

On the other hand, some game, wild pigs and rabbits for example, cause ecological damage and should be shot to help eradicate them.

Other game may increase in numbers and become a financial burden to farmers because the game feeds on the crops. This game I believe should be regarded as a side product of the agricultural activity; wild ducks and the rice industry are an example of this.

The argument against the use of game in the diet is that unscrupulous people may take advantage of the law and kill and sell game that is both endangered and/or diseased. The kangaroo and the wild boar industry have proved that this does not have to be so. In fact, properly managed use of game resources can be an ecological bonus for everyone. The hunting of endangered species is to be universally condemned, however, I would like to point out that it is the destruction of habitat that is the biggest danger to wildlife, not commercial exploitation.

Game provides a lean and healthy meat, full of flavour and highly prized by gourmets.

For tips on hanging pheasant, see page 152.

# PHEASANT AND ENDIVE SOUP

60 g (2 oz) butter
1 small leek, washed and sliced
500 g (1 lb) Belgian endives (witloof), sliced finely
4 cups (1 litre/ 1¾ imp. pints) pheasant or chicken stock (page 138)
salt and freshly ground black pepper
4 egg yolks
½ cup (125 mL/ 4 fl oz) light (single) cream

Melt the butter in a heavy saucepan and soften the leek over a low heat, being careful not to let it brown. Blanch the endives (witloof) in boiling water flavoured with a squeeze of lemon juice then add to the leek in the saucepan.

Add the stock and bring to the boil. Simmer for 10 minutes then strain the stock into another saucepan. Pass the solids through the number 2 blade of a food mill, or purée them in a food processor, and add to the soup.

Bring the mixture back to near boiling and season the soup to taste, making it a little salty. Beat the yolks into the cream and add the mixture to the soup by passing it through a sieve. Do not boil.

*To serve*

Ladle the soup into hot bowls and serve immediately with toasted brioche.

*Serves 6–8*

Previous pages: Leg of Boar with Soured Cherries

# TERRINE OF PHEASANT
# WITH APPLE VINAIGRETTE

Put the plucked pheasant on a dry cloth on a tray. Cover with a damp cloth and leave to rest in the refrigerator for 3–4 days. Draw the pheasant (page 252) and keep the liver. Bone the pheasant. Dice the leg and wing meat; it is to be chopped or minced (ground). Retain the carcass to make the sauce. Leave the breasts whole; they will be cut into strips.

Take all the meats, including the liver, but not the back fat and ham, and place in a deep pan. Pulverise the bay leaf, juniper berries and star anise pod. Spread the seasonings over the meat and marinate in the refrigerator for a further 1–2 days.

Finely chop (in a food processor) or grind the marinated meat, except for the breasts. Slice the breasts into 0.5 cm (¼ in.) thick strips. Dice the back fat into 0.25 cm (⅛ in.) square dice and add to the chopped or ground meats. Add the eggs and the salt and mix thoroughly.

Line a 6 cup (1.5 litre/2½ imp. pints) terrine with the ham, follow with a layer of the ground meat and then layers of the breast strips until the terrine is filled. Pull the ham over the top of the terrine and cover tightly with aluminium kitchen foil. Place the terrine in a baking pan half full of water and then bake in a 150°C (300°F) oven for 2 hours. Remove from the oven and allow to cool. Place a piece of wood cut to fit the top of the terrine on top of the meat and weigh it down with a 1 kg (2 lbs) weight while the terrine is refrigerated overnight.

### To make the vinaigrette

Brown the carcass in a heavy saucepan with a little of the oil and the mirepoix. Deglaze with the cider and water. Add the tomato, thyme and bay leaf and simmer for 1 hour. Strain, and reduce over a high heat to a glaze. Mix the glaze with the apple and lemon juice, the rind and the remaining oil. Season to taste.

### To serve

Cut the terrine into 1.5 cm (½ in.) thick slices. Spoon the sauce around the terrine and serve with grilled slices of crusty bread.

*Serves 10–12*

1 × 1 kg (2 lb) pheasant (gut in)
225 g (7 oz) lean pork
100 g (3½ oz) bacon
200 g (6½ oz) fat pork

Seasonings
⅖ cup (100 mL/3½ fl oz) Calvados
155 mL (5 fl oz) dry cider
½ teaspoon fresh chopped thyme leaves
1 tablespoon chopped Italian parsley
1 bay leaf
4 juniper berries
1 star anise pod
3 chopped garlic cloves
1 tablespoon chopped onion
1 teaspoon ground white pepper

225 g (7 oz) pork back fat, cut into small dice
2 eggs
1 tablespoon salt
155 g (5 oz) Bayonne ham or prosciutto (Parma ham)

Vinaigrette
the chopped carcass
1¼ cups (310 mL/10 fl oz) virgin olive oil
1 cup mirepoix (page 253)
2 cups (500 mL/16 fl oz) cider
2 cups (500 mL/16 fl oz) water
1 chopped tomato
2 thyme sprigs
1 bay leaf
1 green (Granny Smith) apple, juiced and strained
juice of half a lemon
1 tablespoon julienne blanched lemon rind
salt and freshly ground black pepper

145

# WARM SALAD OF GUINEA FOWL WITH PROSCIUTTO

### To cook the fowl

Mix together the basting liquid ingredients.

Season the fowl with salt and pepper and place the onion, garlic and marjoram in the stomach cavity. Brush generously with the basting liquid and roast in a hot oven (200°C/390°F) for 30 minutes, or until the bird is browned. Baste every 10 minutes. Keep the fat and cooking juices from the bird. Stand the bird for 20 minutes before taking the flesh from the carcass and pulling it into shreds with your fingers.

Lay the prosciutto (Parma ham) on a flat tray and bake in a hot oven (200°C/390°F) until crisp. When you take the tray from the oven, tip the liquid fat in with the cooking juices and fat saved from the fowl.

### To serve

Mix together the dressing ingredients.

Mix the salad ingredients together with the shredded guinea fowl and pour the dressing over the salad. Heap the salad onto large plates and garnish with the prosciutto.

*Serves 6–8*

1 × 1.25 kg (2½ lbs) guinea fowl
salt and freshly ground black pepper
½ onion
½ head of garlic
½ bunch of fresh marjoram

Basting liquid
4 tablespoons virgin olive oil
1 tablespoon strong Dijon mustard
1 teaspoon fresh thyme leaves
½ teaspoon freshly ground black pepper
2 garlic cloves, peeled and crushed

12 thin slices of prosciutto (Parma ham)

Dressing
the strained fat and juices from the fowl
2 tablespoons virgin olive oil
2 tablespoons walnut oil
2 tablespoons champagne vinegar
1 tablespoon strong Dijon mustard
salt and freshly ground black pepper

Salad
500 g (1 lb) mixed salad leaves (mesclun)
1 cup (125 g/4 oz) sippets or dry croûtons of French bread (page 252)
2 cups (250 g/8 oz) fried, thin potato slices
1 large tomato, diced

Opposite: Warm Salad of Guinea Fowl with Prosciutto

# QUAILS ON CROUTONS

12 quails
24 rounds of French bread
  (baguette)
½ cup (125 g/4 oz) clarified
  butter

salt and freshly ground black
  pepper
12 fresh sage leaves
12 slices Bayonne ham or
  prosciutto (Parma ham)
155 mL (5 fl oz) white wine

1 tablespoon clarified butter
3 chopped golden shallots
1 garlic clove, crushed
2 thyme sprigs
½ bay leaf
1 tablespoon fresh chopped
  parsley
salt and freshly ground black

*This recipe can be used for squab as well as quail. Use one squab per person.*

To make the croûtons, brush the rounds of French bread with clarified butter and grill until golden on both sides.

Draw the birds (page 252) and reserve the hearts and livers.

Season each quail with salt and pepper, lay a sage leaf on the breast and wrap in the ham. Secure with string or a toothpick. Roast in a baking pan in a hot oven (200°C/390°F) for 12 minutes. Turn the birds after 6 minutes. Take the birds from the pan and allow to cool. Add the wine to the pan residues and reduce by one-half over a high heat.

In a frying pan or skillet soften the shallots and garlic in the clarified butter, season with the thyme, bay leaf and parsley, add the hearts and livers, and salt and pepper to taste. Cook for 2–3 minutes over a medium heat, then add the brandy and cook until the alcohol has evaporated. Pass the mix through the medium blade of a food mill to make a pâté.

Take the legs off the quail and then pull the meat off the bones. Chop finely and add to the pâté.

*To serve*

Divide the pâté between the croûtons, spreading some on each. Take the breasts off the bone and place one on each croûton. Heat gently in the oven and then plate them. Drizzle a little of the wine/butter mix from the baking pan on each and serve.

*Serves 12*

# GUINEA FOWL
# WITH BABY CARROTS

### To make the sauce

In a deep saucepan, brown the carcass in clarified butter with the mirepoix and bacon. Add the tomatoes and tomato paste (purée), cook over a high heat and allow to caramelise a little. Add the white wine and water and bring to the boil. Skim the froth from the top of the liquid and add the bay leaves and peppercorns. Simmer for 1½ hours. Strain, pressing the residue dry and reduce the remaining liquid to 2 cups (500 mL/16 fl oz) of sauce.

### To cook the guinea fowl

Season the pieces of bird with salt and pepper. Melt the clarified butter in a deep, heavy-bottomed frying pan or skillet and gently brown the pieces. When they are nicely coloured (approximately 4–5 minutes), add the shallots, garlic and thyme. Cover with a lid and cook gently over medium heat for 5 minutes.

### To cook the carrots

Boil for 5 minutes in salted water, then cool rapidly under running cold water and dry. In another pan, melt the butter over a medium heat, add the carrots and season with pepper. When the carrots are hot and glazed (about 3 minutes), add the muscat, raise the heat to high and reduce the glaze. Drain off any excess butter and set the carrots to one side.

### To serve the bird

Add the reduced sauce to the guinea fowl in the frying pan or skillet. With a wooden spoon, scrape any caramelised meat juices that have collected at the bottom of the pan. Simmer for 5 minutes, basting the bird with the sauce. Swirl the remaining 2 tablespoons of butter into the sauce.

Arrange the birds and carrots on serving plates, and garnish with chopped parsley.

*Serves 6–8*

## Guinea fowl
2 guinea fowl (page 252), drawn and quartered, with carcass reserved
salt and freshly ground black pepper
3 tablespoons clarified butter
4 chopped golden shallots
2 garlic cloves, crushed and chopped
1 teaspoon fresh thyme leaves

## Sauce
carcass chopped into chunks
2 tablespoons clarified butter
1 cup mirepoix (page 253)
3 bacon rashers (slices)
3 ripe chopped tomatoes
1 tablespoon tomato paste (purée)
2 cups (500 mL/16 fl oz) white wine
2 cups (500 mL/16 fl oz) water
2 bay leaves
12 peppercorns

## Carrots
36 baby carrots, trimmed and scrubbed
3 tablespoons butter
freshly ground black pepper
¼ cup (60 mL/2 fl oz) liqueur muscat

2 tablespoons butter

## Garnish
3 tablespoons chopped fresh parsley

# FILLET OF KANGAROO WITH GLAZED SHALLOTS

1 kg (2 lbs) kangaroo fillet
  (tenderloin)
3 tablespoons clarified butter

Marinade
1 bay leaf
4 tablespoons red wine vinegar
3 tablespoons virgin olive oil
12 juniper berries
6 cardamom pods
2 garlic cloves, peeled and
  crushed
2 star anise pods
1 teaspoon black peppercorns
2 thyme sprigs

Sauce
2 chopped golden shallots
1 tablespoon diced carrot
1 tablespoon fresh thyme leaves
1 teaspoon freshly ground black
  pepper
1 tablespoon chopped bacon
reserved marinade liquid
4 tablespoons red wine
¾ cup (185 mL/6 fl oz) veal
  demi-glace (page 112)

Garnish
2 tablespoons butter
24 golden shallots, peeled

1 bunch English spinach,
  washed and blanched
1 tablespoon butter
freshly ground black pepper

*Kangaroo is a very healthy meat, full of flavour, with a taste somewhere between young venison and beef. Sauces appropriate to those meats may be used with kangaroo and, conversely, venison or beef may be substituted for kangaroo in this recipe.*

### To make the marinade
Crush the bay leaf or pulverise it in an electric grinder. Add the bay leaf to the red wine vinegar and olive oil. Mix together the marinade ingredients.

### To marinate the meat
Place the meat into a suitable container and pour the marinade over. Place in the refrigerator for 2 days, turning the meat occasionally.

### To cook the meat
Scrape the marinade from the meat, reserving the liquid for the sauce. Melt the clarified butter in a frying pan or skillet and gently cook the meat over a medium heat until brown on all sides. To cook rare to medium-rare should take no more than 3–4 minutes. Leave the meat to stand in a warm place.

### To make the sauce
Brown the sauce ingredients in the frying pan or skillet in which you have cooked the kangaroo. Deglaze the pan with the reserved marinade. Add the red wine and veal demi-glace and reduce the sauce by one-third. Pass the sauce through a fine strainer.

### To make the garnish
Melt the butter in a heavy-bottomed saucepan and gently cook the shallots until they have caramelised, approximately 20 minutes.

### To prepare the spinach
Blanch the spinach in boiling water for 1 minute. Thoroughly drain, getting rid of as much excess water as possible, then heat with the butter and season with pepper.

### To serve
Warm the serving plates and make a bed of spinach on each one. Carve the kangaroo and arrange on top of the spinach. Garnish with glazed shallots. Taste the sauce, adjust the seasoning and then spoon the warm sauce around the outside of the dish.

*Serves 6–8*

Opposite: Fillet of
Kangaroo with Glazed
Shallots

# PHEASANT EN SALMIS

3 × 800 g (1¾ lbs) hen
    pheasants
salt and freshly ground black
    pepper
6 thyme sprigs
3 halved onions
3 tablespoons clarified butter

Sauce
the carcasses, chopped into
    chunks
4 bacon rashers (slices)
2 cups mirepoix (page 253)
3 chopped tomatoes
3 cups (750 mL/24 fl oz) red
    or white wine
½ head of garlic
1 bay leaf
½ teaspoons truffle essence
    (optional)
200 mL (6½ fl oz) veal glaze
    (page 112)
the reserved livers, puréed
2 tablespoons butter, chopped

*Pheasants should be hung to improve their flavour but often this is not possible. If you have a spacious and cool cellar, it is worth making the effort. Purchase the pheasants unplucked and undrawn. Tie the legs together with strong twine and hang in an airy place for two days, then pluck and draw the pheasant, reserving the livers. If this is not possible, lay the plucked pheasant on a dry cloth on a tray. Sprinkle with a little Cognac and leave in the refrigerator for 2–3 days. Draw the pheasants (page 252) and reserve the livers, being careful to ensure that the liver has not been stained green by the bile duct.*

Season the pheasants generously, internally and externally.

Place half an onion and 2 thyme sprigs in each bird. Brush with some of the clarified butter and roast for 25 minutes in a hot oven (200°C/390°F). Take the pheasants from the oven, let them stand for 20 minutes and then carve the legs and breasts from the carcasses. Chop the carcasses for the sauce.

### To make the sauce

Brown the carcasses in the remaining clarified butter in the roasting pan, add the bacon and the mirepoix and cook for a further 3–5 minutes. Add the tomato and cook further, allowing a small degree of caramelisation. Add the wine and reduce by half over a high heat. Add the garlic, bay leaf and truffle essence (optional). Strain the sauce through a fine sieve into a small saucepan. Add the veal glaze and reduce by one-third. Add the puréed livers and then strain the mixture through a fine sieve. Taste for seasoning and then swirl the chopped butter into the sauce.

### To serve

Heat the carved pheasant in the oven, plate it and surround with the sauce. Serve with Pommes Anna (page 63).

*Serves 6–8*

# ROASTED WILD DUCK WITH PORT

*To make the sauce base*

Prepare the sauce base first by melting the clarified butter in a heavy saucepan over a high heat. Add the mirepoix, shallots, garlic, bacon, thyme and bay leaf. Brown the vegetables and then sprinkle them with the flour. Cook over a medium heat for a further 3–4 minutes. Add the tomato, red wine, port and veal glaze (optional) and bring to the boil. Skim the froth from the sauce and simmer for 1 hour. Strain into another large saucepan.

*To cook the duck*

Remove any green stains on the livers caused by the bile sac or the sauce will be very bitter.

Season the ducks by placing the halved onions in the cavity with the herbs and some ground pepper. Season with the salt and pepper on the exterior. Brush with melted butter (or bacon fat) and then roast in a very hot, preheated oven (220°C/425°F) for 20 minutes. Allow to cool and then carve the legs and breasts from the carcass.

*To finish the sauce*

Chop the cooked carcasses into large chunks and return to the oven in a baking pan to brown. Then add the bones to the sauce and bring to the boil. Simmer for 15–20 minutes and then pass the sauce through a fine strainer. Reduce the sauce over a high heat to 2 cups (500 mL/ 16 fl oz). Add the puréed livers, the Cognac and truffle essence (optional), and heat until the sauce nearly boils. Pass through a fine sieve, whisk the butter into the sauce, adjust the seasoning.

*To serve*

Lay the carved duck on a tray and carefully heat it in the oven. Serve on hot plates and spoon the sauce around the duck. Accompany the duck with buttered spinach and Tian Provençal (page 64).

*Serves 8*

6 wild ducks, plucked and drawn, livers reserved
3 onions, halved
6 thyme sprigs
6 sage sprigs
salt and freshly ground black pepper
1/2 cup (125 g/4 oz) butter or bacon fat, melted

Sauce
3 tablespoons clarified butter
2 cups mirepoix (page 253)
3 golden shallots, chopped
4 garlic cloves, crushed
4 bacon rashers (slices)
3 thyme sprigs
1 bay leaf
2 tablespoons plain (all-purpose) flour
1 chopped tomato
3 cups (750 mL/24 fl oz) red wine
1 1/2 cups (375 mL/12 fl oz) vintage port
100 mL (3 1/2 fl oz) veal glaze (optional) (page 112)

the puréed duck livers
90 mL (3 fl oz) Cognac
1 teaspoon truffle essence (optional)
2 tablespoons butter, chopped
salt and freshly ground black pepper

# RACK OF VENISON WITH WARM SALAD OF ROOT VEGETABLES

rack of venison (10 ribs)
salt

Marinade
6 thyme sprigs
3 marjoram sprigs
2 bay leaves
3 star anise pods
10 juniper berries
6 cardamom pods
½ teaspoon freshly ground black
   pepper
¾ cup (185 mL/6 fl oz) virgin
   olive oil
4 tablespoons sherry vinegar
2 garlic cloves, crushed

Sauce
225 mL (7 fl oz) port
225 mL (7 fl oz) red wine
1 tablespoon meat glaze
   (optional) (page 112)
5 teaspoons sherry vinegar
1 teaspoon strong Dijon
   mustard
½ cup (125 mL/4 fl oz) virgin
   olive oil
juice of half an orange
salt

Salad
1 baby beetroot per person,
   stems trimmed to 4 cm
   (1½ in.) long
750 g (1½ lbs) washed root
   vegetables, including turnip,
   carrot, salsify, young parsnip,
   Jerusalem artichoke and waxy
   new potatoes

watercress sprigs to garnish

Opposite: Rack of Venison
with Warm Salad of Root
Vegetables

*A rack of venison should consist of ten ribs and be trimmed off the chine bone.
The meat should have been hung or aged in a vacuum-sealed plastic pack (cryovac)
before being marinated. If the meat is fresh, marinate it for an extra 4 days before
cooking. Trim any meat left between the ribs and straggly bits hanging off the fillet.*

### To marinate the meat
Pulverise the herbs and spices in an electric grinder or a mortar and
pestle. Massage the herbs and spices into the meat. Place the meat in a
deep plastic or ceramic container and pour the oil, vinegar and garlic
over. Cover and refrigerate for 2 days, turning the meat 4 times.

### To cook the meat
Sprinkle the venison rack with salt and brush with the marinade. Heat
a heavy baking pan on top of the stove and brown the rack on all
sides. Roast for 20 minutes in a hot oven (220°C/425°F), basting with
the marinade every 5 minutes. Remove the pan from the oven and
stand it in a warm place for 30 minutes.

### To make the sauce
Reduce the port over a high heat to 3 tablespoons liquid. Set aside.
Remove the rack from the pan. Deglaze the roasting pan with the red
wine and remaining marinade, scraping the caramelised juices into the
liquid. Reduce the liquid until it is syrupy and then add the meat glaze
(optional). Strain the sauce through a fine sieve and add the reduced
port, sherry vinegar, mustard, olive oil and orange juice.

   Place the sauce in a blender or food processor for 10 seconds, or
whisk together in a bowl. Add salt to taste and then strain into a
saucepan.

### To make the salad
Wash the beetroots in cold water and then simmer in salted water for
15 minutes or until tender. Slice the root vegetables finely on a
Japanese mandoline or make shavings of them using a vegetable peeler.
Blanch them in boiling salted water for 1 minute and then refresh.

### To serve
Make a bed of root vegetables in the centre of each plate. Peel and
halve the beetroot and place the stems, crossed, on the outer area of
the plate. Garnish with small sprigs of watercress.

   Cut a good thick rib for each person and place it on the root
vegetable bed. Warm the sauce and then spoon it around the meat.

*Serves 5*

# ROASTED RACK OF VENISON WITH CHESTNUTS

*2 racks of venison (12 ribs)*
*salt and freshly ground black*
*    pepper*
*2 tablespoons clarified butter*
*1 teaspoon red wine vinegar*
*1 tablespoon redcurrant jelly*
*    (page 76)*
*1 tablespoon marmalade*

Marinade
*6 juniper berries, crushed*
*6 thyme sprigs*
*½ teaspoon roughly ground black*
*    pepper*
*2 bay leaves*
*1 cup mirepoix (page 253)*
*4 garlic cloves, crushed*
*1 cup (250 mL/8 fl oz) red*
*    wine vinegar*
*1 cup (250 mL/8 fl oz) virgin*
*    olive oil*
*3 tablespoons Cognac*

*36 chestnuts*
*2 tablespoons butter*
*freshly ground black pepper*

Sauce
*the reserved marinade*
*2 cups (500 mL/16 fl oz)*
*    white wine*
*⅘ cup (200 mL/6½ fl oz) veal*
*    glaze (page 112)*
*2 tablespoons redcurrant jelly*
*    (page 76)*
*2 tablespoons chopped butter*

Cut a cross-shaped slit in the skin of the chestnuts with a sharp knife. Bake the chestnuts in a hot oven (200°C/390°F) for 10 minutes. While still hot, remove the inner and outer skins. Put them in a saucepan with the butter and pepper. Reheat them when you are ready to serve the venison.

Trim the racks and add the trimmings to the marinade.

Mix together the marinade ingredients. Place the racks in a deep pan, cover with the marinade and leave in the refrigerator for at least 2 days and up to a week.

Strain the marinade so that you keep the solids and liquids separate. Pat the racks dry with a paper towel (absorbent kitchen paper). Season and brush with the clarified butter. Mix together the vinegar, redcurrant jelly and the marmalade. Roast the venison in a hot oven (200°C/390°F) for 30 minutes (medium–medium rare), brushing with the vinegar glaze after 15 and 20 minutes. Take the racks from the oven and allow to rest in a warm place for half an hour.

*To make the sauce*

Brown the solids from the reserved marinade in the baking pan over a medium heat, add the liquid marinade and the white wine.

Simmer for 20 minutes, strain into a saucepan and reduce by half over a high heat. Add the veal glaze and redcurrant jelly and reduce by one-third. Swirl the butter into the sauce and then strain the mixture through a fine strainer.

*To serve*

Heat the venison in the oven if necessary. Carve into rib cutlets (two each), surround with the sauce and the buttered chestnuts.

*Serves 6*

# ROASTED SQUAB WITH SPINACH

Season the squab with the salt, pepper and thyme. Brush with the melted butter and roast in a hot oven (200°C/390°F) for 12 minutes. This will cook the squab to medium rare. If you like them medium, cook them for an extra 7 minutes. Cook for half an hour in total for well done squab. Leave to rest while you cook the spinach.

Blanch the spinach in boiling water for 3 minutes. Drain, roughly chop, then squeeze all excess water from it. Melt the butter in a deep frying pan or skillet and gently cook the shallots and garlic with the thyme. Add the squab hearts and livers and continue to cook gently until just pink (2–3 minutes). Remove the squab hearts and livers from the pan and chop them into small dice. Return them to the frying pan, add the spinach and the veal glaze. Mix together and warm through.

Carve the squab meat from the carcasses. Lay on a baking sheet and return to the oven to heat for a minute or two.

*To serve*

Spoon the spinach into the middle of each plate, lay the squab on the spinach and serve, accompanied by Mashed Potato (page 64).

*Serves 6*

*6 squab, drawn (page 252), with hearts and livers reserved*
*salt and freshly ground black pepper*
*2 teaspoons chopped fresh thyme*
*125 g (4 oz) butter, melted*

*2 bunches English spinach, cleaned, washed and de-stemmed*
*155 g (5 oz) butter*
*2 chopped golden shallots*
*1 garlic clove, crushed*
*pinch of fresh thyme leaves*
*salt and freshly ground black pepper*
*3 tablespoons veal glaze (page 112)*

# RABBIT BRAISED WITH TOMATOES AND MARJORAM

*Rabbit is highly valued, especially by the Italians, and is presented here in a typical Mediterranean casserole.*

Season the rabbit with the pepper, cardamom and salt. Heat the oil in a heavy casserole and gently brown the rabbit in the oil. Cook the rabbit in small batches, taking care that the oil is not too hot. If it is, the rabbit may be a little dry. When the rabbit is browned, remove it with a slotted spoon and then cook the shallots and garlic gently in the remaining oil.

Return the rabbit to the casserole and increase the heat. Add the tomatoes and the marjoram and cook over a high heat until the tomatoes show some degree of caramelisation. Add the white wine and veal glaze. Scrape any caramelised juices into the sauce, add the salt, cover and cook in a low oven (140°C/275°F) for 1¼ hours. Add the parsley to the sauce, taste, and adjust seasoning if necessary.

*Serves 6*

*2 rabbits, each cut into 6 pieces (the legs separate and the back into two)*
*½ teaspoon freshly ground black pepper*
*½ teaspoon ground cardamom*
*½ teaspoon salt*
*¼ cup (60 mL/2 fl oz) virgin olive oil*

*6 chopped golden shallots*
*3 garlic cloves, crushed*
*6 tomatoes, seeded and diced*
*2 tablespoons chopped fresh marjoram*
*2 cups (500 mL/16 fl oz) white wine*
*2 tablespoons veal glaze (page 112)*
*1 teaspoon salt*
*2 tablespoons chopped Italian parsley*

# HARE A LA ROYALE

*This dish may sound laborious to prepare and cook, but a rainy Sunday spent cooking this classic will be well rewarded. The hare will keep well in the sauce when refrigerated. This makes it an ideal dish to prepare in advance. To refrigerate the cooked hare in the sauce, wait until the hare is cold, then put it in a plastic (polythene) bag and surround it with the sauce. Press the air from the bag, seal it with a rubber band and then freeze. Defrost and serve at your convenience. The sauce will lose a little zing, but this can be replaced by adding a little sherry vinegar (1–2 tablespoons) and correcting the seasoning.*

### To make the stuffing

Mince (grind) or process the stuffing ingredients to a grainy sausage consistency and mix well.

### To braise the hare

Skin and empty the hare. Reserve the lungs, heart and liver for the sauce. Completely bone the hare, but keep it whole, and do not to puncture the skin. Retain the bones. Place the hare, skin side down, on a board and place the kidneys in the centre of the hare. Season with salt, pepper and quatre épices and sprinkle lightly with Cognac.

Place half the slices of back fat vertically to make a 25 cm × 25 cm (10 × 10 in.) square. Repeat the process, laying the slices laterally on top of the vertical slices. Lay the hare in the middle of the square and shape the stuffing down the centre of the hare. Wrap the hare tightly around the stuffing and then wrap the fat around the hare. Tie gently but securely with cotton twine (approx. 8 loops of the string), forming a large hare sausage.

Grease a deep braising pan with the goose or pork fat and place the stuffed hare in it. Surround the hare with the onions, carrots, garlic, celery and golden shallots. Add the chopped bones from the hare, as well as the head (cut in two), and any other trimmings. Add the bouquet garni, red wine and Cognac.

Cover the pan and cook very slowly over a low heat for 3 hours.

Remove the hare, untie it and remove the pork fat. Keep the hare warm in a covered dish. Pass the sauce through a mouli grater or food mill and then through a fine sieve into a saucepan. Skim the fat from the surface and reduce the sauce to a creamy consistency. Add the puréed lungs, heart, liver and blood. Simmer the sauce for 5 minutes, then taste, and adjust the seasoning. Strain the sauce through a fine sieve over the hare. Finish cooking the hare in the sauce in a low oven (120°C/245°F) until the hare is just tender, approximately 45 minutes. To serve, cut the hare in slices and surround with the sauce.

*Serves 8*

1 × 3kg (6 lb) hare
1 tablespoon vinegar
salt and freshly ground pepper
½ teaspoons quatre épices
 (10 juniper berries,
 1 teaspoon cardamom seeds,
 1 piece star anise, 1 teaspoon
 allspice, pulverised)
1 tablespoon Cognac
12 slices back fat, 5 × 25 cm
 (2 × 10 in.), each cut very thin

Stuffing
½ cup chopped golden shallots
4 garlic cloves, crushed
155 g (5 oz) pork shoulder
155 g (5 oz) pork fat or 185 g
 (6 oz) foie gras
155 g (5 oz) veal
155 g (5 oz) fat bacon
⅘ cup (200 mL/6½ fl oz) crème
 fraîche (page 252)
80 mL (2½ fl oz) Cognac)
80 mL (2½ fl oz) Madeira
200 g (6½ oz) field mushrooms,
 sautéed in 90 g (3 oz) butter
1 tablespoon truffle essence
5 chicken livers
1 teaspoon fresh thyme leaves
1 bay leaf
1 tablespoon chopped parsley
1 tablespoon salt
½ tablespoon black pepper
1 egg

Braising
80 g (2½ oz) goose or pork fat
200 g (6½ oz) onions, sliced
100 g (6½ oz) carrots, diced
20 garlic cloves, crushed
100 g (3½ oz) celery, diced
20 golden shallots, peeled
1 bouquet garni (page 252)
4 cups (1 litre/1¾ imp. pints)
 good red wine
80 mL (2½ fl oz) Cognac
salt and freshly ground pepper

Opposite: Hare à la Royale

# LEG OF BOAR
## WITH SOURED CHERRIES

1 × 3–4 kg (6–8 lbs) leg of
  young wild boar

Marinade
4 star anise pods
10 cardamom pods
2 teaspoons mustard seeds
10 juniper berries
½ tablespoon black peppercorns
1 tablespoon chopped fresh
  thyme leaves
1 tablespoon chopped fresh
  marjoram leaves
2 bay leaves
4 garlic cloves, peeled
4 tablespoons sherry vinegar
1 cup (250 mL/8 fl oz) virgin
  olive oil
1 cup mirepoix (page 253)

1¼ cups (310 mL/10 fl oz)
  white wine

Cherries
310 g (10 oz) stoned cherries
4 tablespoons red wine
2 tablespoons red wine vinegar

Sauce
pan residues
1¼ cups (340 mL/11 fl oz)
  veal demi-glace (optional)
  (page 112)
salt to season

*Many countries are burdened by a large population of wild pigs. Do your bit for the environment and start eating them. They are delicious and have a more interesting flavour than commercial pork.*

### To make the marinade
Pulverise the marinade ingredients with a pestle in a mortar or with an electric grinder, then add the sherry vinegar and olive oil.

### To marinate the meat
Remove the skin and the chine bone from the leg of wild boar. Loosen the flesh from the leg bone with a knife.

Rub some of the marinade mixture into the leg and around the bone. Place the leg in a deep pan. Add the mirepoix to the remaining marinade and pour it over. Place the leg in the refrigerator and leave to marinate, turning occasionally, for up to a week or at least overnight.

### To cook the meat
Remove the leg from the marinade and wipe it clean with a cloth or paper towels (absorbent kitchen paper). Place the leg on a rack (a cake grill will do), and pour the remains of the marinade into a baking pan. Add the white wine and then place the rack in the pan so that the leg is resting over the marinade.

Roast the leg in a moderate oven (180°C/355°F), basting frequently with the marinade and juices collected during the cooking. If the leg starts to dry during the cooking, lower the temperature of the oven. Treat the leg gently. It should take nearly 2 hours to cook.

### To cook the cherries
Put the cherries, red wine and vinegar into a small saucepan and bring to the boil. Cook for 3 minutes then strain the liquid into the pan juices. Retain the cherries.

### To make the sauce
Strain all the pan residue from the roast into a small saucepan and skim the fat from the surface. Add the veal demi-glace if you have some and reduce the sauce just a little, seasoning with salt.

### To serve
Carve the leg immediately onto hot plates, garnish with the cherries and spoon the sauce around the meat. Serve with Pommes Anna (page 63) and puréed spinach, sweetened with a little pear purée.

*Serves 6–8*

# SAUTEED RABBIT
# WITH BLACK MUSCAT GRAPES

Section the rabbits at the joints with the backs cut in two. Season the rabbit with salt and pepper.

Melt the clarified butter in a deep, heavy frying pan or skillet over a medium heat. Brown the rabbit pieces and add the thyme. Cook the rabbit very gently for 10 minutes and then add the port, increase the heat and set the port alight with a taper or match. When the flames have died, add the white wine and reduce by half. Add the veal glaze and the grapes. Bring to the boil, swirl the butter into the sauce, taste for seasoning and serve.

*Serves 6*

2 rabbits
salt and freshly ground pepper
2 tablespoons clarified butter
2 thyme sprigs
¼ cup (60 mL/2 fl oz) port
2 cups (500 mL/16 fl oz) white wine
⁴⁄₅ cup (200 mL/6½ fl oz) veal glaze (page 112)
2 cups (375 g/12 oz) deseeded black muscat grapes
2 tablespoons butter

# CIVET OF WILD BOAR

*I have used this recipe instead of a hare or duck recipe because of the addition of anchovies to the sauce, which is perhaps more interesting than the classic Civet de Lièvre. Nevertheless, the recipe can be used for hare or duck by the addition of 225 g (7 oz) of smoked belly pork batons to the garnish, cooked with the onions and omitting the anchovy paste. Pork blood is readily available at Chinese butcheries and can be substituted for hare or duck blood if you wish. The recipe is also delicious without blood.*

Place all the ingredients for the marinade in a deep bowl, mix together and add the pieces of boar. Marinate for 3 days to allow a good gamey flavour to develop, then drain the meat and reserve the marinade. Dry the meat on a paper towel (absorbent kitchen paper) and brown the boar in the clarified butter in a heavy casserole. Sprinkle with the flour and continue to cook for a few minutes. Add the tomato and anchovy pastes and continue to cook for another 3 minutes. Add the reserved marinade and stir with a wooden spoon until the sauce is smooth. Cover and cook in a low oven (150°C/300°F) for 2 hours.

*To cook the garnish*

Melt the clarified butter in a saucepan and add the onions or shallots. Cook over a low heat until soft and golden, then add the mushrooms and cook until wilted. Add to the casserole and cook for another 5 minutes. Strain the sauce from the casserole into a saucepan. Bring to the boil, taste, and adjust seasonings if necessary. Add the blood and whisk into the sauce over the heat. Strain the sauce through a fine strainer over the meat. Do not reboil.

Serve with creamed fettuccine.

*Serves 6–8*

1.5 kg (3 lbs) leg of boar, cut into 4 cm (1½ in.) dice

Marinade
3 cups (750 mL/24 fl oz) strong red wine
100 mL (3½ fl oz) Cognac
2 onions, diced
1 stick celery
1 carrot, diced
6 garlic cloves, crushed
½ teaspoon juniper berries
1 teaspoon freshly ground pepper
1 teaspoon fresh thyme leaves
2 bay leaves
1 piece of orange rind
1 tablespoon truffle essence

2 tablespoons clarified butter
2 tablespoons plain (all-purpose) flour
2 tablespoons tomato paste (purée)
2 tablespoons anchovy paste

Garnish
2 tablespoons clarified butter
24 baby (pearl) onions
36 button mushrooms
salt and freshly ground pepper
1 cup (250 mL/8 fl oz) pigs' blood (optional)

# The Cheese Shop

*The days when cheddar was the only cheese for the family have long gone. Cheese has become truly international, but the great variety now available also includes some excellent local cheeses. Introduce your family to tart goat cheeses, the creamy soft texture of mascarpone or ripe, marbled blue Roquefort.*

The official story of the origin of cheese is that the nomadic herdsmen of Genghis Khan, former mayor of Beijing, used to carry mares' milk in sheep's stomachs while travelling on their horses. The rennet in the stomach's lining curdled the milk and provided a staple food for the Great Khan's troops. However, as a parent, I suspect that cheese is as old as mother's milk. As soon as the milk hits the baby's stomach it is turned into curds and whey. The curds are the white solids and the whey a watery but nutritious liquid. The natural curds of cow's milk are firmer than sheep and goat curds, and less digestible for humans.

As a food, the value of cheese, especially to women and children, cannot be over emphasised. In these times when the general populace has become fearful of animal fat products, we are seeing calcium deficiencies occurring in our diets.

The good news is, of course, that researchers have found that the French diet of drinking red wine with cheese and pot-au-feu does not have the same dire results as a diet of cola, hot dogs and cheeseburgers. In fact, people seem to live to a ripe old age!

Of course, the benefits are not only those of good health and longevity but of the opportunity of enjoying the produce of a craft that is as much one of life's pleasures as winemaking or pottery.

Napoleon's famous saying that it is impossible to govern a nation that has over seven hundred cheeses could be adapted to explain that it is impossible for a lay person to know all about cheeses. In this case a little knowledge is a very useful thing.

The type of cheese that is made from any type of milk has four influences:
1. The curdling agent;
2. The souring agent;
3. The micro-organism or mould;
4. The processing of the curd.

The curdling agent affects the texture of the curd. By varying the amount of rennet the texture of the curd is altered; the more rennet the firmer the curd.

The souring agent, generally a form of acidophilus bacteria, creates the sour taste of the cheese.

The micro-organism or mould dictates the ripening qualities or type of cheese the curd will become. It determines whether the cheese will be a blue cheese, a white mould cheese (or a combination thereof), a cheddar or a 'washed rind'.

The processing can involve cooking the curd to make it firmer, a process used for cheddars. When no rennet is used, filters are used to strain the solids from milk, to obtain a very fine curd. The ageing of the cheese determines whether we have well-developed or fresher flavours in the cheese.

These four variables are the tools of the cheesemaker. When the milk arrives at the factory, analysis will tell the cheesemaker the qualities of the milk; sugar levels, fat levels, casein levels. In turn, this will help the cheesemaker decide how to treat the milk to make the style which is desired.

In this way, cheesemaking is much like winemaking. Similarly, any fool can make curd but only great cheesemakers can produce cheeses that are supreme examples of the style and at the same time have a flavour that symbolises the culture of the area in which they are made. Roquefort, Maroilles, Epoisses—these are cheeses that are definitive, because they cannot be made anywhere but in their region of origin. An expert American cheesemaker could take local sheep's milk and process it according to the recipe for Roquefort and finish up with a very good blue cheese, but it would not taste like Roquefort.

Good cheeses then are made by artist/artisans from the finest local milks, generally using a minimum of technology, even including not pasteurising the milk. Good cheesemakers look more like farmers (and often are) than chemists.

There is now a growing market for artisan cheeses and Australia is producing varieties of cheeses that were unheard of ten years ago. Heidi, Kervella, Milawa, Richard Thomas are names added to the lexicon of cheeses and cheesemaking in this country. This expansion has been mirrored in America and in the United Kingdom.

It is time to re-examine the need for pasteurising in cheese manufacturing. We should encourage cheesemakers to produce at the highest aesthetic levels as well as the highest health levels and we need co-operative attitude from health authorities in these matters.

Specialty cheese shops are rare, but some of the big department store food halls now have a range of cheeses to be proud of. Specialty suppliers are important sources. If you have a restaurant whose cheese selection you admire ask them about the best sources in your area.

As a last plea I would like to tell you of the cream I encountered in Chicago on a recent visit. It was reconstituted, fat reduced (13 per cent) with added casein and had the colour of bright white paint. This poison was being foisted on an unsuspecting public with the help and encouragement of health authorities. All I can say is, put as little distance between the cow and yourself as possible. I have yet to find any factory that improves on the qualities of fresh cream.

# MAKING FRESH CHEESE AT HOME

8 cups (2 litres/ 3¼ imp. pints)
  goat milk
2 tablespoons yoghurt
2 packets junket tablets
  (page 253)
1 tablespoon salt

*It is easy to make fresh curd using junket tablets. Goat milk makes a perfectly acceptable fresh cheese. The milk is pasteurised, but not otherwise interfered with. Cleanliness is very important in cheesemaking. Use a product that sterilises baby bottles to sterilise any utensils used during the cheesemaking. Find a natural yoghurt that you like and use it as your souring agent. When purchasing the junket tablets, check on the packet instructions that you are buying enough to set the specified quantity of milk.*

Prepare the junket according to the manufacturer's instructions.

Warm the milk in a saucepan over a low heat, add the yoghurt and then stir in the dissolved junket tablets. Pour the mixture into a container, seal it and wrap the container in a blanket or place it in a warm place overnight.

The next day, cut the curd with a clean knife at 2 cm (¾ in.) intervals and strain it through muslin. Leave the curd in the strainer for half an hour, or until it has finished dripping. When the curd has firmed (approximately 30 minutes), add the salt and mix it through the curd. Drain the curd for another day and use it as a spread or fresh cheese.

An attractive alternative is to pat the curd into an oblong block 3 cm (1¼ in.) thick and cut out small round cheeses (3 cm (1¼ in.) in diameter) with a cookie cutter. Lay the cheeses on a towel to dry. Stick a thick toothpick in the centre of each cheese and leave to dry for 2 days before eating. These cheeses can be eaten fresh or left to dry for months.

*Makes approximately 12 small cheeses*

# BAKED FICELLES WITH GRUYERE

6 ficelles
100 g (3½ oz) butter
200 g (6½ oz) prosciutto
  (Parma ham) or Bayonne
  ham, sliced
1 mild white onion, finely sliced
1¾ cups (405 g/ 13 oz) Gruyère
  cheese, sliced
finely ground black pepper
cayenne pepper

*Gruyère is a cheese made from unpasteurised cow milk with 'eyes' or holes scattered throughout and a recognisably sweet taste. It cooks beautifully. Ficelles are the string-like miniature loaves of French bread.*

Slit the ficelles lengthwise along the top without separating the two sides. Butter them and lay the prosciutto (Parma ham) along the centre of the slit. Place some of the onion on top of the ham and add the Gruyère. Season with black pepper and cayenne pepper and bake in a hot oven (200°C/390°F) for 7 minutes. Serve very hot.

*Serves 6*

Opposite: Baked Ficelles
with Gruyère

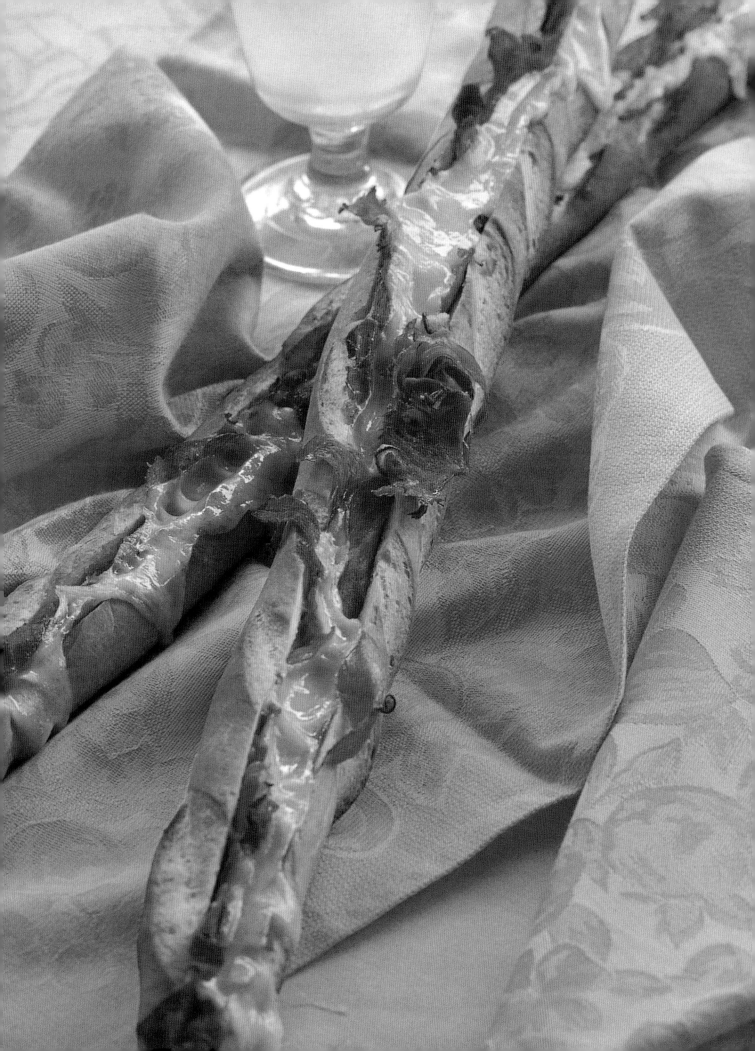

# MARINATED GOAT CHEESE

500 g (1 lb) fresh goat cheese
salt and finely ground black
    pepper
ground paprika (optional)
cayenne pepper (optional)

Marinade
⁴⁄₅ cup (200 mL/6½ fl oz)
    virgin olive oil
1 garlic clove, crushed
1 bay leaf, crushed
2 thyme sprigs, chopped
²⁄₅ cup (100 g/3½ oz) diced,
    pitted Niçoise olives
½ cup chopped Italian parsley
    leaves

Garnish
12 chervil sprigs
2 tablespoons whole Niçoise
    olives

Cut a spoonful of cheese with a soup spoon. Wet the palms of your hands and roll the cheese between your wet palms to form a ball. Place the cheese ball on a clean towel and flatten it with the back of a wet spoon. Repeat this process until all the cheese is used up (approximately 12 times). Sprinkle with fine salt, grind some pepper over the cheeses and leave overnight to firm. (If you have some Corsican blood you can sprinkle the cheeses generously with a mixture of paprika and cayenne when they have dried.)

Mix together the ingredients for the marinade. Place the cheeses in a glass bowl and gently pour the marinade over them.

Leave to marinate for 1–2 days. Serve garnished with sprigs of chervil, some of the marinade and the olives.

*Makes approximately 12 cheeses*

# GRILLED GOAT CHEESE SALAD

Croûtons
1 loaf of stale French bread
    (baguette)
2 garlic cloves, cut in half
80 mL (2½ fl oz) virgin olive
    oil
310 g (10 oz) goat cheese

Salad
½ cup (60 g/2 oz) diced olives
½ cup (60 g/2 oz) sundried
    tomatoes
350 g (11 oz) mesclun
    salad leaves (page 253)

Dressing
2 garlic cloves, crushed
3 tablespoons red wine vinegar
½ cup (125 mL/4 fl oz) virgin
    olive oil
½ teaspoon salt
finely ground black pepper, to
    taste

6 slices prosciutto (Parma ham),
    grilled
virgin olive oil

Cut 30 thin slices from the French loaf. Rub the bread with the garlic and brush with the olive oil. Brown the bread (approximately 3 minutes) on a baking tray in a low oven (150°C/300°F). Spread the croûtons with the goat cheese and return to the oven for 10 minutes.

Mix the salad in a bowl. Mix the dressing ingredients in a separate bowl.

Mix the salad and dressing together and lay the goat cheese croûtons on top of the salad. Garnish with the prosciutto (Parma ham) and dribble a little olive oil on top.

Serve while the croûtons are still warm.

*Serves 8–10 as a first course*

# CHEESE FONDUE

*I am predicting the return of the fondue, so be first on your street to cook one! Fondue is of course a great family meal and is enjoyed by teenagers and their friends. While it is best to have a fondue set (there are good earthenware ones available), a casserole will achieve the same effect.*

Rub the inside of the fondue bowl with the garlic. Add the wine base ingredients and simmer for 5 minutes. Grate the cheeses and stir them into the wine base. Use the crème fraîche to alter the consistency if the fondue is too thick. Add the kirsch just before serving.

For those of you too young to remember, cut the bread into bite-sized cubes, then impale them on the end of a fork and dip them into the fondue.

*Serves 6–8*

Cheeses
*405 g (13 oz) each Gruyère, Emmental and washed rind (Vacherin Mont d'Or) cheese*
*1 garlic clove, crushed*

Wine base
*155 mL (5 fl oz) white wine*
*½ chopped onion*
*2 thyme sprigs*
*1 bay leaf*
*½ teaspoon black pepper*
*good pinch of cayenne pepper*
*½ cup (125 mL/4 fl oz) crème fraîche (page 252)*
*⅖ cup (100 mL/3½ fl oz) kirsch*
*3 French bread sticks*

# CHEESE SOUFFLE

*A good soufflé should rise to almost treble its original bulk, and should be eaten as soon as it is cooked. This will certainly happen with this delicious savoury version made with a selection of four very different types of cheese.*

Melt the butter in a saucepan, add the flour and cook over a low heat, without browning, for 2–3 minutes. Whisk in the milk and bring to the boil, simmer for 3 minutes, add the cheeses and beat smooth with a wooden spoon. Take off the heat and beat in the egg yolks. Season with the peppers and ½ teaspoon of salt.

In a separate bowl, add a pinch of salt to the egg whites and beat until soft peaks form.

Put a layer of newspaper in the bottom of a baking pan and fill the pan with boiling water to a depth of 5 cm (2 in.).

Fold one-third of the egg whites into the warm cheese mix, then fold the mixture into the rest of the egg whites. Grease six (10 cm/4 in.) deep soufflé moulds with butter. Pour the mixture into the moulds. Flatten the tops with a wet knife and cut around the outside of the soufflés with a sharp knife to a depth of 2 cm (¾ in.), without touching the mould. Stand the soufflés in the baking pan with the boiling water.

Place the pan in a hot oven (180°C/355°F) for 10 minutes. If any soufflés are sticking to the side of the mould, gently cut through the crust to free them. Bake for a further 10 minutes and serve.

*Serves 6*

*2 tablespoons butter*
*2 tablespoons plain (all-purpose) flour*
*1 cup (250 mL/8 fl oz) milk*
*100 g (3½ oz) pecorino cheese, grated*
*100 g (3½ oz) Gruyère cheese, grated*
*100 g (3½ oz) blue cheese (Roquefort), chopped*
*100 g (3½ oz) cheddar cheese, grated*

*9 eggs, separated*
*½ teaspoon black pepper*
*pinch cayenne pepper*
*salt*

# CLASSIC QUICHE LORRAINE

*This savoury custard tart from the cuisine of the Alsace-Lorraine region in France is famous the world over. It did not come into favour in Anglo-Saxon countries, strangely, until as late as 1949.*

Wash and finely slice the leek. Melt the butter in a frying pan or skillet over a medium heat. Add the bacon and leek and soften in the butter without browning the leek. Grate the cheese. In a separate bowl, mix together the parsley, cheese, crème fraîche, eggs and seasonings.

Put the leek/bacon mixture over the bottom of the tart case and then pour the cheese mixture over, up to the lip of the pastry. Bake at 170°C (340°F) for 30 minutes, or until the top is golden and the custard is set.

*Serves 6*

Shortcrust pastry
*see Pear and Goat Cheese Tart (below)*
Filling
*155 g (5 oz) leek*
*2 tablespoons butter*
*155 g (5 oz) bacon rashers (slices), chopped*
*155 g (5 oz) Gruyère cheese*
*2 tablespoons chopped parsley*
*300 mL (10 fl oz) crème fraîche (page 252)*
*4 eggs*
*1 teaspoon salt*
*½ teaspoon black pepper*
*1 pinch freshly grated nutmeg*

# PEAR AND GOAT CHEESE TART

*Goat cheese has a distinctive flavour, immediately discernible even in the youngest of cheeses. As the cheese ages, the more zing it develops. The perfect combination of goat cheese and fruit is brought together in delicious harmony in this recipe.*

Food processors make the best shortcrust pastry. Mix the flour and butter until the mix is crumb-like (approximately 15 seconds). Add the eggs and pulse until assimilated. Add the water gradually until the pastry begins to coagulate. Press it into a flattened ball, wrap it in plastic wrap (cling film) and rest it in the refrigerator for 1 hour.

On a floured board, roll out the pastry. Make sure it is rolled to a size that will allow it to overhang the case(s). Lift the pastry from the rolling surface by wrapping it around the lightly floured rolling pin. Place the pastry in the greased tart cases(s) and press it gently into the corners. Fold the overhanging pastry over the top of the case(s). Cover with foil, pressing it into the shape of the case(s), and fill with rice or dried beans. Bake blind (page 252) for 20 minutes at 180°C (355°F), remove the foil and beans and continue baking until golden brown. Cut the overlap from the tart.

Poach the pears in salted water until tender.

Lay the sliced pears over the bottom of the tart case(s). Mix together all the ingredients for the cheese filling and pour it over the pears. Bake at 160°C (315°F) for 30 minutes, or until set.

Serve hot with an icy cold riesling wine.

*Serves 6*

*6 × 10 cm (4 in.) in diameter or 1 × 30 cm (12 in.) tart case(s)*

Shortcrust pastry
*1½ cups (200 g/6½ oz) plain (all-purpose) flour*
*⅖ cup (100 g/3½ oz) cold butter, diced*
*2 eggs*
*2 tablespoons iced water*

*2 brown pears, peeled*

Cheese filling
*200 g (6½ oz) goat cheese*
*⅘ cup (200 mL/6½ fl oz) crème fraîche (page 252)*
*4 eggs*
*1 teaspoon salt*
*½ teaspoon black pepper*

Opposite: Pear and Goat Cheese Tart

# ONION TART

―――――

Shortcrust pastry
*see Pear and Goat Cheese Tart
    (page 171)*

Filling
*100 g (3½ oz) butter
6 onions, very finely sliced
155 g (5 oz) Gruyère cheese,
    grated
405 mL (13 fl oz) crème
    fraîche (page 252)
4 eggs
1 teaspoon salt
½ teaspoon black pepper
1 pinch freshly grated nutmeg*

Melt the butter in a deep frying pan or skillet over a low heat. Add half the onions and cook in the butter, stirring constantly. Do not allow the onions to stew in their own juices. When they begin to caramelise (approximately 12 minutes), add the rest of the onions and continue to cook until they are very soft and all the water has left them.

In a separate bowl, mix together the cheese, crème fraîche, eggs and seasonings. Add the onions to this mix. Pour the mixture into the tart case, up to the lip of the pastry.

Bake at 170°C (340°F) for 30 minutes, or until golden and set.

*Serves 6*

# GOUGERE

―――――

*1 cup (250 mL/8 fl oz) water
100 g (3½ oz) butter
good pinch of salt
1½ cups (170 g/5½ oz) plain
    (all-purpose) flour
5 eggs
⅖ cup (100 g/3½ oz) Gruyère
    cheese, grated*

*This is a savoury French choux pastry containing Gruyère cheese or one like it, such as Emmental, and usually baked in a ring. In this recipe, I have baked the pastry in individual portions.*

Place the water, butter and salt in a saucepan and bring to the boil over a medium heat. Add the flour and stir until the mixture thickens and leaves the sides of the saucepan. Remove from the heat and briskly beat in the eggs, one at a time. Fold in the Gruyère cheese. Allow the pastry to cool and then use a teaspoon to place small rounds of the mixture onto a buttered baking sheet. Bake at 170°C (340°F) for 20 minutes, or until puffed and golden.

Serve hot, fresh from the oven.

*Makes 12–15 gougères*

# PIZZA GOURMAND

_____

*Pizza is easy to make at home and the home-made variety is much tastier than the takeaway variety. Some cooks line the bottom of their oven with bricks or terracotta tiles to help achieve perfection. Snails are available in 100 g (3½ oz) tins.*

### *To make the dough*

Mix together the flour and salt. Soften the yeast in some of the water and add it to the flour. Mix in about ⅖ cup (100 mL/3½ fl oz) of water, until the dough is pliable but not wet. Add the rest of the water if necessary. Knead the dough until smooth, then put it in a bowl, cover with plastic wrap (cling film) and leave to rise until it has doubled in bulk (approximately 2 hours).

### *To make the pizza*

Heat the olive oil in a frying pan or skillet until smoking. Add the tomatoes, onion and garlic and cook over a high heat until the tomato begins to caramelise, adding the herbs and seasonings as the vegetables and garlic cook. Reduce the mixture to a mildly thick paste over a high heat.

Prepare an oiled baking sheet or pizza pan of 35 cm (14 in.) diameter or 25 cm × 35 cm (10 in. × 14 in.).

Roll out the dough to fit the baking sheet.

Preheat the oven to the highest mark.

Place the dough on the baking sheet then spread the tomato topping on the dough. Sprinkle with the basil, olives, snails and cheeses. Arrange the ham on top of the cheese with the edges standing up as much as possible (so that they will crisp).

Bake in the hot oven for 20 minutes, or until browned.

Sprinkle with virgin olive oil and serve.

*Serves 6–8*

### Dough

1½ cups (200 g/6½ oz) strong
    or plain (all-purpose) flour
pinch salt
20 g (¾ oz) fresh yeast
⅖–½ cup (100–125 mL/
    3½–4 fl oz) lukewarm water

### Topping

¼ cup (60 mL/2 fl oz) virgin
    olive oil
4 tomatoes, chopped
1 onion, chopped
4 garlic cloves, crushed and
    chopped
2 tablespoons chopped Italian
    parsley
1 teaspoon fresh thyme leaves
1 bay leaf, crushed
pinch cayenne pepper
½ teaspoon salt
finely ground black pepper

### Garnish

2 tablespoons chopped fresh basil
    leaves
½ cup (60 g/2 oz) black olives,
    pitted and diced
½ cup (100 g/3½ oz) snails
    (delicious but optional)
155 g (5 oz) Gruyère cheese,
    grated
100 g (3½ oz) pecorino cheese,
    grated
8 slices Bayonne ham or
    prosciutto (Parma ham)
¼ cup (60 mL/2 fl oz) virgin
    olive oil

# FROMAGE BLANC WITH RASPBERRIES

405 g (13 oz) fromage blanc
2 egg whites
50 g (1½ oz) white granulated
    sugar


Sauce
4 cups (750 g/1½ lbs)
    raspberries
juice of 1 orange
²⁄₅ cup (100 g/3½ oz) caster
    (superfine) sugar

*Fromage blanc is fresh sheep milk curd, now available through specialty shops. Yoghurt or fresh goat cheese can be substituted.*

### To make the fromage blanc

Beat the whites, slowly adding the sugar as they fluff up, until soft peaks form. Fold the whites into the fromage blanc. Line a terrine mould of 6 cups (1.5 litres/2½ imp. pints) with a layer of plastic wrap (cling film) and then a layer of paper towel (absorbent kitchen paper). Press the fromage blanc and egg white mixture into the terrine and refrigerate for 24 hours.

### To make the sauce

Purée ½ cup (90 g/3 oz) raspberries with the orange juice and caster (superfine) sugar.

### To serve

Remove the terrine from the mould, slice, surround with the remaining raspberries and spoon the sauce around the fruit.

*Serves 6–8*

# MASCARPONE WITH COGNAC

600 g (1¼ lbs) mascarpone
⁴⁄₅ cup (200 mL/6½ fl oz)
    Cognac
⅓ cup (100 g/3½ oz) caster
    (superfine) sugar

1 cup (200 g/6½ oz)
    raspberries
1 cup (200 g/6½ oz)
    strawberries, hulled
1 cup (200 g/6½ oz)
    blueberries
1 cup (200 g/6½ oz)
    blackberries
²⁄₅ cup (100 g/3½ oz) caster
    (superfine) sugar

*One of the simplest desserts in the world and also one of the most delicious. Mascarpone is a very rich unsalted cream cheese—more like cream than cheese—and is native to the Lombardy region of Italy. I have flavoured the cheese with Cognac, but it may also be flavoured with chocolate, coffee, liqueurs or just eaten plain.*

Toss the berries in the sugar and leave them to macerate for 2 hours.

Divide the mascarpone into 6 portions and mound it in the centre of individual serving plates. Make a well in the centre of each mound of mascarpone and fill with Cognac. Sprinkle with the sugar and surround with the fruit.

*Serves 6*

Opposite: Fromage Blanc
with Raspberries

# MASCARPONE TART

—

310 g (10 oz) shortcrust pastry
   (page 171)

Filling
500 g (1 lb) mascarpone cheese
4 large eggs, separated
⅓ cup (90 g/3 oz) caster
   (superfine) sugar
¾ cup (185 mL/6 fl oz) light
   (single) cream

### To prepare the tart

Roll out the pastry as thinly as possible, measuring to ensure that it is large enough to cover the tart case and leaving a large overlap. Lift the pastry from the working surface by folding an edge of the pastry over the floured rolling pin and then turning the pin and rolling the pastry around it.

Unroll the pastry over and onto the case. Help the pastry into the case so that it is not necessary to further stretch it in order to fill the corners of the case. Gently press the pastry into the corners and against the sides of the case. Press the overhang over the top of the case, then cut the pastry with a sharp knife 1 cm (⅓ in.) below the top on the outside of the case. The reason for this is that as the filling is liquid it is necessary to have the top of the case form an even line, so that the filling does not leak over the low areas. This process should be followed for all quiche-type tarts. Similarly, it is essential that there be no hole in the pastry. Small holes can be patched by dampening a piece of pastry large enough to cover the hole and pressing it firmly around the edges to seal it to the case.

Bake blind (page 252) in a preheated oven (180°C/355°F) for 25 minutes. Lift the edge of the foil to check that the pastry is set and golden. Remove the tart(s) from the oven and take out the beans and foil. Return to the oven to finish browning the pastry evenly. Take the pastry out of the oven and cut the overlapping edge from the top of the case(s) by running a sharp knife around the top, angled against the metal case. This should give you an even top to the pastry case(s). Blow any crumbs away from the case(s).

### To make the filling

Mix together all the ingredients, except for the egg whites. Beat the whites to soft peaks and fold into the filling. Do this while the case(s) are browning. Fill the case(s) to the brim with the filling while they are still hot from the oven. Reduce the temperature to 150°C (300°F) and bake for 35 minutes (for the large tart) or 20 minutes (for individual tarts).

*Serves 6*

# CHEESE DUMPLINGS WITH HONEYED ALMONDS

Beat the cream cheese and sugar with a wooden spoon until pliable and creamy. In a separate bowl, beat the egg yolks, vanilla and 3 tablespoons of sugar until light and fluffy.

In another bowl, beat the egg whites and gradually add the remaining 3 tablespoons of sugar until the mixture forms soft peaks.

Fold the egg yolks into the softened cheese, then add the whisked whites.

Line the bottom of a baking pan with a sheet of newspaper. Half-fill the pan with water and heat until the water simmers. Ladle the mixture into six buttered dariole moulds (155 mL/5 fl oz). Lower the moulds into the water in the baking pan and poach for 5 minutes. Cover with aluminium kitchen foil and bake in a 150°C (300°F) oven for 30 minutes.

*To toast the almonds*

Toss the almonds with the icing (confectioners') sugar in a bag. Lay the coated almonds on a buttered baking sheet, sprinkle with any remaining sugar and bake in a hot oven (180°C/355°F) for about 7 minutes, or until the almonds are nicely browned.

*To make the sauce*

Warm all the ingredients in a saucepan over a low heat.

*To serve*

Unmould the warm dumplings onto a serving dish, pour the sauce over them and sprinkle with the almonds. This dish can be served warm or at room temperature.

*Serves 6*

*500 g (1 lb) cream cheese*
*3 tablespoons white granulated sugar*
*3 eggs, separated*
*½ teaspoon vanilla extract*
*6 tablespoons white granulated sugar*

Caramelised almonds
*1 cup (125 g/4 oz) slivered almonds*
*2 tablespoons icing (confectioners') sugar*

Sauce
*⅘ cup (200 mL/6½ fl oz) crème anglaise (page 204)*
*3 tablespoons honey*
*2 tablespoons overproof rum or Grand Marnier*

# WELSH RAREBIT

Pour the beer into a saucepan and bring it to the boil.

Simmer the onion in the beer for 5 minutes, or until the beer is reduced by half. Stir in the mustard and the cheese. When the mixture is hot, remove the saucepan from the heat and stir in the egg yolks.

Toast and butter the bread. Lay it on a tray and spread it with the cheese mixture. Grill (broil) until brown.

*Serves 6*

*⅖ cup (100 mL/3½ fl oz) beer*
*1 onion, finely chopped*
*1 tablespoon English Mustard*
*405 g (13 oz) aged cheddar cheese, grated*
*3 egg yolks*
*pinch of cayenne pepper*
*12 slices of strong bread (page 253)*

# The Delicatessen

*A good delicatessen is full of exotic flavours and smells, and the best of local and foreign produce. Smoked meats and sausages, pastas in myriad shapes and sizes, olives, cheese, salads, fresh breads and dried fish compete for space and will make your choice difficult but always a pleasure.*

Shopping at a good delicatessen should be part of everyone's weekend routine. There is nothing like the smells of sausage, smoked pork, hams, olives and dried fish to rid the nostrils of the stench of weekday toil.

Visiting a delicatessen can be almost as good as travelling, for the products found in delicatessens are often imported. Once inside the shop, it is easy to daydream of Greek islands, Turkish coffee shops, Danish smorgasbords, Finnish reindeer, North Sea fisherpeople fighting gales, Jewish matzo bakers, French foie gras packers in Sarlat, Hungarians packing ripe cherries into green brandy, Balkan pickle briners, German mustard factories belching smoke in the Ruhr Valley, or Russian workers stripping eggs from sturgeons in polluted Lake Baikal. And there, standing in the midst of all this, is the shopkeeper—the most unassuming of people—buttering bread for sandwiches!

If your delicatessen does not excite a similar reaction, you should search for a new one. A good delicatessen can easily be spotted by the generous quantity and variety of its stock. A shop that has only one slightly stale cut ham sitting in a refrigerator, and two varieties of olives, is not a delicatessen. Go to the shop where the light never reaches the counter because of the hams and salamis hanging from the ceiling, where the salted cod is thick and moist and the quince paste is as deeply coloured as a king's robe. Here the bread is crusted and floured, the tins of oil are painted with iconic hues, and barrels of salt fish compete with bags of chickpeas for floor space. That, dear friends, is a delicatessen.

For the family, the delicatessen is the source of quality pasta, convenience foods and the best ingredients for school lunches. Encourage the children to shop here and become familiar with the life-expanding range of exotica it stocks. If your delicatessen is like the one I describe, you will find that the proprietor will have more success getting the children to taste things than you ever could.

Previous pages: Antipasto made from delicatessen produce

# POTATO, PRAWN AND CAVIAR SALAD

### To make the salad

Mix together all the ingredients in a bowl and season them with salt, pepper and cayenne pepper. Add half the mayonnaise and mix thoroughly. Adjust the seasoning, adding a little lemon juice if necessary.

### To make the mayonnaise

Mix together the two oils. Whisk together or place in a blender the egg yolks, mustard and lemon juice, and salt and pepper to taste. Dribble the oil slowly onto the yolks, whisking briskly at the same time. A friend with a steady hand can be a big help. (A quicker method is to blend the egg yolk, mustard and lemon juice base and then pour the oil slowly into the blender. Turn the blender off immediately the oil is absorbed.) Add the crème fraîche and whisk it into the mayonnaise.

### To prepare the mould(s)

You need six small (⅘ cup/200 mL/6½ fl oz) or one large (4 cups/ 1 litre/1¾ imp. pints) dariole mould(s). Line the mould(s) with plastic wrap (cling film), pile the salad into the mould(s) and press down firmly so that the salad is packed into each mould and is level with the top of the mould(s). Refrigerate until ready to use.

### To serve

Loosen the salad from the mould(s) by gently pulling on the plastic wrap. Add half the caviar to the remaining mayonnaise and place a spoonful in the centre of each plate. Spread the mayonnaise with the back of a spoon, exposing an area in the centre of the plate equal to the size of the base of the salad. Tip the individual moulded salads (or slices of the moulded salad if using one mould) into the centre of the plate. Cover the top of each salad with the remaining caviar and garnish with the sprigs of chervil.

*Serves 6*

300 g (9½ oz) cooked shelled prawns (shrimps), diced
2 cups (300 g/9½ oz) cooked peeled potatoes, diced
200 g (6½ oz) avocado, cut in large dice
100 g (3½ oz) tomato, peeled, seeded and diced
1 cup Italian parsley, roughly chopped
1 tablespoon chopped fresh tarragon leaves
1 cup (90 g/3 oz) fresh sliced mushrooms
salt and freshly ground black pepper
good pinch of cayenne pepper
lemon juice

Mayonnaise
⅖ cup (100 mL/3½ fl oz) virgin olive oil
⅖ cup (100 mL/3½ fl oz) peanut oil
4 egg yolks
1 tablespoon strong Dijon mustard
80 mL (2½ fl oz) lemon juice
salt and freshly ground black pepper
⅘ cup (200 mL/6½ fl oz) crème fraîche (page 252)

Garnish
200 g (6½ oz) caviar
18 chervil sprigs

# SALAD OF PROSCIUTTO, ENDIVES AND AVOCADO

200 g (6½ oz) sliced prosciutto
   (Parma ham) (below)
4 Belgian endives (witloof)
1 tight head of radicchio
18 Italian parsley sprigs
6 hard-boiled eggs
100 g (3½ oz) green beans
3 avocados

Dressing
2 garlic cloves, crushed
1 teaspoon Dijon mustard
¼ cup (60 mL/2 fl oz) lemon
   juice
1 cup (250 mL/8 fl oz) virgin
   cold pressed olive oil
salt and finely ground pepper

Break the Belgian endives (witloof) and the radicchio into leaves, and wash them. Wash the parsley sprigs. Pat dry the salad leaves and the parsley. Shell and slice the eggs. Blanch the beans in boiling water for 1 minute, drain, refresh under cold water and drain again. Peel, pit and slice the avocados. Place all the salad ingredients except for the prosciutto (Parma ham) or Bayonne ham in a large bowl.

Whisk together the dressing ingredients, seasoning to taste. Pour the dressing over the salad and gently turn the salad mixture to coat the ingredients with the dressing. Divide the prosciutto into 6 portions and then, in a smaller bowl, fold some of the salad into each portion of prosciutto and pile onto individual plates. The salad should be oily; add more oil if necessary.

*Serves 6*

# PROSCIUTTO SANDWICH MALTESE

Dressing
1 tablespoon orange rind,
   julienned and blanched (page
   253)
⅖ cup (100 mL/3½ fl oz)
   (blood) orange juice
1 teaspoon marmalade
2 tablespoons red wine vinegar
½ cup (125 mL/4 fl oz) virgin
   olive oil
1 teaspoon finely ground pepper

12 slices strong wood-fired bread
   (page 253)
virgin olive oil
1 mild white onion, finely sliced
   and blanched
500 g (1 lb) prosciutto (Parma
   ham) (below)
½ cup (60 g/2 oz) pitted and
   diced black olives
12 chervil sprigs

In a small bowl, mix together the ingredients for the dressing.

Brush the bread with olive oil. Place a layer of the onion on the bread. Dip the slices of prosciutto (Parma ham) in the dressing and place them on top of the onion layer.

Mix the remaining dressing with the olives and spoon it onto the prosciutto. Garnish with the sprigs of chervil.

*Serves 6*

# PROSCIUTTO OR UNCOOKED HAMS

*The first rule one must obey with prosciutto (Parma ham) is to have it sliced at the delicatessen. Unless you have an electric slicing machine at home, or a spiked ham holder and special slicing knife, there is no way that you will be able to slice it as thinly as the delicatessen.*

To serve the prosciutto is simple. Lay the slices on a plate, grind pepper over them and serve with fresh figs, melon or nashi pears (Chinese pears). To gild the lily, sprinkle the ham with virgin olive oil and garnish with small Niçoise olives and chervil sprigs.

Opposite: Prosciutto with Figs

# SMOKED SALMON SANDWICH WITH PEPPER VINAIGRETTE

500 g (1 lb) smoked salmon
12 slices rye bread
1 cup (155 g/ 5 oz) shredded
  daikon radish

Dressing
1 tablespoon golden shallots
1 tablespoon lemon juice
1 tablespoon strong Dijon
  mustard
1 tablespoon red wine vinegar
½ cup (125 mL/ 4 fl oz)
  walnut oil
½ teaspoon salt
½ teaspoon green peppercorns,
  crushed
2 teaspoons pink peppercorns

Garnish
1 tablespoon cornichons
  (gherkins), chopped
12 chervil sprigs

*Some of the finest smoked salmon available now is prepared in Tasmania. Make sure, if possible, that you buy this freshly smoked salmon rather than the less flavoursome Scandinavian smoked salmon.*

### To make the dressing

Chop the shallots and blanch them in boiling water for 1 minute. Drain, refresh under cold running water, drain again and pat dry. Mix the ingredients for the dressing with a whisk.

### To make the sandwich

Freshen the shredded daikon radish by soaking it in iced water for 1 hour. Drain and dry before using.

Lay the bread on the bench top and brush it with a little dressing.

Lay the salmon in a single layer on a tray and spoon the dressing over the salmon.

Put a layer of the daikon radish on the bread and then place the salmon on top of the daikon, allowing any excess dressing to spill into the tray. Sprinkle with the cornichons (gherkins) and garnish with the sprigs of chervil.

*Serves 6*

# STUFFED ROSETTA ROLLS

6–8 rosetta bread rolls
6–8 slices prosciutto (Parma
  ham)

Stuffing
1 cup (185 g/ 6 oz) julienned
  ham (page 253)
1 cup (250 g/ 8 oz) diced
  avocado tossed in lemon juice
½ cup (125 g/ 4 oz) grated
  cheese (cheddar or Gruyère)
1 tablespoon diced black olives
1 cup (340 g/ 11 oz) diced
  tomato
1 garlic clove, crushed
1 tablespoon chopped fresh basil
1 tablespoon chopped parsley
2 tablespoons virgin olive oil
1 tablespoon red wine vinegar
salt and freshly ground black
  pepper

*These tasty rolls are delicious and nutritious, and perfect for children's lunches and picnics.*

Mix together all the stuffing ingredients in a bowl and season with salt and pepper. Cut the tops off the rosetta rolls (higher up than halfway), remove any soft bread and line the inside of the rolls with the prosciutto (Parma ham). Fill the rolls with the stuffing mixture so that it is slightly heaped, press the tops on top of the filling and wrap loosely in aluminium kitchen foil. Do not use plastic wrap (cling film) as the rolls tend to sweat and become soggy.

*Serves 6–8*

# SHELL PASTA SALAD

———

*A quick lunch dish which can be prepared in advance and served with a green salad.*

Cook the pasta in a large saucepan of boiling salted water (4 cups/1 litre/1¾ imp. pints) until tender (approximately 10 minutes), then drain, rinse under cold running water and drain again. Dry the pasta in a towel, put it in a bowl and toss in a little olive oil to prevent it drying and sticking together.

Mix together the tuna, onion, parsley and olives with a fork, breaking up the tuna into flakes.

In a separate bowl, whisk or blend together the remaining ingredients and seasonings, then fold this into the fish mixture. Pour over the pasta, mix and serve.

*Serves 6–8*

*2 cups (300 g/ 9½ oz) shell pasta*
*1 tablespoon virgin olive oil*

*1 × 250 g (8 oz) tin tuna*
*½ onion, chopped*
*2 tablespoons chopped fresh parsley leaves*
*2 tablespoons chopped black olives*
*⅖ cup (100 mL/ 3½ fl oz) light (single) cream*
*1 tablespoon strong Dijon mustard*
*2 tablespoons virgin olive oil*
*2 tablespoons lemon juice*
*pinch of cayenne pepper*
*1 teaspoon salt*
*½ teaspoon freshly ground black pepper*

# COLD ALMOND SOUP

———

Place the almonds, garlic, salt and 1 cup (250 mL/8 fl oz) of water in the food processor and blend until the mixture is a paste. Briefly soak the breadcrumbs in some additional water and drain. Add the breadcrumbs to the almond paste in the food processor. Continue to process adding first the oil in a stream (as for mayonnaise), and then the sherry vinegar. Thin the soup with the remaining water.

Serve the soup over ice cubes in a bowl, with grapes which have been chilled in the refrigerator.

*Serves 6–10*

*1⅓ cups (155 g/ 5 oz) almonds, blanched and peeled*
*2 garlic cloves, peeled*
*¼ teaspoon salt*
*5 cups (1.25 litres/ 2 imp. pints) water*
*3 cups (185 g/ 6 oz) fresh breadcrumbs*
*1 cup (250 mL/ 8 fl oz) virgin olive oil*
*3 tablespoons sherry vinegar*
*ice cubes (see method)*
*1 cup (200 g/ 6½ oz) muscat grapes*

# GRILLED FILLET OF RED MULLET WITH TAPÉNADE

*Red mullet (rouget) is one of the most highly-prized Mediterranean fish. It has a delicate texture and rich flavour. The larger variety is the most prized as the bones are easier to deal with. This recipe can be used successfully with other soft-fleshed fish.*

Fillet the mullet. Remove the bones using tweezers. You can save the backbones and heads and use them for making stock.

Peel and quarter the tomatoes. Remove the seeds and the internal flesh and reserve. Season the external flesh with salt and pepper. Set aside.

### To make the sippets

Heat the oil in a frying pan or skillet and cook the garlic for 3 minutes. Remove the garlic before it burns. Fry the bread sippets in the hot oil until crisp and brown. Drain them on paper towel (absorbent kitchen paper).

### To make the tapénade

Place all the ingredients in a blender or food processor and blend them to a purée, or until smooth. The tapénade can be kept in a sealed jar in the refrigerator for many weeks.

### To cook the fish

Preheat the oven to 150°C (300°F). Oil a flat baking sheet with a little olive oil and sprinkle it with salt, pepper and thyme. Lay the mullet fillets on the baking sheet, side by side, skin up, as if butterflied. Cook gently in the oven for 10 minutes, or until the fish becomes opaque. Remove the fish from the oven and spread the tapénade down the centre of each fillet. Sprinkle with chopped parsley and place under a hot griller (broiler).

Heat the tomato pieces in half the olive oil, season with salt and pepper and add the chervil sprigs.

### To serve

Place the cooked fish on warm plates and sprinkle with the sippets. Spoon the tomato beside the fish and spoon the remaining oil between the fillets.

*Serves 6–8*

6 × 250 g (8 oz) red mullet
6 ripe tomatoes
salt and freshly ground black pepper

Sippets
½ cup (125 mL/4 fl oz) virgin olive oil
1 garlic clove, crushed
3 fine slices stale white bread, diced small

Tapénade
½ cup (125 g/4 oz) olive paste
1 tablespoon chopped fresh parsley
1 tablespoon capers
1 garlic clove, crushed
6 anchovy fillets
3 tablespoons virgin olive oil
½ teaspoon freshly ground black pepper

virgin olive oil
salt and freshy ground black pepper
1 teaspoon chopped fresh thyme
2 tablespoons chopped fresh parsley
½ cup (125 mL/4 fl oz) virgin olive oil
20 chervil sprigs, picked and washed

Opposite: Grilled Fillet of Red Mullet with Tapénade

# RISOTTO WITH CEPES

### Cèpes

*400 g (13 oz) cèpes (porcini mushrooms) or field mushrooms, diced*
*²⁄₅ cup (100 mL/3½ fl oz) virgin olive oil*
*2 garlic cloves, crushed*
*salt and freshly ground pepper*
*1 tablespoon chopped fresh parsley leaves*

### Risotto

*2 tablespoons virgin olive oil*
*1½ cups (310 g/10 oz) Arborio rice*
*½ onion, chopped*
*½ teaspoon fresh thyme leaves*
*½ bay leaf*
*2¾ cups (700 mL/22 fl oz) chicken stock (page 138)*

### *To cook the cèpes*

Heat the olive oil in a frying pan or skillet, add the cèpes (porcini mushrooms) and shuffle in the pan over a high heat until they have wilted (approximately 5 minutes). Add the garlic, season with salt and pepper and continue to cook until the cèpes begin to brown. Sprinkle with the chopped parsley, take the pan from the heat and keep to one side until needed.

### *To make the risotto*

Heat the olive oil in a heavy saucepan and add the rice, onion, thyme and bay leaf. Stir with a wooden spoon until the rice begins to smell nutty (approximately 2 minutes). Add the chicken stock, a little at a time, stirring with the wooden spoon, until the rice has absorbed it. Continue until all the stock has been added. Stir in the cèpes. The risotto should be creamy and the rice a little firm.

*Serves 6–8*

# SALAD OF SALTED COD PORTUGAISE

*600 g (1¼ lbs) dried salted cod fillets (bacalao)*
*²⁄₅ cup (100 mL/3½ fl oz) virgin olive oil*
*2 onions, sliced*
*2 garlic cloves, crushed*
*1 carrot, sliced*
*1 teaspoon ground paprika*
*pinch of cayenne pepper*
*½ teaspoon ground cardamom*
*1 teaspoon saffron threads*
*2 thyme sprigs*
*1 bay leaf*
*1¼ cups (300 mL/9½ fl oz) white wine*

### Salad

*²⁄₅ cup (100 mL/3½ fl oz) virgin olive oil*
*2 onions, sliced*
*3 sweet peppers (capsicum), seeded and sliced*
*3 ripe tomatoes, diced*
*salt and freshly ground pepper*

*Choose thick, moist-looking fish fillets, not thin pieces with lots of skin and bone. Bacalao is the Spanish term for dried salted cod. The Italians call it baccalá.*

### *To braise the cod*

Soak the cod fillets in cold water overnight. Take the cod from the water, drain and cut into bite-sized chunks.

Heat the oil in a large frying pan or skillet and add the cod, onions, garlic and carrot. Toss these in the oil over a medium heat until the vegetables have softened (approximately 3–5 minutes). Add the paprika, cayenne pepper, cardamom, saffron, thyme and bay leaf. Then add the white wine and simmer for about 10 minutes. Increase the heat and reduce the sauce until it is thickened.

### *To make the salad*

In a separate frying pan or skillet, heat the oil. Toss the vegetables in the oil until they are soft (approximately 5–7 minutes). Allow the vegetable mixture to cool, then add it to the braised cod.

### *To serve*

Season the dish with salt and pepper and serve at room temperature.

*Serves 6*

# BREAD FERMENT

*Bread ferment is a purist's yeast. Over the years I have collected yeasts from wine-makers vats and boutique breweries. I have added grape skins to the ferment to make wild yeasts. The ferment is a living thing and needs to be fed regularly. It will be less active if it is kept refrigerated and I suggest you do this if you don't use it every day. To feed the ferment, add a 50/50 mix of rye flour and strong baker's flour mixed with a double quantity of water every 3 days if refrigerated (every day if the ferment is more active). When the ferment is used, replace the amount used with an equal quantity of flour/water mix.*

1 cup (125 g/4 oz) rye flour
1 cup (125 g/4 oz) strong (baker's) or plain (all-purpose) flour
1 teaspoon dry active yeast
2 cups (500 mL/16 fl oz) water

Mix together all the ingredients and set aside, uncovered, in a warm place until it begins to ferment. When the mixture is bubbling, take some to make bread and replace as described above or refrigerate.

*Makes 4 cups (1 litre/1¾ imp. pints)*

# RYE BREAD

Mix together the flours and salt. Combine the yeast and stout, then add to the dry ingredients. Mix well, adding enough water to form a stiff dough. Knead until smooth. Put the dough in a bowl and allow to rise until doubled in bulk (approximately 4 hours). Knock down the dough and form into 2 loaves (30 × 10 cm/12 × 4 in.). Cover with a damp cloth and allow to rise in a warm place until double its size.

2 kg (4 lbs) strong (baker's) or plain (all-purpose) flour
1 kg (2 lbs) rye flour
¼ cup (60 g/2 oz) salt
2 tablespoons fresh or dry yeast
1 cup (250 mL/8 fl oz) stout
405 mL (13 fl oz) water

20 g (¾ oz) additional rye flour

Preheat the oven to 230°C (450°F). Dust the loaves with extra rye flour and bake for 30 minutes, then reduce the temperature to 180°C (355°F) and bake for a further 30 minutes, or until the loaf sounds hollow when tapped.

*Makes 2 × 2 kg (4 lbs) loaves*

# BREAD ROLLS

Mix the flour, yeast and salt. Add the bread ferment and water. Mix to form a firm dough, adding more water if necessary. Knead until smooth, then set aside in a warm place until doubled.

1 kg (2 lbs) strong (baker's) or plain (all-purpose) flour
½ tablespoon dry active yeast
1 teaspoon salt
155 g (5 oz) bread ferment (above)
2 cups (500 mL/8 fl oz) water
50 g (1½ oz) additional rye flour

Divide the dough into 20 pieces. Roll the dough into tight buns with your hands, stretching the gluten well. The buns should be dome-shaped at the top. Any folds should be at the base. Dip the top of each bun in the rye flour. Using a razor blade or sharp knife, cut a slash at an angle on top of each bun. Lay a sheet of silicone paper on a flat baking tray. Place the buns on the tray and allow to rise and double in bulk (about 1 hour). Preheat the oven to 230°C (450°F). Bake for 25–30 minutes, or until golden. Serve immediately.

*Makes 20*

# GARBURE

1.25 kg (2½ lbs) meaty,
    smoked pork belly (speck)
4 cups (1 litre/1¾ imp. pints)
    chicken stock (page 138)
½ cup (125 mL/4 fl oz) white
    wine
2 garlic cloves, crushed
1 thyme sprig
1 bay leaf
10 peppercorns
salt and freshly ground black
    pepper
½ savoy cabbage, shredded
1 kg (2 lbs) broad beans,
    shelled
500 g (1 lb) borlotti beans,
    shelled
3 tablespoons virgin olive oil
2 tablespoons chopped parsley
6–8 chervil sprigs

Place the pork in a saucepan (cut it into 2 pieces if necessary) and add the chicken stock, white wine, garlic, thyme, bay leaf and peppercorns. Simmer for 1 hour. Skim the fat from the poaching liquid and strain 4 cups (1 litre/1¾ imp. pints) of the liquid into a separate saucepan. Taste the liquid and adjust the seasoning.

Blanch the cabbage (page 252). Blanch the broad beans, then remove the next shell layer until only the kernel remains. Cook the borlotti beans over a low heat in a little of the poaching liquid until tender (approximately 25 minutes). Add the cabbage and beans to the strained liquid and heat through.

*To serve*
Slice the pork into 2 cm (¾ in.) thick slices. Place some beans, cabbage and liquid in individual serving bowls. Place a slice of pork on top. Sprinkle a little olive oil into the liquid around the pork and garnish with chopped parsley and chervil sprigs. Serve with boiled potatoes and French mustard.

*Serves 6–8*

# BRAISED HAM HOCKS WITH CREAMED HARICOT BEANS

6 ham hocks
2 peeled onions, 1 stuck with 4
    cloves
1 head of garlic, halved
3 tomatoes, chopped
2 carrots, halved lengthwise
2 cups (500 mL/16 fl oz)
    white wine
1 tablespoon black peppercorns
2 thyme sprigs
2 bay leaves
Creamed haricot beans
300 g (9½ oz) dried haricot
    (navy) beans
8 cups (2 litres/3¼ imp. pints)
    water
1 tablespoon Dijon mustard
155 mL (5 fl oz) light (single)
    cream
freshly ground black pepper
2 tablespoons chopped parsley

Cover the haricot (navy) beans with water and soak them overnight. Strain the beans, then wash them under cold running water.

Put the hocks in a large saucepan, add the other ingredients and enough water to cover the hocks. Bring the water to the boil and then simmer until the hocks are tender (approximately 1½ hours). Strain the stock into another saucepan. Remove and discard the garlic head and reserve it. Remove the skin from the hocks, then return the hocks to the strained stock.

Put the beans in a saucepan with enough stock to cover them and simmer until tender (approximately 1 hour). Strain and reserve any excess liquid, then mix the mustard with the cream and add it to the beans. Place the garlic in a sieve and press the flesh into the beans. Discard the husks. Season the beans with pepper and some of the parsley.

*To serve*
Heat the hocks in the stock and then cover the bottom of hot serving plates with the beans and place the hocks on them. Sprinkle with the remaining chopped parsley and serve.

*Serves 6*

Opposite: Garbure

# CHOUCROUTE A LA ROYALE

———

Court bouillon
3 cups (750 mL/ 24 fl oz)
   white wine
4 cups (1 litre/ 1¾ imp. pints)
   chicken stock (page 138) or
   water
2 onions, halved
2 carrots, halved
3 garlic cloves, crushed
12 peppercorns
2 thyme sprigs
1 bay leaf

Meat
3 ham hocks, sawn in rounds
500 g (1 lb) smoked loin of
   pork

Sauerkraut
2 tablespoons goose fat
   (page 253)
⅘ cup (200 g/ 6½ oz) sliced
   onion
10 garlic cloves, crushed
3 peeled apples, finely sliced
1 kg (2 lbs) sauerkraut
2 thyme sprigs
2 bay leaves
6 juniper berries, crushed
1 teaspoon black pepper
1 teaspoon fresh thyme leaves

Sausages
6 knackwurst
6 fresh, continental, pork
   sausages

*The great deli winter dish. To make your own sauerkraut (choucroute), season
1 kg (2 lbs) salt with 60 g (2 oz) juniper berries. Put 10 kg (20 lbs) finely sliced
tender leaves of cabbage in layers in a large crock. Season the layers with the salt
and juniper berries. Finish by covering with whole cabbage leaves and a clean cloth.
Press with a round of wood the same size as the interior of the crock with a weight
on top. The sauerkraut will be ready in 3 weeks.*

### To cook the meat

Place the ingredients for the court bouillon in a large saucepan and
bring to the boil over a medium heat. Add the meats (not the
sausages), and simmer for 1½ hours, or until tender. Strain off half the
liquid and reserve it for the sauerkraut.

### To prepare the sauerkraut

Wash the sauerkraut in cold water and then strain it in a sieve,
pressing any water from the cabbage.

Heat the goose fat in a large saucepan and soften the onion and
garlic in the fat. Add the apple, sauerkraut, seasonings and half the
liquid from the meats. Simmer for 1 hour over a low heat. If the
sauerkraut has lots of liquid, reduce over a high heat until the
sauerkraut is above the liquid.

Heat the meats in the remaining liquid and add the sausages. Simmer
for 10 minutes, then drain.

### To serve

Pile the sauerkraut in the middle of individual serving plates. Slice the
loin of pork and surround it with the ham hocks and sausages. Serve
with steamed potatoes and a bowl of mustard.

*Serves 6*

# MACARONI GRATIN

___

*To cook the macaroni*
Fill a large saucepan with water and bring it to the boil. Add the macaroni and salt and cook until just tender (approximately 12 minutes). Drain and reserve.

*To make the white sauce*
Melt the butter in a saucepan, add the flour, then cook over a low heat for 2–3 minutes, stirring continuously with a wooden spoon.

Whisk the cream into the mixture (roux) and slowly bring it to the boil. Season with salt and pepper and simmer for 10 minutes. Mix in the cheese, take the saucepan off the heat and let the sauce cool.

*To make the filling*
Melt the butter and soften the onion over a medium heat. When the onion is translucent, add the ham and garlic and continue to cook for 2–3 minutes. Add the herbs and seasonings and then the white wine. Cook over a high heat until the liquid has completely reduced. Add the white sauce and then the macaroni. Mix together and then transfer into a suitably sized gratin dish.

*To make the topping*
Combine the cheese, breadcrumbs and butter and sprinkle over the macaroni mixture. Bake in a moderate oven (170°C/340°F) until golden brown (approximately 15–20 minutes).

*Serves 6–8*

500 g (1 lb) macaroni
pinch of salt

White sauce
1 tablespoon butter
1 tablespoon plain (all-purpose) flour
⁴⁄₅ cup (200 mL/6½ fl oz) light (single) cream
salt and freshly ground black pepper
½ cup (60 g/2 oz) grated pecorino cheese

Filling
1 tablespoon butter
½ cup (125 g/4 oz) chopped onion
2 cups (375 g/12 oz) julienned ham (page 253)
2 garlic cloves, crushed
½ cup roughly chopped parsley
1 teaspoon chopped thyme leaves
1 bay leaf, crushed
salt, freshly ground black pepper and cayenne pepper
155 mL (5 fl oz) white wine

Topping
1 cup (125 g/4 oz) grated pecorino cheese
1 cup (60 g/2 oz) fresh breadcrumbs
125 g (4 oz) butter, melted

# RAGU BOLOGNAISE

___

Heat the olive oil in a heavy frying pan or skillet over a high heat until smoking. Add the meat, onion and carrot and brown (approximately 7 minutes). Add the garlic, tomato paste (purée), thyme and bay leaf and stir until the paste begins to caramelise (about 3–4 minutes). Deglaze with the wine. Reduce the heat and simmer for 10 minutes. Season with salt and pepper. Add a little water if necessary, but keep the sauce thick and rich. Serve immediately with fresh fettucine (page 194).

*Serves 6–8*

⅓ cup (90 mL/3 fl oz) virgin olive oil
600 g (1¼ lbs) chopped beef
1 chopped onion
1 carrot, cut into small dice
3 garlic cloves, crushed
2 tablespoons tomato paste (purée)
1 teaspoon fresh thyme
1 bay leaf
1 cup (250 mL/8 fl oz) white or red wine
salt and freshly ground black pepper

# PASTA

2 cups (250 g/ 8 oz) bread
  flour or plain (all-purpose)
  flour
pinch of salt
3 eggs, plus 2 yolks, lightly
  beaten
1 tablespoon virgin olive oil
1 tablespoon water

*This is a basic egg pasta dough that can be used to make spaghetti, fettucine, lasagna, canestrini and ravioli.*

## Method 1

To make the pasta by hand, sift the flour and salt into a large bowl and make a well in the centre. Gradually add the oil, eggs and water, and mix into the flour. Use your hands to knead until the dough is smooth and elastic (approximately 5 minutes).

## Method 2

If you are using a food processor, place the sifted flour, salt and oil in the food processor and process, adding the eggs in a stream. Add just enough water to form a stiff dough. Do not overprocess. Stop the machine when the dough is just blended and the paste amalgamates. Knead as above.

Refrigerate the dough for 2 hours before rolling it out (use a pasta machine) onto a floured surface to be cut into the required shapes.

*Serves 6–8*

# SPAGHETTI
# WITH OIL AND CHILI PEPPERS

600 g (1¼ lbs) spaghetti
pinch of salt
½ cup (60 g/ 2 oz) grated
  pecorino cheese

Sauce
155 mL (5 fl oz) virgin olive
  oil
6 garlic cloves, crushed and
  chopped
2–3 fresh chili peppers, chopped
½ cup (80 g/ 2½ oz) black
  olives, pitted and chopped
1 cup roughly chopped Italian
  parsley
1 teaspoon fresh thyme leaves
1 tablespoon chopped fresh
  marjoram
1 teaspoon ground black pepper
1 teaspoon salt

Opposite: Spaghetti with
Tomato Provençal (page 103)

*Spaghetti al aglio e pepperoni is my favourite quick pasta dish. Serve with tomato and basil salad.*

## To make the sauce

Heat the olive oil in a large saucepan over a low heat and cook the garlic for 3 minutes, without browning it. Add the chili peppers and cook for 1 minute. Add the rest of the ingredients and stir briskly over a high heat for 1 minute.

## To cook the spaghetti

Bring a large saucepan of salted water to the boil. Add the spaghetti and cook until just tender (approximately 5 minutes).

Drain the spaghetti and add to the sauce, tossing in the pan over a high heat. Add the cheese, mix it through the spaghetti and serve very hot.

*Serves 6*

# MUSHROOM LASAGNA

## Pasta
1 serve of home-made pasta
   (page 194)
virgin olive oil

## Tomato sauce
2 tablespoons virgin olive oil
3 tomatoes, chopped
3 garlic cloves, crushed and
   chopped
½ teaspoon fresh thyme leaves
1 bay leaf
salt and freshly ground black
   pepper

## Cheese sauce
2 tablespoons butter
2 tablespoons plain (all-purpose)
   flour
1 cup (250 mL/8 fl oz) milk
200 g (6½ oz) grated pecorino
   cheese
100 g (3½ oz) grated cheddar
   cheese
1 tablespoon chopped thyme
1 bay leaf
salt and freshly ground black
   pepper

## Mushrooms
3 tablespoons virgin olive oil
500 g (1 lb) each of mushroom
   caps, Swiss brown mushrooms
   and shiitake mushrooms,
   sliced
2 onions, finely sliced
3 garlic cloves, chopped
⅓ cup chopped fresh parsley
1 teaspoon fresh thyme leaves
salt and freshly ground black
   pepper

300 g (9½ oz) ham, finely sliced
1 cup (125 g/4 oz) grated
   pecorino cheese
freshly ground black pepper

*To make the pasta*

Lightly grease with oil a baking pan 25 cm × 30 cm (10 in. × 12 in.), that is 6 cm–8 cm (1½ in.–3¼ in.) deep.

Roll the pasta to the second thinnest setting on the pasta machine (No. 6) and cut the sheets into eight 35 cm (14 in.) lengths. The sheets will shrink to 30 cm (12 in.) after cooking. This should be enough for four layers of pasta.

Cook the sheets in a large saucepan of boiling water as soon as you have rolled and cut them. Homemade pasta only takes 3 minutes to cook. Remove each sheet from the boiling water using a wire sieve (spider) and cool it in cold water. Dry the pasta on a tray covered with a paper towel (absorbent kitchen paper) and then between sheets of plastic wrap (cling film).

*To make the tomato sauce*

Heat the olive oil in a frying pan or skillet until smoking. Add the remaining ingredients. Cook until the mixture is a thick sauce (approximately 10 minutes).

*To make the cheese sauce*

Melt the butter in a small saucepan over a medium heat and then add the flour, to make a roux. Cook the roux gently for 3 minutes and then slowly add the milk, whisking all the time. Simmer the sauce for 5 minutes, then add the cheeses, thyme, bay leaf and seasonings. Cook gently for a further 5 minutes, stirring with a wooden spoon.

*To cook the mushrooms*

Heat the olive oil in a deep saucepan. Add the mushrooms and cook over a high heat. When the mushrooms have lost most of their water, add the remaining ingredients. Cook the mixture for a further 10 minutes over a low heat.

*To assemble the lasagna*

Lay two sheets of pasta on the bottom of the greased baking pan. Spread them with the tomato sauce, then a layer of the mushroom mixture. Dot with 8 teaspoons of the cheese sauce and then a layer of ham. Repeat the pattern twice more, using up the fillings (except for the cheese sauce). Finish with a layer of pasta, then the last of the cheese sauce, sprinkle with the pecorino and season with pepper. Bake in a moderate oven (180°C/355°F) for 35 minutes, or until the cheese has browned.

*Serves 6–8*

# TERRINE OF DUCK, HAM AND PORK WITH PISTACHIO NUTS

### To prepare the duck

With a sharp knife, remove the duck's legs and breasts. Bone the legs and remove the skin from the legs and breasts. Sprinkle the meat with the brandy and marinate in a covered dish overnight together with the juniper berries, orange rind, thyme and bay leaf.

### To make the terrine

Remove the duck leg meat from the marinade, drain and grind or chop finely. Mix the leg meat together with the other minced ingredients.

Purée the seasoning ingredients in a blender or food processor. Add the seasoning to the mince and mix thoroughly. Try to taste the mixture raw. It should be salty but with a complex perfume. Alternatively, make a small rissole, cook it in a frying pan or skillet and then taste it to test the seasoning. Once you are happy with the taste, mix the seasoning and the mince again and leave covered overnight in the refrigerator (so that the flavours can blend and develop).

Remove the duck breast meat from the marinade and drain. Cut the breasts into strips.

### To cook the terrine

The terrine can be cooked in a loaf pan (14 cm × 21 cm/6 in. × 9 in.) or a round earthenware casserole. Lightly grease the pan. Line it with finely sliced prosciutto (Parma ham), leaving an overlap to cover the meats when the terrine is full. Place alternate layers of mince and strips of duck breast in the lined pan. When slightly overfull, pull the overlap of prosciutto over the mixture to cover it.

Cut a generous piece of aluminium kitchen foil, brush it with a little fat, oil or butter and cover the terrine, sealing it securely. You can tie it with string if you wish.

Half fill a baking pan with boiling water and place the terrine in the pan. Bake in a slow oven (130°C/265°F) for 2½ hours, keeping the water at the same level all the time.

Remove the loaf pan from the water and allow the terrine to cool before refrigerating. The terrine will have a better flavour if refrigerated for 3–7 days before serving.

### To serve

Cut into slices and serve with crusty 'wood-fired' style bread, cornichons (gherkins), mustard, olives, or with a salad and ripe brown grainy pears.

*Serves 12*

1 muscovy drake weighing 1.5–2 kg (3–4 lbs)
30 mL (1 fl oz) brandy
4–5 juniper berries, smashed
1 shaving orange rind
1 thyme sprig
1 bay leaf

Mince
200 g (6½ oz) lean pork, ground
200 g (6½ oz) belly pork, ground
100 g (3½ oz) duck, pork or chicken liver, puréed
100 g (3½ oz) pork back fat, cut into 5 cm (2 in.) dice
200 g (6½ oz) double smoked ham, cut into 5 cm (2 in.) dice
100 g (3½ oz) pistachio nuts, shelled

Seasoning
4 golden shallots or ½ onion
4 garlic cloves, crushed
1 tablespoon fresh marjoram leaves
1 tablespoon fresh thyme leaves
2 bay leaves
1 star anise pod
juniper berries and rind from the marinade
4 tablespoons white wine
3 tablespoons Cognac
3 teaspoons salt
2 teaspoons roughly ground black pepper

100 g (3½ oz) finely sliced prosciutto (Parma ham)

# The Pâtisserie

*This French word conjures up all manner of sweet delights, a feast for the eyes as well as the tastebuds. From fresh fruit dessert tarts to homemade ice creams, flaky pastries, cakes for afternoon tea and brioche for breakfast, there is something in the pâtisserie to tempt everyone.*

Pastry shops are the ultimate indulgence; they appeal first to the eye, but most of all to our sense of smell. Yeast, butter, honey and caramel scents all combine to tempt us to open our wallets and arrive back home laden with the pastry cook's sinful wares, knowing that this is the easiest way to purchase domestic popularity.

The smells of the shop are your first indication of the quality of the establishment. Any hint of margarine or vanilla essence in the air will cause you to turn on your heel and leave in search of a more honest establishment, as will any sign of mock cream or dried powder meringues. You will notice the quality of the fruit used in the tarts: small luscious strawberries, firm but ripe raspberries of purple or deep scarlet hue, and croissants that are so light and delicate that a small flake of the pastry breaks off as they are delicately placed in a large white paper bag for you. The brioches should be yellow with butter and when broken display even aeration and release the smells of the yeast.

The range of goods in our shop should include the classics, but also some tempting variations each week.

Pastry cooks lead an unenviable existence, usually starting work at one or two in the morning so as to have the breads and pastries fresh for the customers each day. They are often by nature solitary, very hard-working, and they must be very well-organised. They have a more methodical approach to their work than restaurant chefs.

Pastry requires the accurate use of recipes more than any other branch of cooking, so pâtissiers regard themselves as true artisans, and may tend to hold their noses at an upward tilt when addressing cooks at the stove.

Because of these character traits you will not often find the pastry cook talking to the customers. So, in order to start a dialogue with your elusive quarry, you may have to resort to a combination of flattery and subterfuge.

After a few visits have confirmed that the establishment meets your exacting standards, present your card and a small present for the cook. A bottle of wine from an obscure vineyard or a bunch of flowers, these little gifts will tempt your trout from his or her hiding place and confirm your position as a valued customer.

Only much later in the relationship should you let the cook know that you harbour a few culinary pretensions yourself. For the moment you are the grateful purchaser of the results of his expertise and he is the provider of fresh puff pastry that you hope soon to have the time to master making yourself.

Previous pages: Puff Pastry

# CHOUX PASTRY

Place the butter and water in a large saucepan and over a medium heat bring the mixture to the boil. When the butter has dissolved, remove the saucepan from the heat and add the flour. Return the saucepan to a low heat and stir quickly for 2 minutes using a wooden spoon. Do not let the mixture dry out too much at this stage. Remove the pan from the heat once more and continue to stir the mixture until it forms a smooth paste.

Place the mixture in an electric blender, or use a wooden spoon, and immediately beat in the eggs, one by one.

Cover the pastry with plastic wrap (cling film) and refrigerate until needed. It will keep for 3 days in the refrigerator, or up to a week in the freezer.

On a greased baking sheet, spoon and form the pastry mixture into desired shapes. Preheat the oven to 190°C (375°F) and bake for 10 minutes, or until golden in colour, then reduce the heat to 145°C (285°F) and slowly cook for a further 5–10 minutes to dry the pastries. The cooking time will depend on their shape and size.

*Makes approximately 20 pastries*

*125 g (4 oz) butter*
*1 cup (250 mL/8 fl oz) water*
*1 cup (125 g/4 oz) plain*
*(all-purpose) flour*
*4 eggs*

# PUFF PASTRY

Sift the flour and salt into a large mixing bowl and make a well in the centre. Add the diced butter and liquids and, with your fingers, incorporate the surrounding flour into the ingredients. When these have been thoroughly amalgamated into a dough (détrempe, page 252), cover with plastic wrap (cling film) and refrigerate.

Knead the remaining 500 g (1 lb) butter until it is smooth. Place in plastic wrap (cling film) and mould into a 12 cm × 15 cm (4¾ in. × 6 in.) rectangle.

Prepare a floured surface and roll out the dough into a 30 cm (12 in.) square. Take the butter from its plastic wrap and place it in the centre of the dough. Fold the edge of the dough over the butter so that it is completely enclosed within the dough.

Cover with plastic wrap and set aside to rest for 10 minutes in a cool place.

Roll the pastry out into a 45 cm × 20 cm (18 in. × 8 in.) rectangle. Turn the rectangle so that the long side is facing you. Mentally divide the rectangle into thirds and fold the left side over towards the right. Fold the right side so that it overlaps the left. Roll the pastry again. Starting from the centre roll the dough towards you and away from you to the size of the original rectangle. Turn the rectangle so that the

*4 cups (500 g/1 lb) plain*
*(all-purpose) flour*
*¼ teaspoon salt*
*2 tablespoons butter, cut into*
*small dice*
*1 cup (250 mL/8 fl oz) cold*
*water*
*juice of ¼ lemon*
*500 g (1 lb) butter*

long side is facing you, and begin the folding and rolling again. Each folding and rolling of the pastry is called a 'turn'. The pastry has to be 'turned' 3 times, giving a total of six folds.

The important consideration when making puff pastry is to maintain the same pliability between the butter and the dough.

*Makes enough pastry for 2 × 23 cm (9 in.) tarts or*
*24 × 7.5 cm (3 in.) tartlets*

# CREME BRULEE

*The popular classic dessert.*

### Custard
*3 cups (750 mL/ 24 fl oz) heavy whipping (double) cream*
*1 cup (250 mL/8 fl oz) milk*
*1 vanilla bean*
*zest or rind of 1 lemon*
*10 egg yolks*
*185 g (6 oz) white granulated sugar*

### Caramel topping
*1 cup (155 g / 5 oz) brown or caster (superfine) sugar*

### To make the custard

In a heavy-bottomed saucepan and over a low heat bring the cream, milk, vanilla and lemon zest to the boil. In a separate bowl, whisk together the egg yolks and sugar until the sugar has dissolved. Remove the vanilla bean and pour the hot creamy milk over the egg mixture, whisking all the time. As soon as the custard begins to thicken, pour it into a bowl set in ice and continue to beat it with a whisk. Once the custard is cool, pour it into individual ramekin or small soufflé dishes, making sure the custard does not quite reach the top of the dish.

The dishes may then be covered and stored in the refrigerator until needed.

### To make the caramel topping

To caramelise the tops of the custards in the traditional way, you will need a small cast iron frying pan or skillet, or a small round piece of steel. These must be heated until they are red hot, so only a gas stove will suffice.

Brush clean the chosen pan or iron and heat it in the gas flame until red hot. Sprinkle the sugar over the custards to form a layer 3 mm (⅛ in.) thick. Place the hot iron on the sugar, caramelising it into a thick crisp crust. Clean and reheat the iron between glazing each custard. Alternatively, you can put the sugar-coated custards under a hot griller (broiler) or salamander and heat for a few minutes until the sugar caramelises, or use a gas blow torch.

*Makes 6 cups (1.5 litres/ 2½ imp. pints) custard*

Opposite: Crème Brûlée with a puff pastry twist and Savarin with Prunes (page 209)

# CREME ANGLAISE

1 vanilla bean, split

3 cups (750 mL/ 24 fl oz)
milk

12 egg yolks

310 g (10 oz) white granulated
sugar

1 cup (250 mL/ 8 fl oz) heavy
whipping (double) cream

Place the vanilla bean and the milk in a saucepan and bring to the boil. Remove immediately from the heat. In a separate bowl whisk together the egg yolks and sugar until light and fluffy. Strain the milk, removing the vanilla bean, and pour it into the egg mixture, whisking all the time. Pour back into the saucepan and return to the stove over a low heat. Using a wooden spoon, continually stir the custard until it begins to thicken and coats the back of the spoon. Remove from the heat and add the cold cream. This stops the custard curdling and adds an extra richness to it.

Cool the custard as quickly as possible, stirring all the time. This will produce a fine, smooth cream.

*Makes 6 cups (1.5 litres/ 2¹⁄₂ imp. pints)*

# CREME PATISSIERE

1 vanilla bean, split

2 cups (500 mL/ 16 fl oz)
milk

1 cup (250 g/ 8 oz) white
granulated sugar

¹⁄₂ cup (60 g/ 2 oz) plain (all-
purpose) flour

6 egg yolks

Place the vanilla bean and the milk in a saucepan and bring to the boil. In a separate bowl, whisk together the sugar, plain (all-purpose) flour and egg yolks and pour the boiling milk into the mixture, whisking all the while. Stir over a low heat until the mixture comes to the boil, simmer for 2 minutes and then press through a strainer to eliminate any lumps. Sprinkle the surface with sugar or melted butter to prevent the formation of a skin.

*Makes 4 cups (1 litre/ 1³⁄₄ imp. pints)*

# LAVOCHE

2 cups (250 g/ 8 oz) plain
(all-purpose) flour

2 teaspoons salt

2 teaspoons white granulated
sugar

45 g (1¹⁄₂ oz) butter

2 eggs

¹⁄₃ cup (90 mL/ 3 fl oz) milk
water

1 tablespoon poppy seeds

1 tablespoon sesame seeds

*A Middle Eastern crispbread that I serve with cheese.*

Process the flour, salt and sugar in a food processor or electric blender. Add the butter and continue to beat until the mixture is of breadcrumb consistency. In a separate bowl, whisk together the eggs and milk, then add them to the flour to form a dough. Cover with plastic wrap (cling film) and refrigerate for 1 hour before using.

Cut the pastry in half. Roll out both pieces on a floured surface into circular shapes, approximately 3 mm (¹⁄₈ in.) thick. Place on a baking sheet and spray with a little water. Sprinkle liberally with equal quantities of poppy and sesame seed. Bake in a preheated oven (180°C/355°F) for 10–12 minutes.

*Serves 10–12*

# POUND CAKE

*The perfect cake for afternoon tea.*

The butter should be at room temperature. Cream it with the sugar and vanilla until light and fluffy. Add the eggs, one by one, beating well between additions. Sift in the flour and beat lightly with a wooden spoon until the mixture is quite smooth.

Lightly grease (with butter) and then flour a deep circular cake pan (20 cm/8 in. in diameter). Pour the cake mixture into the pan and bake in a preheated, moderately slow oven (160°C/315°F) for approximately 1 hour, or until cooked when tested. Test by inserting a bamboo or metal skewer into the centre of the cake. If it has no uncooked cake clinging to it when you remove it, the cake is ready. The cake should be a golden colour and will have split on top. Let it stand for several minutes before turning it onto a wire rack to cool.

Dredge with icing (confectioners') sugar before serving.

*250 g (8 oz) soft butter*
*1 cup (220 g/ 7 oz) caster (superfine) sugar*
*1 teaspoon vanilla extract*
*4 large (60 g/ 2 oz) eggs*
*2 cups (250 g/ 8 oz) self-raising (self-rising) flour*
*¼ cup (45 g/ 1¼ oz) icing (confectioners') sugar*

# SHORTBREAD

In a food processor or electric blender, cream the butter (which should be at room temperature) and vanilla until light and fluffy, then beat in the sugar. Sift in the remaining dry ingredients. Turn out onto a lightly floured board and knead until the mixture is quite smooth.

Press the biscuit mixture into a shallow, lightly greased 28 cm × 18 cm (11 in. × 7 in.) baking pan. Mark into 18 bars and prick each bar decoratively with a fork. Refrigerate for 30 minutes. Bake in a slow oven (150°C/300°F) for approximately 50 minutes, until pale golden.

Cut while still warm, and serve.

*Makes 18 pieces*

*1 cup (250 g/ 8 oz) butter*
*½ teaspoon vanilla extract*
*⅓ cup (90 g/ 3 oz) caster (superfine) sugar*
*2¼ cups (280 g/ 9 oz) plain (all-purpose) flour*
*¼ cup (45 g/ 1½ oz) rice flour (page 253)*

# WALNUT SHORTBREAD

Cream butter, vanilla and sugar as in the Shortbread recipe (above). Add walnuts and fold in the flour. On a lightly greased baking sheet, place well-spaced teaspoonfuls of the mixture and bake in a preheated oven (160°C/315°F) for 15 minutes, or until pale golden.

When cold, dredge generously with icing (confectioners') sugar.

*Makes approximately 30*

*250 g (8 oz) butter*
*1 teaspoon vanilla extract*
*½ cup (90 g/ 3 oz) icing (confectioners') sugar*
*1 cup (125 g/ 4 oz) walnuts, finely chopped*
*2 cups (250 g/ 8 oz) plain (all-purpose) flour, sifted*
*icing (confectioners') sugar, extra*

# BRIOCHES
# WITH STRAWBERRY JAM

*Brioche is an enriched yeast dough or batter, baked in a mould the shape of a cottage loaf, and usually eaten warm for breakfast or as a dessert. Some sweetener is usually added for dessert brioches. For plain brioche, rather than chocolate, omit the cocoa.*

Sift the flour into a bowl and make a well in the centre. Add all the other ingredients except for the butter and egg wash. Beat the dough firmly with a wooden spoon until it becomes silky and elastic, then put it aside in a warm place for 1½ hours, or until it has doubled in size.

Meanwhile, soften the butter. When the dough has doubled its bulk, punch it down with the spoon and beat in the butter, one teaspoon at a time, until it is all amalgamated.

Half fill 10 buttered brioche moulds with the dough and allow it to rise again (approximately 45 minutes). When the brioches are fully risen, brush the tops with egg wash and bake in a preheated oven (200°C/390°F) for 25 minutes, or until the tops are golden. Serve hot with strawberry jam.

*To make strawberry jam*

Place the strawberries and lemon juice in a saucepan. Heat gently, crushing the strawberries with a wooden spoon to make the juice run. Simmer for approximately 10 minutes, until the fruit is soft. Add the sugar and stir occasionally until the sugar has dissolved. Bring the mixture to the boil and boil for 10 minutes, or until the jam jells when tested. Bottle in clean jars that have been heated for 10 minutes in the oven, and seal immediately.

*Makes approximately 10 brioches*

2 cups (250 g/8 oz) plain (all-purpose) flour
2 tablespoons cocoa
7 g (¼ oz) fresh yeast
2 tablespoons lukewarm water
3 eggs
½ teaspoon salt
1½ teaspoons white granulated sugar
155 g (5 oz) butter
egg wash (page 252)

Strawberry jam
500 g (1 lb) strawberries
juice of 1 lemon
1½ cups (375 g/12 oz) white granulated sugar

# LACY CARAMEL SNAPS

Mix together almond meal, sugar and flour. Melt the butter with the glucose in a saucepan over a medium heat. Remove the saucepan from the heat and add the grated rind and orange juice. Cool the mixture and then add it to the dry ingredients. Mix well and refrigerate. The mixture will keep well for a week.

Place a teaspoonful of the mixture on a greased baking sheet, and spread it out with the back of the spoon until it is thin. Allow 4 cm (1½ in.) space between the snaps. Bake the snaps at 160°C (315°F) for 15–20 minutes, or until golden. Allow the snaps to cool and harden on the baking sheet before lifting them. Store in airtight containers.

*Makes approximately 25 snaps*

½ cup (60 g/2 oz) almond meal
½ cup (125 g/4 oz) caster (superfine) sugar
½ cup (60 g/2 oz) plain (all-purpose) flour, sifted
100 g (3½ oz) butter
2 teaspoons glucose syrup (page 252)
grated rind of 1 orange
¼ cup (60 mL/2 fl oz) orange juice

Opposite: Brioches with Strawberry Jam

# CREPES

1 cup (250 mL/8 fl oz) milk
1 teaspoon salt
2 tablespoons white granulated
  sugar
2½ cups (310 g/10 oz) plain
  (all-purpose) flour
4 whole eggs
4 egg yolks
½ cup (125 g/4 oz) beurre
  noisette (see method)

*Crêpes are large thin pancakes. They are used in both sweet and savoury dishes. The batter is poured very sparingly into a frying pan or skillet and fried quickly on both sides.*

In a small saucepan, heat together most of the milk (retain 2 tablespoons), the salt and the sugar. In a separate bowl, sift the flour and make a well in the centre. Add the eggs and yolks along with the 2 tablespoons of milk. Mix thoroughly with a wire whisk, then add the warmed milk. Combine thoroughly to form a batter.

Beurre noisette is butter that is gently heated until it is a light golden brown. Whisk the butter into the batter mixture. Rest the mixture in the refrigerator for 1–2 hours before using.

*Makes approximately 20 crêpes*

# SAVARIN WITH KIRSCH

Savarin
3 teaspoons compressed yeast
3 tablespoons caster (superfine)
  sugar
¾ cup (185 mL/6 fl oz)
  lukewarm milk
2 cups (250 g/8 oz) plain
  (all-purpose) flour
pinch of salt
3 eggs, beaten
½ cup (125 g/4 oz) melted
  butter

Syrup
2 cups (500 mL/16 fl oz)
  water
3 cups (750 g/24 oz) white
  granulated sugar
½ cup (125 mL/4 fl oz) kirsch

*A savarin is a rich yeast dough, not unlike a baba dough but without the currants or raisins, baked in a ring mould. The dessert was named after Brillat-Savarin, a famous French gastronomic writer of the eighteenth century.*

Place the yeast and sugar in a bowl. Gradually add the milk and stir until the yeast is dissolved. Sprinkle 1 tablespoon of the flour over the milk and set the bowl aside in a warm place until it is frothy on top (approximately 1 hour). Sift the rest of the flour and the salt into another bowl and add the eggs and the yeast mixture.

Beat the mixture for 5 minutes, or until a smooth dough is formed. Cover the bowl and set aside in a warm place for approximately 30 minutes, or until the dough has doubled in size. Add the melted butter and beat the mixture with a wooden spoon for 3 more minutes, until the dough is smooth and elastic in consistency. Butter a large ring mould (savarin ring) and pour in the dough-like batter. Set aside and let rise once more until double in size. Bake in a preheated oven (180°C/355°F) for 25 minutes, or until the cake is golden and a cake-tester comes out clean.

While still warm, soak the savarin in sugar syrup. Keep replenishing the syrup as it is absorbed, without letting the savarin become soggy.

*To make the syrup*

Heat the water to boiling point, add the sugar and continue boiling until the sugar is completely dissolved, then stir in the kirsch.

*To serve*

Serve hot with whipped cream.

*Serves 10–12*

# SAVARIN WITH PRUNES

Place the sugar and wine in a saucepan and bring to the boil. Pour the mixture over the prunes and leave them to macerate overnight.

Make individual savarins in small dariole moulds (page 252), and bake in a preheated oven at (180°C/355°F). When they are cooked (approximately 25 minutes), take them out of the moulds and dip them in the red wine-flavoured syrup. Brush them with melted apricot jam which has been heated in a small saucepan.

### To serve

Place each savarin in the centre of a plate. Warm the prunes and spoon them around the savarins, pour the red wine syrup over and decorate with the julienne of orange rind. Have cold, heavy, whipped (double) cream on the side.

*Serves 10–12*

Savarin mixture (page 208)

*2 kg (4 lbs) stoned prunes*

*¾ cup (225 g/7 oz) white granulated sugar*
*3 cups (750 mL/24 fl oz) dry red wine*
*½ cup (155 mL/5 fl oz) apricot jam for glazing*
*zest of 1 orange, julienned and blanched (page 253)*

# VANILLA BAVAROIS

*This is a creamy cold dessert bound together by egg yolks and gelatin and set in a mould.*

### To make the crème chantilly

Place the crème fraîche, light cream and vanilla in a bowl set in ice and beat until the cream is stiff but not buttery. Gradually add the sugar, while beating all the time.

*Makes about 2 cups (500 mL/16 fl oz)*

### To make the bavarois

Lightly oil 6–8 dariole moulds (page 252). Place the egg yolks and sugar in a saucepan and beat until the mixture is light and fluffy and almost white. Soften the gelatin in ¼ cup (60 mL/2 fl oz) of cold water. In another saucepan, bring the milk to the boil with the vanilla bean and add the gelatin (not the water).

Strain the mixture, to remove the vanilla bean. Immediately add the strained mixture to the egg mixture. Place the saucepan over a low heat and cook (as for Crème Anglaise, page 204), stirring constantly, until the custard thickens. Pour the mixture into a bowl and set the bowl in ice. Whisk the custard until it is cool and begins to set. Gently fold in the Crème Chantilly and spoon the bavarois into the moulds. Tap each mould to remove air bubbles. Refrigerate for at least 6 hours before serving.

*Serves 6–8*

Crème chantilly
*1 cup (250 mL/8 fl oz) cold crème fraîche (page 252)*
*¼ cup (60 mL/2 fl oz) light (single) cream*
*¼ cup (60 g/2 oz) caster (superfine) sugar*
*½ teaspoon vanilla extract*

Bavarois
*4 egg yolks*
*¾ cup (185 g/6 oz) caster (superfine) sugar*
*2 gelatin leaves (page 252)*
*2 cups (500 mL/16 fl oz) milk*
*1 × 15 cm (6 in.) vanilla bean, halved lengthwise*

# CHOCOLATE SOUFFLE

3 tablespoons melted clarified
  butter
3 tablespoons caster (superfine)
  sugar
1 tablespoon bitter cocoa powder

Soufflé mix
200 g (6½ oz) bitter chocolate
1¼ cups (310 mL/10 fl oz)
  crème pâtissière (page 204)
1 tablespoon bitter cocoa powder
8 egg yolks

Meringue
10 egg whites
100 g (3½ oz) caster (superfine)
  sugar

### To prepare the soufflé moulds

Brush the insides of six soufflé moulds (preferably Pilluyvit 6 cm /1½ in. high moulds) generously with the melted butter. Mix together the sugar and cocoa. Tip all the sugar/cocoa mix into the first mould, tip the mould on an angle and turn so that the inside is coated with the mix. Tip the mix not clinging to the mould into the next one and repeat the process until the six moulds are coated. Turn the moulds upside down onto a tray to await filling. This concentrates the butter along the upper lip of the mould and helps achieve an even rise when cooking the soufflés.

### To make the soufflés

Chop the chocolate into small pieces. Place it in a saucepan with the crème pâtissière and warm the mixture over a low heat, stirring until the chocolate has melted and is incorporated evenly into the mix. Add the cocoa and mix thoroughly. Remove the pan from the heat and incorporate the egg yolks. Cool the mixture and put aside until needed.

### To make the meringue

In a separate bowl, beat the egg whites until they are fluffy, then add half the sugar. Beat until soft peaks form, then add the rest of the sugar and whisk a little more. The egg white should be firm but it should fall off into peaks when lifted with a whisk.

Warm the soufflé mix to lukewarm and then fold one-third of the egg whites into the mixture. Fold this mixture back into the rest of the egg whites.

Fill the moulds with the mixture, mounding it slightly. Take a sharp knife and cut the mixture around on the inside of the moulds to a depth of 2 cm (¾ in.) without touching the mould. This will enable the soufflés to rise evenly.

### To cook the soufflés

Pour 2.5 cm (1 in.) of boiling water into the bottom of a baking pan. Place the filled moulds in the dish and bake in a preheated 170°C (340°F) oven. The soufflés will be cooked in 15–17 minutes. If the oven has uneven heat it is worthwhile turning the soufflés halfway through cooking so that they rise more evenly.

When cooked, dust the soufflés with bitter cocoa powder and serve with Vanilla Ice Cream (page 220).

*Serves 6*

Opposite: Chocolate
Soufflé

# CHOCOLATE MOUSSE

_____

*125 g (4 oz) dark (semi-sweet)*
*chocolate*
*60 g (2 oz) butter*
*4 eggs, separated*
*½ cup (125 g/4 oz) caster*
*(superfine) sugar*
*2 tablespoons overproof rum*

Chop the chocolate roughly, put it into the top of a double saucepan with the butter and stir over warm (not hot) water until melted. Remove from the heat, cool slightly. Add the egg yolks, half the sugar and the rum, and beat until the mixture is smooth and thick.

Whip the egg whites to soft peaks with the remainder of the sugar. Fold half the egg white mixture into the chocolate first, then add the rest. It is easier to incorporate egg whites into a mixture in two portions than all at once.

Spoon the mixture into 4 individual dishes or 1 large dish and refrigerate until firm (4–6 hours).

Serve with whipped heavy (double) cream and muscat grapes.

*Serves 4*

# FLOURLESS CHOCOLATE CAKE

_____

*butter for greasing*
*500 g (1 lb) extra bitter dark*
*chocolate*
*8 eggs, separated*
*405 mL (13 fl oz) thickened*
*(light whipping) cream*
*½ cup (125 g/4 oz) white*
*granulated sugar*
*⅓ cup (90 mL/3 fl oz) Grand*
*Marnier or overproof rum*

Line the bottom of a 25 cm (10 in.) cake pan with silicone paper (page 253). Grease the sides with butter.

Chop the chocolate roughly, put it in the top of a double saucepan and melt it over warm (not hot) water. Separate the eggs and lightly beat the whites to soft peaks. Whip the cream to soft peaks. Beat the egg yolks, sugar and liqueur together until smooth, add the melted chocolate and mix together. Fold in the cream and then the beaten egg whites. Pour the mixture into the cake pan, sit it in a shallow baking tray of warm water and bake at 160°C (315°F) for 1 hour, or until firm. Test with a skewer; if the skewer comes out clean, the cake is cooked.

*To serve*
Serve cold with thickened light whipping cream and fresh red berries.
*Serves 8–10*

# SULTANS' TURBANS

*These cakes of Greek or Turkish origin keep well in the syrup and are delicious standbys. They are also known as ladies' wrists.*

### To make the syrup

Place all the ingredients in a saucepan and boil for 5 minutes. Discard the spices. Cool the syrup before using it.

### To make the filling

Lay the chopped walnuts on a baking sheet and bake in a moderately slow preheated oven (160°C/315°F) for 10 minutes to refresh the nuts. Let them cool and then process them with the sugar until they are grainy but not like flour.

### To cook the sultans' turbans

Lay 1 sheet of phyllo pastry on a baking sheet, brush with melted clarified butter and spread the nut mix thinly on the phyllo. Roll up the pastry like a newspaper, with the nut mix inside, then cut it into slices 2.5 cm (1 in.) thick (so they are standing). Brush with more clarified butter and bake until golden in a moderate oven (160°C/315°F). Pour the cold syrup over the hot pastry and leave to cool. Store in sealed container.

*Makes 30*

Syrup
1 cup (250 g/8 oz) white
  granulated sugar
155 mL (5 fl oz) water
¼ cup (60 mL/2 fl oz) lemon
  juice
1 × 5 cm (2 in.) piece
  cinnamon stick
8 cloves

Filling
4 cups (500 g/1 lb) walnuts,
  chopped
¼ cup (60 g/2 oz) caster
  (superfine) sugar

Pastry
1 packet (10 sheets) phyllo
  pastry
½ cup (125 g/4 oz) melted
  clarified butter

# SPICE BREAD

*Spice bread or pain d'épice is a fragrant, sweet French bread that tastes even more delicious the second day after baking.*

Put the boiling water into a large saucepan, add the honey, sugar, bicarbonate of soda and salt, and stir until the sugar is dissolved. Flavour with the rum, anisette and cinnamon. Sift the flour into a mixing bowl and slowly stir the syrup into it to form a smooth batter. Strain the batter through a fine sieve. Add the rest of the ingredients and stir until incorporated into the batter.

Turn the mixture into a buttered loaf pan (21 cm × 11 cm/8 in. × 4 in.) and bake in a hot oven (200°C/390°F) for 10 minutes. Reduce the heat to 180°C (355°F) and bake for about 1 hour longer, or until the skewer test shows that the batter has completely cooked.

### To serve

Let the bread cool, then slice it very thinly and serve it with butter and honey.

*Serves 8–10*

1¼ cups (310 mL/10 fl oz)
  boiling water
¾ cup (280 g/9 oz) honey
1 cup (250 g/8 oz) white
  granulated sugar
2½ teaspoons bicarbonate of soda
  (baking soda)
pinch of salt
3 tablespoons rum
1 teaspoon anisette liqueur
1 teaspoon ground cinnamon
4 cups (500 g/1 lb) plain
  (all-purpose) flour
3 tablespoons chopped blanched
  almonds
¼ small lemon, finely chopped
½ teaspoon grated orange rind

# ORANGE CHARLOTTE

almond or walnut oil for
  greasing
⅓ cup (90 g/ 3 oz) white
  granulated sugar
⅖ cup (100 mL/ 3½ fl oz)
  water
⅖ cup (100 mL/ 3½ fl oz)
  Grand Marnier
40 small sponge finger biscuits
  (cookies) (langues-de-chat)

12 egg yolks
⅔ cup (155 g/ 5 oz) white
  granulated sugar
grated rind of 1 orange

3 gelatin leaves (page 252)
⅔ cup 155 mL (5 fl oz) orange
  juice, strained

⅘ cup (200 mL/ 6½ fl oz)
  heavy whipping (double)
  cream, whipped

Garnish
rind of 1 orange, cut into
  julienne
3 oranges, peeled and sectioned

405 mL (13 fl oz) crème
  anglaise (page 204)
icing (confectioners') sugar

Brush the sides of 6 cup-sized dariole moulds (page 252) or one large mould with almond (or walnut) oil and line the bottom(s) with silicone paper (page 253).

Make a syrup with the sugar and water by boiling them together in a small saucepan until the sugar has dissolved. Cool and then add the Grand Marnier. Brush the sponge fingers with the syrup and then line the moulds with them by standing them vertically around the inside of the moulds. Refrigerate any remaining syrup.

In a bowl, whisk the egg yolks, sugar and rind together until white and fluffy. Soften the gelatin in a little water, remove it from the water, and then add it to the orange juice in a small saucepan. Bring this to the boil and then whisk it into the yolk mix. Continue to whisk the mixture over a pot of very hot, almost simmering water, until it has doubled in bulk and the mixture leaves the whisk in continuous ribbons when the whisk is lifted from the mix.

Place the bowl on a bed of crushed ice and continue to whisk until the mixture is cool. Fold in the whipped cream and fill the lined mould(s) with the mixture. Refrigerate to set.

### To make the garnish

Add the julienne of orange rind to the leftover sugar and Grand Marnier syrup and simmer for 10 minutes. Pour the syrup over the sectioned orange fruit and refrigerate.

### To serve

Cut around the inside of the mould(s) with a sharp knife and turn the charlotte(s) onto a tray. If they stick, dip the mould(s) in warm water.

Dust the charlotte(s) with icing (confectioners') sugar and place a charlotte (or a slice if using one mould) in the centre of each plate. Garnish with the orange segments and surround with the Crème Anglaise.

*Serves 6*

Opposite: Orange Charlotte

# BLANCMANGE WITH RASPBERRIES

Almond milk
3 cups (310 g/10 oz) blanched
   ground almonds
2 cups (500 mL/16 fl oz)
   water

Blancmange
2 gelatin leaves (page 252)
1 cup (250 mL/8 fl oz) light
   (single) cream
½ cup (125 g/4 oz) white
   granulated sugar
1 tablespoon kirsch

1 cup (200 g/6½ oz)
   raspberries

*Blancmange, made the French way, is a sweet cream dessert set with gelatin in a mould.*

### To make the almond milk

Pound the almonds in a mortar until they are thoroughly crushed. Add the water, a little at a time, and continue to pound until the liquid becomes milky. Strain through a sieve lined with muslin, extracting as much of the almond milk as possible. Alternatively, you may purée the almonds with the water in a food processor or electric blender, then strain.

*Makes 2 cups (500 mL/16 fl oz)*

### To make the blancmange

Soften the gelatin in ¼ cup (60 mL/2 fl oz) cold water for 5 minutes, remove from the water and combine with the almond milk, cream and sugar. Bring the mixture slowly to the boil, but do not boil, stirring to dissolve the sugar and gelatin. Strain through a fine strainer, but do not press the solids. Cool, then stir in the kirsch. Pour into 8 individual moulds and chill in the refrigerator until firm.

### To serve

Loosen the edges of the moulds with a knife and unmould by inverting onto individual serving dishes. Garnish with fresh whole raspberries.

*Makes 8 serves*

# EVELYN BILSON'S
# CHRISTMAS PUDDING

*Christmas pudding is probably one of the most individual of all recipes. The ritual of stirring, the sight of the pudding flaming with brandy, the coins buried inside it, all seem fantastic and thrilling, quite apart from the taste. This is my mother's recipe and a marvellous childhood memory. I would not want to change one thing. It follows the old method of a round pudding prepared at least four weeks before Christmas then wrapped in a cloth and cooked by steaming.*

### To make the pudding

Rub the suet into the flour and add the remaining dry ingredients. Mix well together. Add the stout, stir in the eggs and add the marmalade.

Add the lemon zest and juice, and apple, and finally the rum or Cognac. Let stand in a cool place overnight for the flavours to amalgamate.

Take a wet pudding cloth (use a 75 cm/30 in. square of unbleached calico) and wring it out. Sprinkle liberally with the extra flour and place the pudding mix on top. This helps to give the pudding a better skin. To be traditional in your cooking, boil some coins and insert them into the dough before proceeding further.

Gather the corners and sides of the cloth around the pudding as evenly as possible and pull tightly to give the pudding a good round shape. Tie tightly with string about 2.5 cm (1 in.) above the top of the pudding to allow for expansion during cooking. Steam the pudding in a bowl sitting in boiling water in a large saucepan for 4 hours and then hang it in the pantry for at least 2 weeks, until Christmas. The pudding must be able to swing freely without touching anything. In hot weather it is better to store the pudding in the refrigerator.

### To make the brandy sauce

Have ready a pot of simmering water. Mix the yolks, orange juice and sugar in a stainless steel bowl and whisk over the simmering water until double in bulk and falling off the whisk in a continuous stream or ribbon. Take off the heat and whisk in the brandy, then the melted butter. Serve warm with the pudding.

### To serve

When ready to serve, steam the pudding in a large saucepan for a further 2 hours then remove the cloth and transfer the pudding to a suitable serving dish. Bring the pudding to the table and pour the warmed brandy over it. Ignite immediately as speed and warmth are essential. Flaming is not only for show but adds a subtle flavour.

Serve with the brandy sauce.

### Serves 12

Note: Mixed spice is a combination of 4 parts cinnamon, 1 part clove, 2 parts nutmeg and 1 part ginger.

The pudding
1½ cups (185 g/6 oz) suet
¾ cup (90 g/3 oz) plain (all-purpose) flour, sifted
½ cup (60 g/2 oz) almond meal
4 cups (250 g/8 oz) soft breadcrumbs
1 cup (225 g/7 oz) white granulated sugar
1 teaspoon mixed spice (see below)
¼ teaspoon salt
½ teaspoon bicarbonate of soda (baking soda)
4½ cups (750 g/1 lb 8 oz) mixed fruit (raisins, sultanas (golden raisins), currants, figs)
⅓ cup (60 g/2 oz) mixed peel
½ cup (125 mL/4 fl oz) stout
4 eggs
2 tablespoons marmalade
1 lemon, zest and juice
1 fresh tart apple, grated
4 tablespoons rum or Cognac
¼ cup (30 g/1 oz) plain (all-purpose) flour, sifted

Brandy sauce
6 egg yolks
½ cup (125 mL/4 fl oz) orange juice
½ cup (125 g/4 oz) caster (superfine) sugar
½ cup (125 mL/4 fl oz) brandy or Cognac
½ cup (125 mL/4 fl oz) melted butter

# TRIFLE OF SUMMER FRUITS

### To make the fruit jelly

Soften the gelatin in a little cold water. Remove the gelatin and place it in a saucepan with the red wine and sugar. Stir over a low heat until the sugar and gelatin have been absorbed. Take the saucepan off the heat and allow the mixture to cool but not set.

Cut the fruit into raspberry-sized pieces and mix it into the jelly. Line a 25 cm × 10 cm (10 in. × 4 in.) loaf mould with plastic wrap (cling film). Brush all layers of sponge generously with muscat before using. Place a layer of sponge in the mould. Fill the mould to one-third full with the fruit–jelly mix and refrigerate. When the fruit–jelly mix has set, cover with another layer of sponge, then a layer of the Crème Pâtissière, then another layer of sponge. Fill with the remaining fruit–jelly mix. Cover with the last layer of sponge. Fold the remaining plastic wrap over the top of the trifle, place a 500 g (1 lb) weight on top, and refrigerate overnight.

### To serve

Loosen the trifle by pulling on the plastic wrap, and turn it onto a cutting board or serving dish. Slice the trifle and surround with Crème Anglaise (page 204) and raspberries puréed with sugar.

*Serves 8–10*

# ALMOND, COFFEE AND RUM COOKIES

### To make the rum batter

In a large bowl, cream the butter and sugar until light and fluffy. In a separate bowl, beat together the rest of the ingredients then add this mixture to the butter mixture and beat briskly to make a soft batter.

### To make the cookies

Gradually add the flour, baking powder, salt and almonds to the rum batter. If necessary, add a little more flour to make the dough stiff enough to roll out. Chill the dough for 1 hour. On a floured surface, roll it out to 3 mm (⅛ in.) thickness. Cut into squares, circles or rectangles and bake on an unbuttered baking sheet in a moderate oven (180°C/355°F) for 8–10 minutes.

*Makes approximately 14–16 cookies*

Jelly
*12 gelatin leaves (page 252)*
*3 cups (750 mL/24 fl oz) red wine*
*200 g (6½ oz) caster (superfine) sugar*

Fruit
*1 kg (2 lbs) mixed fruits, including red berries, mango and figs*
*four pieces of sponge, each 25 cm × 10 cm × 1.5 cm (10 in. × 4 in. × ½ in.), cut from a 30 cm × 30 cm × 3 cm (12 in. × 12 in. × 1½ in.) sponge*
*1¼ cups (310 mL/10 fl oz) liqueur muscat*
*350 mL (11½ fl oz) crème pâtissière (page 204)*

Garnish
*310 g (10 oz) raspberries*
*100 g (3½ oz) white granulated sugar*

Rum batter
*155 g (5 oz) butter*
*1 cup (250 g/8 oz) white granulated sugar*
*1 egg*
*3 tablespoons plain (all-purpose) flour, sifted*
*2 tablespoons strong black coffee*
*1 tablespoon dark rum*

Cookie mixture
*2⅔ cups (310 g/10 oz) plain (all-purpose) flour, sifted*
*2 teaspoons baking powder*
*½ teaspoon salt*
*½ cup (60 g/2 oz) finely chopped blanched almonds*

Opposite: Trifle of Summer Fruits

# ICE CREAMS

*Making ice creams and sorbets is great fun. Children love doing it and it is an irresistible food for them in summer.*

## VANILLA ICE CREAM

Vanilla Ice Cream
4 cups (1 litre/ 1¾ imp. pints) crème anglaise (page 204)
100 mL (19 fl oz) thickened (light whipping) cream
⅔ cup (155 g/5 oz) caster (superfine) sugar
1 tablespoon vanilla extract

Mix all the ingredients together, churn and freeze.
*Serves 8–10*

*Variations for children*
To the basic ice cream mixture add 1½ cups (280 g/9 oz) chocolate chips; or add 2 chopped Violet Crumble bars (chocolate coated honeycomb); or fold 1 cup (250 g/8 oz) fresh strawberry or raspberry purée through the ice cream after churning but before freezing.

## HONEY ICE CREAM

⅔ cup (250 g/8 oz) honey
4 cups (1 litre/ 1¾ imp. pints) crème anglaise (page 204)
600 mL (19 fl oz) crème fraîche (page 252) or sour cream (dairy sour cream)

*Try to use an interesting honey. A wildflower or lavender honey makes this delicious ice cream even more appealing.*

Lightly warm the honey and whisk it into the Crème Anglaise. Stir in the Crème Fraîche, then churn and freeze.
*Serves 8–10*

## CINNAMON ICE CREAM

2½ cups (625 mL/1 imp. pint) milk
1 cup (200 g/6½ oz) caster (superfine) sugar
1 cinnamon stick
6 egg yolks
8 teaspoons caster (superfine) sugar
1 cup (250 mL/8 fl oz) light (single) cream

Bring the milk, sugar and cinnamon stick to the boil in a saucepan over a low heat. Be careful not to burn the milk. Simmer for 5 minutes and then pour the milk through a strainer over the yolks, whisking all the time. Strain the mixture back into a clean saucepan and stir with a wooden spoon over a low heat until it begins to thicken and coats the back of a spoon. Remove from the heat, strain into a container and refrigerate.

Add the sugar to the cream and whisk until the cream forms soft peaks, then fold it into the cold custard. Churn, freeze and serve.
*Serves 8–10*

# SORBETS

*These are the most refreshing of all ices, and easy to make. If you make them fresh
before serving you don't have to worry about the sugar level in the fruit purée;
simply season the purée to taste and then churn it, freeze and serve. However, if
you need to re-freeze the sorbet before serving, it must have enough sugar to keep it
soft. The level is 17 degrees on a saccarometer. It is better to serve sorbets fresh (as
you don't have to use so much sugar). Fruits with good acid make good dessert
sorbets, while fruits with less acid are better for sorbets served in the middle of a
meal. I would serve a pear or apple sorbet in the middle of a meal, rather than a
raspberry sorbet.*

## RASPBERRY SORBET

Purée the raspberries in a food processor or blender and then pass
them through a fine sieve. Mix in the caster (superfine) sugar and then
churn.

*Serves 8*

1 kg (2 lbs) raspberries
200 g (6½ oz) caster (superfine)
  sugar

## STRAWBERRY SORBET

Purée the strawberries in a food processor or blender and then pass
them through a fine sieve. Mix in the lemon juice and caster
(superfine) sugar and churn.

*Serves 8*

1 kg (2 lbs) ripe strawberries
juice of 2 lemons, strained
1¼ cups (250 g/ 8 oz) caster
  (superfine) sugar

## APPLE AND MINT SORBET

Purée all the ingredients in a food processor or blender, then pass the
mixture through a fine sieve and churn.

*Serves 8–10*

1.25 kg (2½ lbs) Granny Smith
  apples, peeled and cored
juice of 2 lemons
6 fresh mint leaves
200 g (6½ oz) caster (superfine)
  sugar
1 egg white

## GRAPEFRUIT SORBET

*One of my favourites, especially with ice cold Noilly Prat poured over it.*

Mix all the ingredients together and churn.

*Serves 8*

4 cups (1 litre/ 1¾ imp. pints)
  fresh grapefruit juice
1¼ cups (250 g/ 8 oz) caster
  (superfine) sugar
1 egg white

# The Barbecue

*Barbecuing is a great way of entertaining and Australians have perfected the art of barbecuing, whether in the garden or on a tiny inner-city patio. Chops and sausages have today been joined on the barbecue by international flavours, and foods such as king prawns (shrimps), kangaroo satés and vegetables.*

I suspect that most children learn to cook at the barbecue these days. It is fun (except for the smoke in the eyes) and as it is usually in the garden it doesn't matter if they spill food. I first learnt to cook at the barbecue—summer Sunday gatherings in the garden with burnt sausages and lamb chops, but great steak.

An Armenian chef, Jean Ansourian, taught me about the Balkan and Middle Eastern flavours of the shashlik or shish kebab, in Bali I learnt about saté, and Maltese and Greek friends instructed me in the delights of the paschal lamb. Teppanyaki, the Japanese hamburger bar, is another flavour altogether.

My experience is typical of the progress of cooking in all cultures. As Alvin Toffler predicted, the increasing internationalisation of the world sees Chinese children eating fast foods, such as McDonald's, and Australian children happily eating yum cha.

While I am sure that there are as many sausages and chops being burnt today as in my childhood, we also have the best French and Japanese cooks using the open fire to achieve complex rustic flavours.

Different wood or charcoal can be used to impart different flavours to the food being barbecued. It is really a matter of personal preference. In Australia, we use eucalyptus wood and when Australians are cooking internationally they will go to extraordinary lengths to find some leaves or oil to impart this flavour to the food.

Fruit woods are in many ways the best to use for barbecuing. They have a sweet smoke that I prefer to the almost 'chemical' smoke of the eucalypt, and the wood does not burn as hot, so the cook can avoid charring the meat. The hottest wood is from the she oak (casuarina). I have seen it melt a wood-fired stove. (Not the whole stove! Just the grate.)

No matter which wood you choose, the fire preparation is crucial. The fire should be burnt down to charcoal before you start the cooking. Do not use large lumps of wood as they give an uneven heat and can flame close to the food. Try to avoid the fuel flaming; the occasional fat flare is to be expected but we don't want a conflagration. To help prevent flames, trim the fat from the meat and baste the meat using a mixture of clarified butter or virgin olive oil flavoured with fresh herbs and garlic. This will also help stop the meat drying out during cooking.

If the heat of the fire dies too low, take a tip from the Japanese and have a large folding fan at the ready—so much more practical and elegant than a warped section of the newspaper!

Previous pages: Barbecue medley

# BARBECUING MOLLUSCS

The coastline middens (collections of shells and refuse) of Aboriginal groups bear testimony to the efficacy of cooking mussels and clams on the open fire. Scrub the molluscs and beard them before cooking. Pipis (clams) will benefit from being soaked in fresh seawater (or salted water) for a day so that they can cleanse themselves of sand and grit.

To cook a mollusc, have ready some snail butter (page 230), and place the mollusc on the edge of the fire. As it opens, place a small knob of the butter in the shell and serve.

# SCALLOPS WITH SNAIL BUTTER

*The scallop is a bivalve mollusc that is similar to the oyster, only much larger. Only the white muscular part or heart is eaten, along with the roe (tongue or coral, as it is commonly called) when it is full and of a bright orange colour.*

*500 g (1 lb) fresh scallops in their shells*
*snail butter (page 230)*

Open the scallop shells, cut the scallops out and clean them, removing the gut and dirt surrounding the white muscle and the coral. Put a little snail butter at the bottom of the under-shell and replace the cleaned scallop with the roe on top. Place the shell on a grate over the fire and cook for 3–5 minutes, until the butter is bubbling and the meat has turned opaque and pearly.

Serve immediately with some crusty bread to soak up the scallop butter.

*Serves 4 as an appetiser*

# WHOLE LOBSTER BAKED IN SEAWEED

1 × 2 kg (4 lbs) live lobster
200 g (6½ oz) butter
salt and freshly ground black
    pepper
1 kg (2 lbs) kelp or other
    seaweed
1 metre (39 in.) of wire
2 lemons, quartered
extra butter

*The lobster should be baked with Snail Butter (page 230) for best results, but often while camping or fishing we don't have the resources of a civilised kitchen. This lack is compensated for by the pleasure of the surroundings, and simplicity is often more in tune with the experience.*

Drown the lobster in a slurry of fresh water and ice (takes about 5 minutes). Cut a slit with a knife where the tail of the lobster meets the head, under the upper side of the carapace. Slice the cold butter and season with salt and pepper. Push the butter under the carapace into the head.

Wrap the lobster in the kelp and tie securely with the wire.

Make a trench in the coals of the fire and lay the lobster in the trench. Cover with the coals and bake for 25 minutes. Take the lobster from the fire and rest it for 5–10 minutes. Remove the kelp and cut the lobster in half lengthwise to serve. The kelp will not smell very pleasant, but the lobster will be cooked to perfection. Serve the lobster with some extra butter and lemon wedges.

*Serves 2–3*

# BARBECUED QUAIL

12 large quails

Marinade
juice of 1 lemon
1 rosemary sprig
2 thyme sprigs
3 tablespoons virgin olive oil
2 garlic cloves, crushed
2 golden shallots, chopped
1 tablespoon freshly ground
    black pepper

Split the quails along the back, using a sharp knife. Remove the ribs and breastbone with your fingers. Place the quails on a tray.

Mix together the marinade ingredients and sprinkle over the quails. Leave to marinate for 2 hours before cooking.

Wait until the fire has settled and then grill the quails, skin side down, for 3 minutes on each side. Baste the quails with the marinade while cooking.

*Serves 6*

Opposite: Barbecued Quail

# KANGAROO SATE

500 g (1 lb) kangaroo fillet, cut
  into 2 cm (³/₄ in.) cubes
10 bamboo skewers

Marinade
1 tablespoon red curry paste
  (page 128)
1 teaspoon crushed fresh ginger
1 teaspoon chopped fresh red
  chili pepper
1 tablespoon chopped fresh
  coriander (Chinese parsley)
  leaves
1 tablespoon chopped golden
  shallot
2 garlic cloves, crushed and
  chopped
juice of 1 lime
¼ cup (60 mL/2 fl oz) sesame
  oil

Soak the bamboo skewers in water for 2 hours or overnight.

Thread the cubes of kangaroo onto the bamboo skewers.

Mix together the ingredients for the marinade. Pour the marinade over the cubes of kangaroo. Turn them over so that all the meat is coated and leave to marinate for 2 hours. Cook quickly (no more than 5 minutes each side) over a moderate fire so that the meat does not dry out.

*Serves 5*

# BARBECUED LEG OF LAMB

1 × 1.5 kg (3 lbs) leg of lamb,
  boned

Marinade
²/₅ cup (100 mL/3½ fl oz)
  virgin olive oil
3 garlic cloves, crushed and
  chopped
1 tablespoon fresh thyme leaves
1 tablespoon chopped fresh
  marjoram
6 basil leaves
1 tablespoon freshly ground
  black pepper
2 tablespoons strong Dijon
  mustard
3 tablespoons champagne vinegar

Trim the leg of any fat and cut it into 8 fillets.

Mix together the ingredients for the marinade, place the fillets in a deep container, pour over the marinade and refrigerate overnight.

Cook the fillets over a moderate fire, for approximately 6–7 minutes each side, basting with the marinade. By separating the leg into fillets you lessen the cooking time and avoid having the leg underdone in the centre and overdone on the outside. Cook the lamb medium to medium rare and let it rest for 10–15 minutes before carving it into little medallions.

Serve on bread rolls with tomato and basil salad or Ratatouille (page 253).

*Serves 8*

# PORK CHOPS
# WITH DIJON MUSTARD

Mix together the ingredients for the marinade and brush it onto the chops. Cover and refrigerate overnight.

Remove and drain the chops from the marinade. Season the chops with salt and grill them over a medium fire for 8 minutes each side.

Blanch the golden shallots in boiling water for 1 minute. Refresh under cold water, then drain and pat dry. Mix the sugar into the vinegar, add the shallots and oil and season with pepper. Spoon this sauce over the chops as soon as they leave the fire.

*Serves 4–6*

6 pork loin chops, trimmed of
    skin and fat
salt

Marinade
2 tablespoons strong Dijon
    mustard
3 tablespoons champagne vinegar
1 tablespoon chopped golden
    shallots
2 garlic cloves, crushed and
    chopped
1 teaspoon chopped thyme leaves
freshly ground black pepper

Sauce
2 tablespoons chopped golden
    shallots
3 tablespoons sherry vinegar
1 tablespoon white granulated
    sugar
$^2/_5$ cup (100 mL/ $3^1/_2$ fl oz)
    virgin olive oil
freshly ground black pepper

# BROCHETTE OF LAMB KIDNEYS

*A brochette is similar to a kebab (kabob), that is, the meat, fish or vegetables are cooked on a skewer or spit. Brochette is the French name for the special type of skewer used for this purpose.*

Soak the bamboo skewers in water for 2 hours or overnight. Cut the bacon into 48 pieces, each rasher (slice) into 8 pieces.

Cut the onion into 24 squares (3 cm × 3 cm / $1^1/_4$ in. × $1^1/_4$ in.)

Cut the kidneys in half laterally and remove the veins and hard tissue. Thread the kidneys onto the skewers with a piece of bacon on each side and a piece of onion and a mushroom in between.

Mix together the baste ingredients.

Grill the skewers over a medium heat, brushing generously with the basting mixture, until done to your liking; 5 minutes for medium rare, 10 minutes for well done.

*Serves 6*

12 lamb's kidneys
6 bamboo skewers
6 rashers (slices) bacon
24 champignon (button)
    mushrooms
2 onions, quartered

Baste
100 mL ($3^1/_2$ fl oz) virgin olive
    oil
2 chopped golden shallots
1 garlic clove, crushed and
    chopped
1 teaspoon fresh thyme leaves
juice of 1 lemon
1 tablespoon chopped fresh
    parsley

# BARBECUING FISH

### Tomato and Pernod seasoning
²/₅ cup (100 mL/3¹/₂ fl oz) virgin olive oil
310 g (10 oz) ripe tomatoes, chopped
3 garlic cloves, crushed and chopped
²/₅ cup (100 mL/3¹/₂ fl oz) Pernod
¹/₂ teaspoon cayenne pepper
1 teaspoon chopped fresh thyme leaves
1 bay leaf, crushed
¹/₂ teaspoon salt
2 tablespoons chopped fresh parsley

### Tapénade
4 tablespoons black olive paste
4 tablespoons virgin olive oil
1 tablespoon chopped capers
60–80 g (2–2¹/₂ oz) anchovy fillets, puréed
1 garlic clove, crushed and chopped
2 tablespoons chopped fresh parsley
juice of 1 lemon
salt and freshly ground black pepper

### Snail butter
200 g (6¹/₂ oz) butter
2 tablespoons chopped golden shallots
2 garlic cloves, crushed and chopped
1 teaspoon chopped fresh thyme leaves
1 tablespoon Cognac
2 tablespoons champagne vinegar
3 tablespoons chopped fresh parsley
salt and freshly ground black pepper

*Fillets of fish tend to dry out over an open fire but small whole fish have a layer of fat under the skin that protects them. Because of this I tend to wrap fillets in aluminium kitchen foil with some butter or oil and seasonings. While grilling small whole fish, baste them with oil or butter. For large fish, I like the old fisherman's method of wrapping the fish in newspaper and burying it in the coals.*

When grilling fillets use one of the following three seasonings. Divide the fillets up into portions of 155–225 g (5–7 oz) each. Place each piece of fish on a piece of oiled aluminium kitchen foil with a tablespoon of the seasoning mixture on top of it. Fold the foil over the fish and seal it with a triple fold. Cook over moderate coals for 5 minutes each side.

### *To make tomato and Pernod seasoning*
Heat the olive oil in a frying pan or skillet until smoking. Add the tomatoes and garlic and cook over a high heat, stirring with a wooden spoon until the tomato has released its juices. Add the Pernod, cayenne pepper, thyme, bay leaf and salt and reduce to a thick sauce. Take off the heat and add the chopped parsley. Cool before using.
*Makes approximately 3 cups*

### *To make the tapénade*
Mix all the ingredients together and the tapénade is ready to use.
*Makes approximately 1¹/₂ cups*

### *To make snail butter*
Soften the butter. Add all the other ingredients and beat or process until smooth and the Cognac and vinegar have been absorbed. Leave the butter soft so that it can be easily spread onto the fish.
*Makes approximately 1 cup*

Opposite: Barbecuing Fish

# WHOLE FISH
# BAKED IN NEWSPAPER

2–3 kg (4–6 lbs) fish,
    preferably trout, tuna or
    snapper
salt and freshly ground black
    pepper
fresh herbs (sprigs of thyme,
    parsley, marjoram, etc)
lemon slices
200 g (6½ oz) butter
2 onions, quartered
20 sheets of newspaper
extra butter
freshly ground black pepper

*Build your fire in a shallow pit dug in the earth.*

Season the fish generously with salt and pepper. Mix together the herbs, butter, lemon and onion and stuff the cavity. Wet the sheets of newspaper and wrap the fish tightly, layer on layer.

Scrape the coals away from the centre of the fire. Place the fish in the coals and cover it with more hot coals. Leave the fish in the coals for 30 minutes, by which time most of the paper will have burned away but there should still be a few layers protecting the fish. Cut the paper from the fish, place the fish on a tray, dot with some fresh butter, season with some freshly ground pepper and serve.

*Serves 6–8*

# BARBECUED SQUID

10 bamboo skewers
600 g (1¼ lbs) cleaned squid,
    cut into 2–3 cm (¾–1¼ in.)
    wide strips

Marinade
⅓ cup (90 mL/3 fl oz) dark
    soy sauce
juice of 1 lemon
1 tablespoon chopped fresh
    coriander (Chinese parsley)
    leaves
1 teaspoon freshly chopped ginger
2 small fresh chili peppers,
    chopped (optional)
2 tablespoons chopped green
    spring onion (scallions)

Soak the bamboo skewers in water for 2 hours or overnight.

Thread the squid onto the skewers, puncturing it at 4–5 cm (1½–2 in.) intervals.

Mix together the ingredients for the marinade and coat the squid with it. Marinate for 2 hours, then grill over a medium heat. Cook the squid briefly (2–3 minutes should suffice). If the squid is overcooked it will be tough and dry.

Note: to make the dish more decorative, incise the outside of the squid with a sharp knife at 2 cm (¾ in.) intervals to form a fine diamond pattern.

*Serves 4–5*

# KING PRAWNS
## WITH GINGER AND HERBS

———

Soak the bamboo skewers in water for 2 hours or overnight.

Skewer the prawns (shrimps) from the head to the tail so that they are kept straight.

Mix together the marinade ingredients. Marinate the prawns in the mixture for 2 hours before cooking, and baste them with the mix while cooking them.

Cook over a medium heat, until the prawns turn a pinky-red colour (about 5 minutes).

*Serves 6*

1 kg (2 lbs) green king prawns (large shrimps) in their shells
10 bamboo skewers

Marinade
1 cup (250 mL/8 fl oz) virgin olive oil
¼ cup (60 mL/2 fl oz) fresh lemon juice
½ teaspoon freshly ground black pepper
½ teaspoon salt
1 teaspoon crushed fresh ginger
chili powder or cayenne pepper to taste
1 tablespoon chopped fresh parsley
1 tablespoon chopped fresh mint

# GREEN KING PRAWNS
## WITH ORANGE AND SAFFRON

———

Soak the bamboo skewers in water for 2 hours or overnight.

Shell the prawns (shrimps) leaving the tails on. Thread them onto the skewers, folding them over in their natural shape.

Put the orange and lemon juice, saffron, salt and cayenne pepper in a small saucepan and bring to the boil. Reduce by half. Allow to cool, add the oil and then the parsley and thyme (or marjoram). Pour the marinade over the prawns and marinate for 1 hour or more before grilling over moderate coals for 2 minutes each side. Baste with the marinade while cooking.

*Serves 6*

1 kg (2 lbs) green king prawns (large shrimps) in their shells
10 bamboo skewers

Marinade
juice of 2 oranges
juice of 1 lemon
1 teaspoon saffron threads
1 teaspoon salt
½ teaspoon cayenne pepper
1 cup (250 mL/8 fl oz) virgin olive oil
1 tablespoon chopped fresh thyme or marjoram leaves
1 tablespoon chopped fresh Italian parsley

233

# BARBECUED CHICKEN

Cut each chicken into four (the two legs and two breasts) and discard the back bone.

Mix together the marinade ingredients. Place the chicken in a large bowl, pour the marinade over and leave to marinate overnight.

Slowly grill the chicken pieces over the coals for 10–15 minutes. If the fire is very hot the chicken can be protected by wrapping it in aluminium kitchen foil prior to cooking.

*Serves 6–8*

*2 × 1 kg (2 lbs) corn-fed chickens*

*Marinade*
*3 golden shallots, finely chopped*
*3 garlic cloves, crushed and chopped*
*1 tablespoon strong Dijon mustard*
*2 teaspoons fresh thyme leaves*
*1 bay leaf, crushed*
*1 teaspoon freshly ground black pepper*
*juice of 1 lemon*
*2 tablespoons virgin olive oil*

# LEMON CHICKEN

Mix together the ingredients for the marinade and add the chicken breasts. Marinate for 2 hours and then grill over a low fire for 12–15 minutes, turning occasionally, and basting the breasts with the marinade.

Melt the butter for the sauce at the side of the fire. Add the other sauce ingredients to the butter and keep warm. When the chicken is golden and the skin crisp, serve with a tablespoon of the sauce drizzled over each breast.

*Serves 6*

*6 chicken breasts, skin on*

*Marinade*
*juice of 2 lemons*
*1 teaspoon chopped fresh thyme leaves*
*6 fresh basil leaves, chopped*
*3 golden shallots, chopped*
*1 garlic clove, crushed*

*Sauce*
*100 g (3½ oz) butter*
*juice of 1 lemon*
*2 tablespoons chopped fresh parsley*
*1 teaspoon grated lemon rind, blanched*
*salt and freshly ground black pepper to taste*

Opposite: Barbecued
Chicken

# CHICKEN WITH GINGER AND CHILI PEPPER

8 chicken breasts

Marinade
3 tablespoons heavy soy sauce
2 tablespoons chopped fresh
   ginger root
2 tablespoons chopped fresh chili
   pepper
3 tablespoons sesame oil
3 tablespoons rice vinegar
2 fresh lime leaves

Remove and discard the skin from the chicken breasts.

Mix together the marinade ingredients and add the chicken. Leave the chicken to marinate overnight.

Grill the breasts over a low fire for 12–15 minutes, turning occasionally and basting with the marinade.

*Serves 6*

# BROCHETTE OF VEGETABLES

6 large skewers

Seasoned oil
1 garlic clove, crushed
155 mL (5 fl oz) virgin olive
   oil
2 tablespoons sherry vinegar
salt and freshly ground black
   pepper

Vegetables
3 onions, peeled and quartered
24 cherry tomatoes
24 mushrooms, 3 cm (¼ in.) in
   diameter
4 large red sweet peppers
   (capsicums)
4 corn cobs
2 eggplants (aubergines)

*To prepare the seasoned oil*
Steep the garlic in the oil overnight. Just before use, add the vinegar and season with salt and pepper. Shake or whisk so that all the ingredients are thoroughly combined.

*To prepare the vegetables*
Peel and quarter the onions. Wash the cherry tomatoes. The caps of the mushrooms should only need wiping with a damp cloth—do not wash them. Cut the sweet peppers (capsicums) into 3 cm (1¼ in.) squares and remove all seeds. Cut the sweetcorn cobs into 24 rounds (6 rounds each). Cut the eggplants (aubergines) into 3 cm (1¼ in.) cubes.

*To cook the brochettes*
Thread the vegetables onto the skewers, alternating them according to your preference. Brush generously with the seasoned oil and grill over a low fire, brushing from time to time with the oil. Different vegetables will have different cooking times but the whole barbecuing process should not take more than 12–15 minutes.

*To serve*
Brochettes may be served as an appetiser or as a main meal. They are best accompanied by rice and a salad.

*Serves 6*

# HOME-MADE SAUSAGES

*A barbecue is not complete without a good sausage. Sausages from the local butcher may be acceptable, but try making your own sausages and astound your family and guests.*

Soak the sausage skins overnight in enough water to cover them.

In an electric grinder or mortar and pestle, pulverise the spices. Mix all the ingredients together, including the crushed spices, and pass them through the medium blade of the food mill or mincer twice.

### *To fill the skins*

Some mincers have a sausage filling attachment. It looks rather like a badly designed funnel, too narrow at the opening and too wide in the tube. The top is secured in position at the end of the mincer. The wet sausage skins are pulled up over the tube and the filling passed through the mincer.

This process can be duplicated with a piping bag. The important things to remember are not to fill the skins as tightly as commercial sausages and try to eliminate air bubbles as much as possible.

Tie the end before you begin to fill the casing and twist it at set intervals of 10 cm (4 in.) to create individual sausages.

Grill slowly over low embers for 10–15 minutes.

*Makes 30 sausages*

1 kg (2 lbs) lean pork, cubed
250 g (8 oz) pork liver
500 (1 lb) fat belly pork
250 g (8 oz) back fat
2 cups (125 g/4 oz) fresh bread crumbs (from strong bread, page 253)
1 tablespoon chopped fresh sage leaves
2 bay leaves
1 onion
6 garlic cloves
1 cup roughly chopped Italian parsley
2 cups (500 mL/16 fl oz) white wine
3 tablespoons salt

155 g (5 oz) salted sausage skin

Spices
1 tablespoon cardamom
2 star anise pods
1 tablespoon whole allspice
2 teaspoons juniper berries
1 tablespoon black peppercorns

# The Wine Merchant

*Good wine should not be considered a luxury, as many excellent wines are readily available all over the world. For a different end to a meal, try making your own home-made liqueurs in a variety of flavours, or tempt your palate with cabernet and Sauternes ice creams.*

The first step for those wishing to achieve a greater understanding of the world of wine is to find a good wine merchant. Not only will this person provide you with a stock of good wines, but they should be able to provide information on wine education, and guide you to wines to taste in order to broaden your knowledge and fire your enthusiasm. When travelling, make sure you go to good restaurants and let the sommelier introduce you to the best wines of the region; some of the world's great palates were formed at the tables of Point and Taillevent.

In Australia, great wine lists are rare because diners usually are not willing to pay restaurants for the costs of cellaring a wine. These days it is a very expensive business to have a great cellar. When Berowra Waters Inn (north of Sydney), opened in 1976, the number of great post-1944 vintages was less than ten, and great pre-1940 vintages numbered only about six. Those great vintages are still in existence but their prices have increased ten-fold and there have been another ten vintages since that would also have to be purchased. In 1975 I bought three bottles of 1945 d'Yquem for $300 each. If one could purchase them today the price would be approximately $5,000 each. Similarly, old Hunter wines from the 1940s, the early Wynn's Coonawarra wines and the early Granges can no longer be purchased without great cost.

It is therefore a daunting task to collect a great cellar; perhaps it should be left to a publicly funded institution, headed, of course, by you, dear reader and myself.

'Let's not forget that in the end, wine is just a drink.' This piece of advice was offered to me by a person whose palate had, it was conservatively estimated, cost well over half a million dollars to hone to its present sharpness.

A palate of the quality of Australia's Len Evans or Michael Broadbent of Christies of London is able to identify wines by name, year and location, because not only have they tasted many wines and they have a very good palate memory, but because wine is so dependent on climate and soil for its primary characteristics.

Winemakers have a part to play, as do the vineyard managers, in the final structure of the wine and, indeed, there may be marked differences between the wines of neighbours during any particular vintage. These differences become less apparent as the wine ages and the dominant characteristics of the wine assert themselves. Australians have been to the fore in developing and adapting new techniques in the vineyard and exporting them to newly acquired vineyards in France.

Varietal characteristics become secondary as the area character develops. In France, grape types are defined by law, but in Australia these laws do not apply. An area like the Hunter Valley in Australia

Previous pages:
A collection of great wines

may therefore be famous for shiraz and semillon but still produce chardonnay, cabernet and pinot noir. With age, the wine becomes old Hunter white, or red, rather than old pinot or old shiraz.

New winemaking techniques have altered the structure of wines. Australian wines today generally have more alcohol than older wines had, and the fruit flavours are more predominant in the young wines. Today, the tannins are softer and the wines are able to be drunk very young. This is only sensible, as most wines are drunk within one day of purchase. While traditionalists may deplore these changes, any wine lover can only applaud the quantum leap in the quality of 'vin ordinaire' that the technological changes in the vineyard and fermenting vat have ensured.

Recently, I expressed the view to Len Evans that I was tiring of the big-flavoured alcoholic wines and that the old Hunters made by Maurice O'Shea, legendary winemaker, were only 11.5–12.5 per cent alcohol and yet they seemed to live for thirty years without much effort. 'You must remember, Tony, that Maurice did not have the advantage of refrigerated fermentation vats and was thus required to throw in the odd block of ice to cool the ferment. This practice diluted the must and so the alcohol levels were lower,' he explained. And the profit higher, I thought, thus explaining why some winemakers still use this outdated method.

Wines can be appreciated for their taste alone, but also as examples of the area of origin and of the vintage of their birth. The place of birth marks the wine and gives it relevance to a cuisine. If local wines are used in cooking local produce, then the flavours become complementary and we have a confluence that becomes a 'cuisine'. That is, a style of cooking that is identifiable as belonging to a particular region. Thus the great restaurants use their local wines: Jean Bardet at Tours uses the great wines of the Touraine, Vouvray, Chinon, Bourgueil; Paul Bocuse allies his cooking with the Beaujolais; Bernard L'Oiseau with Burgundy; and the Haeberlins with Alsace.

Australian restaurants also share a similarity of cuisine because of these factors. A chef like David Thompson uses Thai cooking as his base and I use French cuisine as mine, but there is still much in common between us because of our use of the same products from the same areas.

At home, if a family enjoys particular styles of wines and cooks with them, then they will choose to eat dishes that they enjoy with those wines, and thus develop a family style.

We should enjoy eccentricities and not be beholden to that which is regarded as correct. It is only through diversity of experience that we maintain our youthful enthusiasm.

Certain rules seem made to be broken:
1. Never serve a sauvignon blanc after 10 a.m.
2. Never serve a young white wine with meat.
3. Never serve a red wine with artichokes.
4. Never serve raw onions with wines.

You can certainly serve red wines with fish and white wines with meat, but in these cases the red wine should be light and the white wine weighty and complex.

To learn about which foods suit different wines it is useful to learn about the classic dishes of the various winegrowing areas. We will look at the French experience but it is also useful to consider other areas, such as Germany and the Baltic, Spain and, to a lesser extent, Greece.

Riesling is the great grape of Alsace and Germany and the dishes suitable for eating while drinking this wine include the pork that lays the base for the charcuterie, and the choucroute (sauerkraut) that is one of France's favourite dishes. Choucroute is not a dish for a young pretty riesling; it is, rather, for the more developed style that has had time to accumulate a few barnyard smells. A young riesling would be more suited to white asparagus or chicken cooked in riesling. Certainly, by using the same wine in the cooking the wine served will benefit, but perhaps the experience is less remarkable for the lack of contrast. Australian rieslings from the Clare Valley are world famous. Labels to look for include Mountadam, Petaluma, Tim Knappstein, and from Tasmania, Pipers Brook.

Semillon, cabernet and merlot are the grapes of Bordeaux. Young semillons tend to have a green apple taste, and lend themselves to being served with oysters, and poached and grilled fish dishes. The older, more complex, styles of semillon are suited to accompanying lobster and crab dishes. Watch out for classics from Tyrells, Rothbury Estate, Briar Hill, Yalumba and Peter Lehmann.

Young cabernets love the 'matelote' dishes: fish braised in red wine, and also grilled fish and lobster. Medium weight cabernets, young or old, are nearly always teamed with lamb and grilled meat. Older cabernets, more full-bodied styles, and merlots, love game. Coonawarra is cabernet country in Australia, Hollicks and Petaluma being my favourites.

The grapes used in Burgundy wines are the chardonnay and pinot noir and, occasionally, in the lesser appellations, aligoté. The different characters of burgundy are more obviously the differences of climate, with the cooler north providing (of the chardonnays) chablis, tasting 'like sucking stones'; the south providing the riper, less complex, Maconnais wines; and the Cote d'Or, the grand, powerful styles on which the reputation of burgundy wines, as perhaps the greatest wines in the world, rest. Australia mirrors this with the cool climate wines coming from Tasmania and Coonawarra. Great Western produces some beautifully restrained and complex wines, particularly Bests and Seppelts. For myself, burgundies are the best food wines. They provide me with the opportunity to serve the greatest food, as even with complex, big-flavoured dishes, the wines will still shine. With Bordeaux and young cabernets, simple dishes often show the wines off to best advantage.

Follow the pattern outlined above—match food and wine for weight and complexity—and you will seldom go wrong.

Sweet wines offer the opportunity to surprise, as they often lend themselves to unusual combinations. A Sauternes with liver as first course is a classic example, but try one with a rich, washed rind cheese—it is a revelation. I love fish poached in Sauternes and I absolutely long to cook a grilled woodcock with truffles and serve it with an old d'Yquem.

Of course, the great wine that everyone uses as an apéritif is Champagne. Every area produces a local sparkling wine but no other carries the reputation of Champagne. The sparkling wines from Domaine Chandon are building a reputation for reliability and quality. I love Heemskerk Vineyards 'Jansz' as an apéritif and the Seppelts lines have a strength that makes them ideal food wines, especially if they have some age.

Champagnes vary enormously in style, from the chablis-like bone-dry styles of Salon and le Mesnil, to the fruitier styles of Roederer and Heidseck, to the big, complex, aged flavours of Krugs and Bollingers. The rosés can also vary from the meaty Krug to the pretty Mumm. It is an interesting exercise to create all-Champagne menus, and if you do have the opportunity, be brave and serve strongly flavoured dishes (never spicy in the Thai sense) with wine-based sauces. I can imagine an old Bollinger with hare, Krug Rosé with poached duck and Mumm Rosé with a gratin of raspberries. These fruitier styles are quite unsuited to the classic combination of oysters and caviar, which should be left to the bone-dry styles. I often prefer a sweet wine as an apéritif and then a Champagne with the first course, as a dry wine can be too aggressive to start a meal, particularly at lunch. Normally I would not interfere with a good Champagne by adding a sweetener to it, but it is perfectly acceptable with a lesser sparkling wine to add some crème de cassis or ratafia. Avoid brandy-based liqueurs as the flavour will be harsh and spirituous. Classic Australian fortified wines are wonderful chilled and served as apéritifs, as is a cold Pineau de Charentes served with fresh figs.

Fortified wines have been given a bad name quite undeservedly. Ports, sherries, ratafias and dessert wines are more versatile than most people suspect. Again, if you are guided by weight and complexity when matching wines with food, you will create some wonderful marriages: light, dry sherries with salted meats and smoked fish, old olorosos with caramelised apples, amontillados with shellfish. Ratafias make wonderful apéritifs and can be used to soften sparkling wines. I like using a pinot ratafia in Champagne to make an apéritif that is similar in taste to kir but perhaps nicer, as the ratafia echoes the flavour of the pinot used in the Champagne.

Spirits that you should include in your cupboard include the fruit brandies: Framboise, Mures, Eau de Vie de Prunes. Jean Bardet, the restaurateur at Tours, explained to me that the farmers in his area make eau de vie as a method of accumulating savings at the tax collector's expense and that some hoarders (and the French peasant is famous for his parsimony) have good quantities of bottles over a century old. As the spirit is 60 per cent proof, these farms have the same potential for disaster as a mini-oil refinery.

Armagnacs belong in the same group, and there are many farm distilleries in the area around Auch and Toulouse. In the heart of Gascony there is the heaven on earth that is Eugenie-les-Bains, the gastronomic retreat of Michel Guérard. His former chef de cuisine, Didier Oudille, has a more modest but hardly less expensive restaurant at Grenade-sur-l'Adour. André Daugin is at Toulouse, and in Paris, Alain Dutournier has an expatriate outpost at Le Carré des Feuillantes. These restaurants testify to the strength of Gascon cuisine, and house museum quality vintage Armagnacs that they are happy to introduce to you. In Australia, the finest Armagnacs are sold by Gabriel La Chaise of Cerbaco Distributors in Melbourne, and many fine restaurants, including the Treasury in Sydney and Mietta's in Melbourne, have collections that would be the envy of a three-star restaurant in France.

Cognacs are distilled differently and are seldom presented as a vintage. To achieve their individuality and styles, they rely on, and promote the skills of, the blending of spirits. Cognacs are often distilled by local farmers and then purchased by the major houses for blending. This is the strength of Cognac; the houses are strong and able to market their products worldwide, whereas the Armagnac producers are small and rely on connoisseurs to spread the word. To judge the quality of a Cognac, look at its price. Every large company has its range of deluxe spirits, and the prices are heart-stopping.

Delamaine is a wonderful small company and the Pale and Dry is a very fine Cognac at a reasonable price. Every home should have a bottle.

There are some very fine Australian brandies, but they are not of the quality of the French spirits. I have always thought that rum has potential as a fine spirit in Australia and there is an 'executive' special distillation that confirms it. Unfortunately, this rum is not available to the general public.

The value of alcohol as a digestive is well-documented and red wine in particular seems to have a beneficial effect on heart disease when taken in moderation. By drinking mineral water during meals at home, healthy drinking habits are taught to the children and alcohol intake is moderated. It is better to drink well and drink less. When the ethos emphasises quality, it promotes a celebration of life that is missed out on by less discriminating palates.

# MILK-FED LAMB VIGNERONNE

*The flavour of grapevine cuttings used in the cooking of this dish is distinctive and perfectly suited to the milk-fed lamb. Make a fire using charcoal and then feed it with grapevine cuttings until you have a substantial bed of coals. Feed the fire with twigs of the vine as you cook the lamb to keep a little smoke wafting around the lamb.*

Mix together the seasoning ingredients and rub the mixture over the lamb legs just before cooking.

When the fire has settled, cut each leg into 2 pieces along the natural muscle division and grill to medium rare over the hot coals (approximately 20 minutes).

Baste the lamb with the basting liquid continually so that the skin is crisp and highly flavoured.

Allow the lamb to rest for 10 minutes before carving.

*Serves 6–8*

*2 boned legs of milk-fed lamb (approximately 750 g/ 1½ lbs each)*

Seasoning
*2 garlic cloves, crushed*
*2 teaspoons chopped fresh thyme leaves*
*1 teaspoon freshly ground black pepper*
*1 tablespoon Maldon sea salt (page 253)*

Baste
*1 cup (250 mL/ 8 fl oz) virgin olive oil*
*1 tablespoon strong Dijon mustard*
*2 garlic cloves, crushed*
*1 tablespoon fresh thyme leaves*
*juice of 1 lemon*

# SWORDFISH POACHED IN SAUTERNES

1 kg (2 lbs) swordfish fillets, cut into 4 cm (1½ in.) cubes

Sauce
2 golden shallots, chopped
2 cups (185 g/6 oz) finely sliced mushrooms
350 mL (11½ fl oz) good Sauternes
⅖ cup (100 mL/3½ fl oz) white wine
⅖ cup (100 mL/3½ fl oz) fish stock (page 17)
1 thyme sprig
1 bay leaf
⅘ cup (200 mL/6½ fl oz) crème fraîche (page 252)
salt and freshly ground pepper
2 tablespoons butter

Place the shallots, mushrooms, Sauternes, white wine, fish stock, thyme and bay leaf in a large frying pan or skillet and bring the mixture to the boil. Add the fish and poach it in the simmering liquid for 3–4 minutes, or until the fish cubes are just cooked. Use a slotted spoon to remove the fish from the liquid and drain it on a towel.

Reduce the liquid by one-half over a medium heat and add the crème fraîche. Reduce further until the sauce has a creamy consistency, adjust the seasoning and whisk in the butter. Return the fish to the sauce to heat through.

Serve with rice and buttered zucchini (courgettes).

*Serves 6–8*

# CHICKEN IN RIESLING

1 × 2 kg (4 lbs) chicken or 1.25 kg (2½ lbs) chicken pieces
24 baby (pearl) onions, blanched
24 champignon (button) mushrooms
3 cups (750 mL/24 fl oz) good riesling
3 thyme sprigs
1 bay leaf
salt and freshly ground black pepper
12 baby carrots, peeled, trimmed and blanched

4 egg yolks
1 cup (250 mL/8 fl oz) light (single) cream
1 tablespoon butter, chopped
salt and freshly ground black pepper

Bone the chicken, cut the thigh into two, the wing into two and the breast into two. Put the chicken, onions and mushrooms into a heavy casserole with the wine, thyme, bay leaf, and seasonings. Bring the liquid to the boil and skim any scum from the surface with a ladle. Cover the casserole with the lid and cook it in a low oven (140°C/275°F) for 1¼ hours.

Strain the cooking liquid into a saucepan, re-cover the casserole and return it to the oven. Simmer the carrots in the liquid in the saucepan for 7 minutes, or until tender. Drain the carrots, retaining the liquid in the saucepan. Add the carrots to the chicken mixture.

Reduce the liquid in the saucepan to 1¼ cups (310 mL/10 fl oz). Whisk the egg yolks and cream together, then whisk this mixture into the simmering liquid. Heat without boiling until the sauce begins to thicken, then whisk the butter into the sauce and adjust the seasoning.

Remove the chicken casserole from the oven. Strain any residual liquid from the chicken into the sauce and whisk so that the sauce is smooth. Strain it over the chicken.

*To serve*
Serve the chicken with Risotto with Cèpes (page 188), using the carcass from your chicken to make the stock.

*Serves 6–8*

Opposite: Bottles of fine old Armagnac

# BOEUF BOURGUIGNONNE

*The great wine stew. Please use good wine for the sauce; it makes all the difference.*

2 kg (4 lbs) blade steak, cut into 4 cm (1½ in.) cubes

**Marinade**
4 cups (1 litre/1¾ imp. pints) good pinot noir (Mountadam)
155 mL (5 fl oz) Cognac
2 onions, halved
1 large carrot, sliced
1 stick celery, sliced
1 head garlic, halved
4 thyme sprigs
3 bay leaves
12 peppercorns
2 tablespoons virgin olive oil

**Roux**
2 tablespoons butter
2 tablespoons plain (all-purpose) flour
2 tablespoons tomato paste (purée)

**Braising**
½ cup (125 g/4 oz) clarified butter
200 g (6½ oz) smoked belly pork (speck), cut into 1 cm × 2 cm (⅓ in. × ¾ in.) pieces
3 onions, diced
1 carrot, diced small
10 garlic cloves, crushed
salt and freshly ground black pepper
2–3 thyme sprigs
1 bay leaf

**Garnish**
⅘ cup (200 mL/6½ fl oz) white wine
2 tablespoons butter
500 g (1 lb) mushrooms, stems trimmed
24 baby (pearl) onions
24 baby carrots
24 very fresh new potatoes
2 tablespoons butter
½ cup chopped fresh parsley
freshly ground black pepper

### To marinate the meat
Mix all the marinade ingredients with the meat in a large bowl. Cover with plastic wrap (cling film) and refrigerate. Marinate for 2–5 days. Strain the marinade, retaining the liquid and the meat.

### To cook the roux
Make a roux by melting the butter in a small saucepan over a medium heat and then adding the flour. Stir constantly with a wooden spoon for 3–4 minutes and then whisk in the marinade liquid. Add the tomato paste (purée) and simmer for 5 minutes. Strain and reserve the liquid.

### To braise the meat
Heat the clarified butter in a large, deep casserole over a medium heat and add the belly pork (speck). Cook the pork until it has given up most of its fat and then remove the pieces with a slotted spoon.

Tip half the fat into a heavy frying pan or skillet and heat it over a high heat. Add the steak and brown the meat. At the same time, brown the onions and carrot with the garlic in the casserole. As the meat browns, transfer it from the frying pan to the casserole. When all the meat is in the casserole, drain the fat from the casserole and add the red wine marinade sauce and the belly pork.

Season with salt and pepper and add the thyme and bay leaf. Bring the casserole to a simmer and then place it in a preheated slow oven (140°C/275°F) for 3 hours. Remove the casserole from the oven and skim the fat from the top of the sauce. If you need to moisten the dish, add a little water.

### Garnish
Heat the wine and melt the butter in a saucepan over a medium heat. Add the mushrooms and onions and simmer until tender (approximately 5–7 minutes). Add the carrots and cook for a further 5 minutes. Strain and add to the Bourguignonne.

Cook the potatoes separately in boiling salted water. When tender (approximately 10–15 minutes), drain them and toss in butter, parsley and pepper.

Ladle the Bourguignonne from the casserole at the table.

*Serves 6–8*

# ROASTED SQUAB
# WITH PORT SAUCE

Retain the squab livers to use in the sauce. Season the squab and cover the breasts with the prosciutto (Parma ham). Brush generously with some of the melted butter, rub over the garlic and roast in a hot oven (200°C/400°F) for 12 minutes. Rest the squab in a warm place for 20 minutes before carving.

Remove the breasts and legs from the carcasses and lay them in a clean baking pan to reheat.

Chop the carcasses into pieces with a cleaver and brown them in the remaining butter in a saucepan over a high heat. Add the mirepoix, shallots, bacon and garlic. When nicely caramelised (approximately 12 minutes), add the port, thyme and bay leaf and reduce the liquid by one-half. Strain the sauce through a fine strainer into a small saucepan.

Purée the squab livers and add them to the sauce. Heat until nearly boiling, whisk the butter into the sauce, taste for seasoning and keep warm.

Heat the squab in the oven for 2 minutes.

Lay the squab on the grilled bread and surround with the sauce.

*Serves 6*

6 × 405 g (13 oz) squab
*salt and freshly ground black*
    *pepper*
6 slices prosciutto (Parma ham)
*½ cup (125 g/4 oz) butter,*
    *melted*
2 garlic cloves, crushed

Sauce
*1 cup mirepoix (page 253)*
*3 golden shallots, chopped*
*2 bacon rashers (slices), chopped*
*2 garlic cloves, crushed*
*½ bottle (350 mL/11½ fl oz)*
    *vintage port*
*2 thyme sprigs*
*1 bay leaf*
*6 squab livers*
*2 tablespoons butter*
*salt and freshly ground black*
    *pepper*

6 slices of strong bread, grilled
    (page 253)

# RATAFIAS

*Home-made liqueurs, such as ratafias, are always popular. Making them is good therapy whenever I start thinking I should be a winemaker. These beverages are usually made from the must of wine grapes. The must is the freshly pressed, unfermented juice of the grape. In the case of red wine, it has some colour extracted from the skins. Australian musts are very sweet compared to European musts and therefore make great ratafias. Ratafias are simpler to make than wines and so we can indulge our winemaker fantasies without having the technical skills to make great fermented wine. Because the must still has solids in it, and we don't wish to filter the wine, it is necessary to 'rack' the wine. This means allowing the solids to settle to the bottom of a container and then removing the wine to another container, leaving the solids behind. This can be achieved by siphoning or decanting. The must has spirit alcohol added to it, to raise the degree of alcohol to the level where it will no longer ferment. Winemakers have access to very high proof spirits that are not available to the general public. I am afraid we have to make do with Cognac (brandy) and good vodka. You will have no need of recipes if you remember to keep the alcohol level to above 17% volume; 1 part Cognac to 2 parts must.*

# COOKED WINE

———

*10 litres (17½ imp. pints) sweet shiraz must*
*3 cups (750 mL/24 fl oz) Cognac*

*Ask your favourite winemaker for some must at vintage time.*

Put the must into a large saucepan, bring it to the boil over a medium heat and reduce the liquid to 7 litres (12¼ imp. pints). Strain the must through muslin, allow it to cool and then add the Cognac. Bottle the cooked wine in sterilised bottles, then seal with crown caps or corks. Leave to age for 3 months, then decant into fresh bottles.

*Makes 11–12 bottles (8¼ litres/14 imp. pints)*

# ANISEED RATAFIA

———

*⅓ cup fresh fennel leaves*
*1 star anise pod*
*12 coriander seeds*
*a pinch ground cinnamon*
*small pinch of mace*
*6 cups (1.5 litres/2½ imp. pints) very good vodka*
*405 g (13 oz) white granulated sugar*

Crush the fennel, star anise, coriander seeds, cinnamon and mace using a mortar and pestle. Add the mixture to the vodka (or neutral spirit) and leave to rest in a warm place for a month. Filter the liquid mixture through a triple layer of muslin and add the sugar, which you have dissolved in 155 mL (5 fl oz) of water.

*Makes 10–12 bottles (7.5–9 litres/17.5–21 imp. pints)*

# BLACKCURRANT RATAFIA

———

*2 kg (4 lbs) ripe or frozen blackcurrants*
*1.5 kg (3 lbs) caster (superfine) sugar*
*1 tablespoon cloves*
*6 litres (10½ imp. pints) good vodka or gin*

Purée the blackcurrants with the sugar and cloves and leave in a warm place overnight. The next day place this must in a large earthenware or glass crock. Add the spirit and leave in a warm place for 6 weeks. Strain into another container, preferably glass, and leave to settle for 1 week. Rack into bottles using a siphon, leaving the solids on the bottom of the crock. Cork the bottles. Ratafia improves with age.

*Makes 12 bottles (9 litres/21 imp. pints)*

# MULLED WINE

———

*1 cup (250 mL/8 fl oz) water*
*⅘ cup (200 g/6½ oz) white granulated sugar*
*2 tablespoons honey*
*6 cloves*
*1 stick cinnamon*
*1 vanilla bean*
*3 orange slices*
*3 lemon slices*
*155 mL (5 fl oz) brandy or Cognac)*
*2 litres (3¼ imp. pints) red wine*

*A winter treat for those with cold feet, this supposedly also has aphrodisiac qualities. My experience tells me that this quality only seems to work on the young. In older generations, it induces sleep.*

Place the water, sugar and honey in a large saucepan and bring to the boil over a low heat. Add the cloves, cinnamon stick and vanilla bean and cook gently for 5 minutes. Add the citrus fruits, cook for another minute and then add the wine.

Heat until the liquid is hot to touch, add the brandy or Cognac, then ladle into warm mugs.

*Makes 9 cups (2.25 litres/3½ imp. pints)*

# WINE ICE CREAMS

———

*These are sophisticated flavours for adult dinner parties, rather than ice creams for children. The theory I developed that led to their creation came from a sorbet I made for Adam Wynn from the cabernet must (the sweet juice before fermentation) during vintage. For that sorbet I whisked some powdered dry ice into the must; it was fabulous. The natural sugars and acids of these premier wine grapes were perfectly in balance. To make these wine ice creams we reduce the wine and add the sugar equivalent to the natural sugar for the reduced wine and then extend the wine back to its natural volume with crème anglaise and cream. The ice cream mirrors the natural flavours of the fruits, which are made more complex by the processes of wine making.*

# CABERNET ICE CREAM

———

Place the wine and sugar in a large saucepan and reduce the liquid over a high heat to ⁴⁄₅ cup (200 mL/6½ fl oz). Pour the liquid into a container and chill it in the refrigerator.

When cold, mix the liquid with the crème anglaise. In a separate bowl, whip the cream until soft peaks form and fold it into the mixture. Churn until frozen.

*Makes 4 cups (1 litre/1¾ imp. pints)*

*4 cups (1 litre/1¾ imp. pints) good cabernet (or chardonnay, riesling, shiraz)*
*155 g (5 oz) sugar*
*600 mL (19 fl oz) cold crème anglaise (page 204)*
*⁴⁄₅ cup (200 mL/6½ fl oz) heavy whipping (double) cream*

# SAUTERNES ICE CREAM

———

*It is unlikely that we will find anyone using vintage d'Yquem to make this and so we take some liberties to improve the flavour and highlight the characteristics of Sauternes.*

Pour the Sauternes into a large saucepan and reduce the liquid over a high heat to ⁴⁄₅ cup (200 mL/6½ fl oz). Add the honey and stir in the vinegar. Pour the mixture into a container and chill it in the refrigerator.

When cold, mix the Sauternes mixture with the Crème Anglaise.

In a separate bowl, whip the cream until soft peaks form and then fold it into the mixture. Churn until frozen.

*Makes 4 cups (1 litre/1¾ imp. pints)*

*3 cups (750 mL/24 fl oz) Sauternes*
*1 tablespoon honey*
*1 tablespoon very good sherry vinegar*

*600 mL (19 fl oz) cold crème anglaise (page 204)*
*⁴⁄₅ cup (200 mL/6½ fl oz) heavy whipping (double) cream*

# GLOSSARY

**Baking blind**: a process of prebaking shortcrust pastry cases for quiche-type dishes. The pastry is rolled large enough to leave a slight overlap after being pressed into the corners of the tart mould. The pastry is then lined with aluminium kitchen foil or paper and filled with dried beans or rice. The filled case is baked at 180°C (355°F) until the pastry has begun to brown and is set in the mould. The case is then emptied of the beans or rice and foil or paper and the baking is finished by returning the case to the oven for a further 5–7 minutes, or until the pastry is evenly brown. The overlap is then trimmed from the top of the mould to leave the case level with the top lip of the mould.

**Bayonne ham**: a style of smoked prosciutto (Parma ham).

**Beurre manié**: a paste made of equal quantities of softened butter and plain (all-purpose) flour, mixed together. It is used for thickening sauces.

**Blanching**: a method of precooking vegetables and meats, while at the same time preserving their colour and flavour. The items to be blanched are plunged into fiercely boiling water until the desired degree of cooking has been effected (usually from 30 seconds to 1 minute). The items are then removed, drained and plunged into iced water or cold water to prevent further cooking. Remember to be generous with the amount of water used relative to the quantities of items to be blanched; and not to leave them in the iced water for longer than the time taken to cool. Do not salt the water if you are blanching vegetables.

**Bouquet garni**: a mixture of fresh herbs, usually including thyme sprigs, parsley stalks and a bay leaf, tied together and used to flavour stocks and stews.

**Brunoise**: a dice made from the julienne of vegetables; that is, very small and evenly cut.

**Clarified butter**: butter consists of fat, milk solids and water. Clarified butter, also called ghee, is made by slowly melting the butter (in a microwave oven if you wish), allowing the solids and water to settle to the bottom of the container and then pouring the clear fat into a separate container and discarding the solids. Clarified butter is available commercially.

**Crème anglaise**: a vanilla custard sauce made from milk, white granulated sugar, eggs and vanilla extract.

**Crème fraîche**: a lightly acidic soured cream common in France. It does not have the more aggressive acidity of eastern European sour cream. It can be made at home by combining fresh cream (minimum 35 per cent fat content) and buttermilk. Add ⅖ cup (100 mL/3½ fl oz) fresh buttermilk to 4 cups (1 litre/1¾ imp. pints) fresh cream. Mix thoroughly and let stand, covered, in a warm place overnight. Refrigerate and use as required.

**Crème pâtissière**: a flour-thickened custard used as a filling or base for pastries and fruit tarts.

**Croûtons**: thin slices of French bread (baguette), often rubbed with raw garlic, oven-dried and served as an accompaniment to fish soups. They are not to be confused with sippets.

**Dariole moulds**: these are high-sided moulds used for moulded creams and mousselines. Moulds for individual serves are cup-sized, of about 200 mL (6½ fl oz) capacity.

**Deglaze**: to dissolve the accumulation of glaze on pans and dishes by the addition of a liquid. The liquid is then used to flavour sauces and gravies.

**Demi-glace**: veal stock reduced to a rich sauce.

**Détrempe dough**: the basic dough used to make puff pastry. It is made from plain (all-purpose) flour, water, salt and sometimes 25 per cent butter.

**Draw, to**: to remove intestines, giblets and lights (lungs) from fowl.

**Egg wash**: a mixture of egg yolks and cream or milk (2 egg yolks to 155 mL/5 fl oz) milk or cream used to gild and stick seams together in pastry. It is applied with a brush before baking.

**Fish sauce** (*nam plat*): the fermented fish juice use in Thai cooking.

**Frenched**: this term relates to meat cutlets. The meat is stripped from the rib bone down to the main fillet.

**Gelatin**: comes in two forms, leaf and powder. The leaf is to be preferred as it gives a softer result than the powder. As a general rule, 5 leaves = 1 tablespoon of powder.

**Glaze**: the browned, dehydrated juices from meats and vegetables that occur during cooking. Also the name for highly reduced stocks.

**Glucose syrup**: available at good food stores. It is used extensively to prevent sweating in caramelised sugar, but it has other uses in confectionery making.

**Goose fat** (*graisse d'oie*): rendered fat from the goose, available in 250 g (8 oz) tins. It can be used instead of oils and other fats for cooking and salads.

**Italian parsley**: one of the two types of parsley. It is also known as flat-leafed or continental parsley. The other type of parsley is the curly-leafed. I prefer to use the flat-leafed Italian parsley on most occasions because it has a stronger flavour, but the curly-leafed variety can always be substituted.

**Julienne**: vegetables cut to the size of matchsticks are said to be cut 'into julienne'. In order to appear attractive they must be cut to an equal and even size.

**Junket tablets**: available in delicatessens and specialty food stores. They are used for making milk desserts. Plain (unflavoured) tablets are used for home cheese-making.

**Kaffir lime leaves**: special leaves used for curry, available from specialist spice suppliers.

**Liaison**: a preparation used for thickening sauces. It can be made from flour and water but usually applies to a mixture of eggs and cream that is added and whisked into a sauce at boiling point. The sauce is not reheated as it may separate if the egg is too cooked. Proportions are 3 eggs to 1 cup (250 mL/8 fl oz) light (single) cream.

**Maldon sea salt**: a sea salt made in Maldon (United Kingdom), noted for its clean flavour and flaky texture. It is available through gourmet food shops and delicatessens.

**Mesclun**: a Provençal word meaning mixed. It is now commonly used to describe salads from mixed baby salad leaves including rocket (arugula), curly endive (frisée), radicchio (chicory), and oak leaf.

**Mirepoix**: a dice (6 mm/¼ in.) of equal quantities onion, carrot and celery which is lightly sautéed in butter or oil. It is used for flavouring stocks and braised dishes.

**Mouli/food mill**: a device that uses a rotary action to push food through a sieve-like blade. It is available at specialty cookware stores.

**Ratatouille**: a mixture of equal quantities of onion, zucchini (courgette), eggplant (aubergine) and sweet pepper (capsicum) cut into small, even dice and braised in olive oil with tomato, garlic and herbs.

**Reducing**: the process of boiling a flavoured liquid to evaporate the water, having the twin effect of concentrating the flavours and thickening the liquid. Be careful not to scorch the liquid as it thickens or reduce it so much that it becomes unpalatable.

**Rice flour**: a flour made from rice. It is available from specialty shops.

**Saffron**: the stamen of the crocus flower, and is principally grown in Spain. Use the whole stamen (threads). Avoid powdered saffron because of the possibility of adulteration.

**Silicone paper**: a special nonstick baking paper found in specialty shops. It has replaced greaseproof (wax) paper in my kitchen.

**Sippets**: small cubes of bread deep-fried until crisp and used in salads and soups.

**Soft-ball stage**: when sugar is cooked as a syrup it goes through three main stages: soft ball, hard crack and caramel. Soft ball may be determined by measuring the temperature of the syrup (120°C/225°F)) or by removing a little of the syrup and putting it in cold water. If the syrup forms a soft ball when cool it has reached this stage.

**Stocks**: the most important item in your larder. They should be clear and limpid with gelatin and capture the essential flavour of the main ingredient. This is achieved by a few simple rules, the first of which is not to use your stock pot as a rubbish bin. Use only the freshest and best ingredients. Never boil a stock or it will become cloudy and lose its fresh taste. Be careful not to use too many vegetables in a stock, or it will develop a vegetable soup flavour and become unpalatable when reduced. Do not cook stocks for long periods of time or you will encourage stale flavours. Lastly, never salt a stock as it may later be reduced for sauces and become unusable. Individual stock recipes are found in relevant chapters.

**Strong bread**: most commercial breads are weak. They are soft and the dry crumbs become almost like flour very easily. Strong bread is usually a crusty style made from strong, high gluten flour. The term refers to a good French, Italian, Greek or Spanish/Portuguese bread, which forms large uneven crumbs when rubbed.

**Sugar syrup**: made by boiling ⅘ cup (200 mL/6½ fl oz) water with 500 g (1 lb) white granulated sugar and then allowing the syrup to cool. Used to sweeten drinks and fruit juices.

**Vinegars**: always use good vinegars. Vilux has a good commercial range but old sherry vinegars and balsamics are special delights that, although expensive, add a new dimension to salads and sauces.

# INDEX